How To Write SO PEOPLE CAN UNDERSTAND YOU

By ROBERT S. BURGER

Backstopped by CHARLES N. MYERS

R. S. BURGER & ASSOCIATES, INC.
GLEN MILLS, PENNSYLVANIA

Library of Congress Catalog Card No. 74-79378

FIRST PRINTING: MAY, 1969
SECOND PRINTING: JANUARY, 1971

PRINTED BY TINICUM PRESS
West Chester, Pennsylvania

CONTENTS

PART 1 – THE LEAD

Chapter 1

OUR PURPOSE, AND HOW WE'LL TRY TO ACHIEVE IT

My purpose in this book is to show you how to turn out better reports –with

"report" having the special meaning "any piece of informative writing, whatever its form," and

"informative writing" being the kind that's intended either

- just to inform – that is, to convey information and/or ideas–or
- (1) to inform, and (2) to persuade by informing.

So a letter, a memo or any other kind of written document may be for our purposes a report.

My method will be

- to identify the major "writing diseases" and their "agents,"
- to eliminate the agents, one by one, from a piece we'll call the "Sloane Report" (a somewhat doctored version of a report once written by an internal auditor to his boss), and
- to show how each disease disappears as its agents are eliminated.

Beginning with Chapter 5, almost every chapter will end with a group of sentences for you to practice on; each–except that I'll have changed some names–will have been taken word for word from a real-life report. But you can practice best on your own reports. So I suggest you now pull one out of your files–one totaling, say, five hundred to a thousand words–and after each chapter you check it, too, for the agent or agents you'll just have been introduced to.

But you must always wait till a report's "finished" before you try to "cure" it; while you're *writing* it, you must just *get the words on paper, however they occur to you first.* The reason: If you try to cure it while you're writing it, you may never *get* it written. (More on this in Chapter 32.)

To understand some agents you'll have to understand some grammatical terms and concepts, and if you're like most adults you'll need to have most of these redefined. Therefore I'll define each that I use–some when I discuss the agents they relate to, the others in the last chapter, called "Grammatical Glossary," which I urge you to refer to whenever you need to.

I'll assume throughout that you write as most do, and for the same reasons.

PART 2 – THE BACKGROUND

Chapter 2

WHY YOU WRITE AS YOU DO, THE FIRST STEPS TOWARD IMPROVING, AND ABOUT GRAMMAR

You know perfectly well that the one good reason for writing a report is to deliver a message–to "communicate."

Yet the chief reason your reports communicate so badly is that you consistently choose and arrange your words *not* chiefly to communicate, but rather

(1) to impress, and
(2) to conform.

And this for an equally simple reason: You've been trained to.

The first to so train you were your schoolteachers.

No, they never *told* you to write to impress and conform. They didn't even realize they wanted you to. Rather they believed they were trying to teach you to *communicate*–or, as your English-comp teachers probably put it, to "express yourself"–and that the better you communicated in any report, the higher they graded it.

But from fifth grade through graduate school, in English-comp, science, social-science and even phys-ed courses, with few exceptions at most and quite possibly with none, if ever you just told a story clearly, simply and concisely they thought you'd communicated badly, and discouraged you with a C or C- from doing it again. Your A's and B's, on the other hand, you got for the reports in which you most impressively

(1) avoided "grammatical errors,"
(2) displayed your "vocabulary,"
(3) avoided short, simple sentences, and combined your compound and complex sentences into massive paragraphs,
(4) poured out words, and
(5) proved you could organize your material as they had taught you to: into three-headed monsters–the heads called "introduction," "main body" and "conclusions"–in *any* of whose beards you could conceal the main point or points of any story.

Your English teachers stressed all five about equally; your others, chiefly the last two.

So it's chiefly because you were a *good* student that you still, today,

(1) consistently choose a "correct" word or construction–that is, one some teacher once *said* was "correct"–over the one that would tell your story best;

(2) load your reports with countless indefensible fancy words, including even many inaccurate ones;
(3) average far too many ideas per sentence, and too many sentences per paragraph;
(4) tell every story in *far* too many words, and
(5) so organize that a reader can never guess in advance where he'll find the key points in your message; and sometimes never does find them; and sometimes, when he finds them, doesn't recognize them; and sometimes must waste precious time reading all the way through a report that, had it been organized properly, he'd have stopped reading after the first paragraph.

Since you left school, your trainers have been your seniors in your business or profession, and especially those you've had to write *through*, whom we'll call your "middlemen." (Your boss, for example.) They, too, have continually *told* you you need to write to communicate. But actually they've reinforced you in the habits and attitudes you developed in school, and persuaded you also that you must always strive also to "sound professional": to so write that no one can distinguish your copy from anyone else's in your field.

Partly, of course, they've been able to do this just by example. But mostly they've done it by the way they've "edited" you, and especially by the fact that any time one of your reports has sounded *really* "unprofessional," they haven't even bothered to edit it, but have just bounced it back.

Which is why, today, you do always strive to "sound professional"—to write as you think people in your field are "supposed" to.

So as Step 1 toward writing better you must understand that it isn't your fault—chiefly—that you write badly now. Your only sin—almost—has been not to realize what others were doing to you.

Step 2 must be to resolve to rise above your past training and start to really write to communicate.

Now clearly, however earnestly you want to communicate, you won't be able to till your middlemen let you. So you'll need to persuade them *to* let you. And every middleman is unique, and no one can tell you just how to handle yours.

But if you're just reasonably lucky, your middlemen will not be impervious to reason; if they weren't intelligent, they could hardly have risen to be middlemen. Their trouble is just that they've been victimized by their own teachers and middlemen; if you can just find a tactful way to show them this, and persuade them to look at the situation through their own eyes, you can be confident they'll at last see it as it really is.

Your *big* fight will be with yourself. However determined you think you are to break free of the old habits and attitudes, you'll find they cling mighty tenaciously. You'll find all sorts of excuses, for example, for not splitting infinitives, or changing "obtain" to "get."

But you can win it. And you'll give yourself an edge if you memorize the following definition, and make yourself really believe it, and try hereafter to look at every word you write in its light alone:

> **A writer's only proper objective is just to so choose and arrange his words that his readers can most clearly and easily understand his message, and are most likely, as a result of reading it, to do what he wants them to.**

Despite what some say, you *won't* achieve that objective if you

- write *only* short, simple sentences;
- use *only* short, common words;
- always provide absolutely the fewest words possible, and/or
- "forget about grammar."

I'll elaborate later on the first three. As to the last:

First let's define grammar–and if your teachers defined it much differently they just proved they didn't understand it: It's the rules and conventions governing word forms and relationships that have developed in any language so its users *can convey and receive messages, clearly and confidently, through permutations and combinations of words* instead of individual words alone. For example, I can expect you to understand

"John loves Mary" only because we've both accepted subject-verb-object as the normal word order in English, and

"The boy jumped" only because we've agreed that "-ed," added to most verbs, will show the action is past.

So grammar is important. When you violate a grammatical rule–a *real* grammatical rule–your reader must at least expend extra energy to understand you, and at worst *won't* understand you.

But it's important only as a tool, a means to an end–only because, when and to the extent that it *helps someone communicate*. In and of itself, it's no more important than a saw, chisel, hammer, any other tool.

So as part of recovering from your past training you must stop valuing it for its own sake alone.

Further, much of what you now regard as grammar isn't grammar at all, but just a lot of nonsense that some schoolteachers–and some of their victims–*call* grammar. And this part, unhappily, includes most of the "rules" you now continually sacrifice communication to–for example, those that forbid you to split infinitives or end sentences with prepositions.

Now anyone can distinguish between a real grammatical rule and a mere schoolmarms' whim; the only reason you haven't is that you haven't realized you could, and so haven't tried. The criterion is so clearly sound that I can't believe even any schoolmarm will seriously challenge it: Since the whole purpose of grammar is to promote communication, a real grammatical rule is just one that *promotes communication.* For example, the one that says a participle at the beginning of a sentence must modify the subject of its sentence (which you'll see violated, quite typically, in Sloane): Without it we could only *guess what the message was.*

On the other hand, the one that "forbids" split infinitives can *never* help anyone communicate; it can only get in the way. Far from rising to meet a communicative need, it's been decreed; and not by communicators, but by dilettanti: by people who regard writing–at least chiefly–as just an intellectual pastime, which, they apparently feel, isn't quite tough enough till you've complicated its practice with a few arbitrary thou-shall-nots.

Actually, I hope you'll pay more attention, rather than less, to real grammar.

The mere schoolmarms' whims, on the other hand, you must totally disregard.

Now you can expect that your middlemen, till you've enlightened them, will notice your violations of the alleged rules, and "correct" them, and maybe even point them out to you.

But *readers,* except a tiny minority–even your middlemen, when they read to *get your messages,* rather than as critics and censors–just want to be communicated to. And when the result of your violating an alleged rule is that your message comes through more clearly and easily, your typical reader won't even realize you *have* violated it–but will like your report better because you have.

Chapter 3

YOUR MOST IMPORTANT WRITING TOOL, AND THE ONE FACTOR THAT TAKES PRECEDENCE OVER IT

However thoroughly you may understand the principles of informative writing, and however skillfully you may learn to use the techniques, your *most* important writing tool will always be your *judgment*.

And for your judgment to serve you best, you must always apply it in the light of the "four W's": the terribly important considerations, in any report, of

WHO
writes WHAT
to WHOM
and WHY

That is: However theoretically right a word or construction may be, you must *not* use it if, or when,

(1) you're personally uncomfortable with it;
(2) something special about your particular story or context calls for some alternative;
(3) you've good reason to not use it to your particular reader, or
(4) some alternative seems likely to better promote your *purpose.*

(3) and (4) apply most often, (3) often in combination with (2) and/or (4).

For example, (3) might govern your decision about splitting a particular infinitive. You've a perfect right to split it, and let's say your construction will clearly be smoother if you do. But if you happen to know your reader is one of the few you *would* disturb by splitting it, you'd better not.

(4) is especially likely to justify your including something that—except for the fact that readers aren't pure thinking machines—is really irrelevant. For example, suppose you're writing to persuade someone that your company should automate a certain operation. If the move offers

- only one advantage—it would save $25,000 a year—but
- no disadvantages,

nothing else is really relevant, so you should theoretically provide these two facts—documented, of course, to whatever extent they need to be—and nothing else. But since readers are just people, you may have reason to believe yours will be more likely to decide favorably if you tell him also—for example—how some competitor has solved a similar problem; and if you have, you should.

I've never been able to satisfactorily illustrate (2) except in face-to-face conversation with particular writers about their own reports, so I'll not try here. But I'm sure that if you just look, you'll begin quickly to find spots in your reports where it applies.

I'll be able to illustrate (1) several times in relation to the Sloane Report.

The One Factor That Takes Precedence Over Your Judgment

This is your "ground rules": the thou-shalts and thou-shalt-nots imposed on you in any situation by whoever controls the situation, however much or little he knows about writing. Yours probably seriously hinder you from communicating.

Yet I don't recommend you mount an all-out crusade against them. They're usually best attacked from the outside, by people like me.

On the other hand, if your situation is like most you can get *some* repealed quite easily, and I think you should be willing to invest a *little* effort, from time to time, in trying to.

And finally: Before you obey a ground rule you owe it to yourself and your readers to make reasonably sure it *really exists*—and I think you'll find you've been obeying *many* that don't. For example, the letter of the type that, going out of your office, "must" begin "Thank you for bringing this matter to our attention": Maybe the only reason it always does is that no one's ever *tried* to start it differently.

But whenever you find one really exists, and you can't easily get it repealed, and whoever imposed it does control the situation:

Do the best you can within the limits it imposes on you . . .

But obey it!

Otherwise you risk getting your head chopped off. And your responsibility to your readers doesn't go *that* far.

PART 3 – ELABORATION OF THE LEAD

Subsection 1 - THE DISEASE OF WORDINESS

Chapter 4

GENERAL

I believe wordiness is by far the most serious of the writing diseases.

One reason is that most of us are *so* wordy. Of a hundred reports picked at random, probably

- ninety to ninety-five will be 35% to 100% longer than they should have been–that is, their authors will have used 135 to 200 words to convey every hundred words' worth of relevant, significant meaning;
- at least half the others will be *more* than 100% too long;
- the average will be about 60% too long.

But also, every agent of wordiness is also an agent of other diseases; and *every* other disease–including, I'm convinced, even any that haven't been discovered yet–at least includes among its agents some that are also agents of wordiness. So when you've cured yourself of wordiness you've largely cured yourself of every writing disease.

But in trying to cure wordiness, you must distinguish between conciseness, which is good, and brevity, which–at least as I'd like us to define it–is not. A concise report contains all the words it needs to deliver its message smoothly and easily, but few *superfluous* words. A "brief" one, on the other hand,

(1) contains too *few* words–that is, doesn't contain some that would have made it *easier* to read and understand–and/or

(2) doesn't convey all the *facts and ideas* it should.

(In Case 1, it suffers from the disease of terseness; in Case 2, from arrogation.)

So a long report may be beautifully concise, a short one terribly wordy. For example, this, a complete report out of a New York company:

> It would be appreciated if you would contact the undersigned by telephone at your earliest convenience.

Only sixteen words–but 78% too long. Because the message would have been conveyed *better* in nine:

> Will you please phone me when you conveniently can?

On the other hand, just "Phone me" would have been terribly terse, and "Phone me when you can" not much better. Not because a two-word report is necessarily too short–in fact, just "Yes" or "No" might be a perfect report–but because in this case every word of the nine would have *individually promoted the likelihood that the reader would do as the writer wanted him to, and as happily as possible.*

The thirty-nine agents on the next page account for every possible superfluous word in English. The ranking is of course my own, and totally subjective, so anyone may disagree with it; and it's in terms of the "average" writer rather than any one in particular. But the top twenty-three appear on page after page of virtually everyone's writing, and it's a rare five hundred words that don't contain examples of at least twenty-five or -six of the top twenty-nine.

On the other hand, 30 through 39 appear maybe once each every ten thousand words, maybe once every fifty thousand. (So you may find *none* of them in your thousand-word sample.) In fact, I've really just numbered these, rather than ranked them; and only so that as we go through Sloane—and you go through your copy—you can mark each correction with the agent's number instead of its name.

But while all thirty-nine *are* agents of wordiness, at least over all, for 1 through 29 the ranking reflects *total* importance—importance in relation to *all* diseases—rather than merely how many superfluous words each produces. For example, the one we'll rank first isn't even among the top seven in relation to wordiness, and 4 isn't among the top dozen. In fact, maybe half a dozen of the thirty-nine sometimes even "save" words—in which case you must still eliminate them.

The thirty-nine fall into eight families, and we'll attack them by family so far as we conveniently can. But we'll shuttle around among families as we've reason to.

THE AGENTS OF WORDINESS

SLOANE REPORT - Stage 1

September 9, 1957

To : H. B. Dawson

From : N. B. Sloane

Subject : Audit of Payroll Deduction Funds, Exville Plant

The audit last week of the records of those employees at the
Exville plant who have deductions for U. S. Savings Bonds withheld from
their wages or salaries indicated that the account in which these funds
are held at the First National Bank-- the account R. J. Wright, Cashier--
5 was in balance with the individual account cards of the employees' deductions. However, there has been a mishandling of the funds which represents
what might be considered collusion between Mr. R. W. Smith, the plant
manager, and the cashier, although both of them advise that, while the
procedure in which they have been engaging is admittedly not a very
10 common one, each of them fails to see how his own actions in the matter
can be considered in any way improper or otherwise deserving of censure
Smith has authorized payroll deductions for savings bonds since July 1,
1950, at which time Miss Platt informed the writer that it was decided
by this company to undertake a concentrated buy-savings-bonds campaign
15 for the purpose of convincing all of our employees to sign up to purchase
bonds under the payroll deduction plan. Upon examination of Mr. Smith's
deduction card it was indicated that although deductions from Smith's
pay check have continued to be made since that time, Mr. Smith has not
purchased any bonds. Smith is on a bimonthly payroll that is made up
20 here at the main office. As you know, the total of all of the deductions
on every payroll is forwarded to the cashier on every payday in order to
be deposited by him in this account. It then becomes the duty of the
cashier to purchase a bond for any individual employee whenever the
individual accounts indicate that an employee has accrued a sufficient
25 purchase price for one. As of the present time the plan is being taken
advantage of by nearly 1,000 of our employees, 997 to be exact, therefore
it has clearly achieved a considerable degree of success.

As was mentioned in the above paragraph, however, Smith has
never purchased any bonds. The bimonthly payroll is written very early
30 in the payroll period, and as soon as this payroll is written the bond

deductions which are listed on it are posted to every individual employee's account. Therefore, very early in the month in each payroll period,
Smith's bond deduction card has been credited with his regular $100
deduction. However, upon investigation of his individual deduction card
35 it was ascertained that Smith has consistently requested of the cashier
that the latter grant a refund to him of this $100 before the actual
date of the payday for that period, the cashier always acceding to the
request. This means that whenever the cashier has done this there was
not really any money in the bank for Mr. Smith's refund and therefore
40 Smith, the plant manager, was actually obtaining advances in every single
payroll period. The cashier, of course, would not have been able to
accede to the request if it had not been for the presence in the account
R. J. Wright, Cashier, of funds that had been deducted on earlier payrolls from the pay of the other employees.

45 Feeling that this is not a proper procedure, it has been
brought to the attention of the plant manager and also to the attention
of the cashier. Mr. Wright, the cashier, says that he does not consider
himself to have done anything for which anyone can justifiably censure
him inasmuch as he was merely acting pursuant to the instructions to
50 give Mr. Smith the refund that he has regularly received from the plant
manager. Mr. Smith says that he does not feel that there have been any
violations of the company's rules and/or policies and for this reason
I have apprised him that I would include it in my audit report. Mr.
Wright will be 65 years of age on the 12th of October of this year and
55 has been in the employ of this company since shortly after the First
World War. In addition there is the further complication that the records indicate that Mr. J. J. Blake, the assistant plant manager, who
was formerly at our Chicago, Ill., plant, while he has not utilized this
procedure as frequently as Smith, on one or two occassions during the
60 past several months, when for some reason or another he has been financially embarassed, he has in effect likewise provided himself with a
payroll advance through the same means. Mr. Blake, too, is on the
bimonthly payroll that is made up here at the main office, whereas all
of the other employees who have bond deductions withheld from their pay
65 are on a weekly payroll that is made at the plant. There is not much
doubt in my mind that you will agree with the two following conclusions:

1. That the actions of the above named personnel in this matter have not been within the intended results desired to be achieved by the ''Buy U. S. Savings Bonds'' campaign, and that

70 2. There is a loophole here by which it will be equally possible for any additional plant manager who might be so minded to perhaps also follow the Smith procedure, thereby also obtaining an improper advance on his salary prior to the day on which it actually becomes due.

Chapter 5

THE WRONG-WORD-ORDER FAMILY

What characterizes these five agents is that each produces a construction you can eliminate one or two words from by just rearranging the other words.

30. Failure to Use Indirect Objects

Some verbs–"give," "bring," "send," "tell" and the like–may simultaneously take direct and indirect objects. But to be an indirect object, a word must come *right* after its verb; if it doesn't, it must instead be the object of a preposition–usually "to"–which you must insert to take care of it.

So you can sometimes eliminate a preposition just by so relocating a potential indirect object that it does immediately follow its verb:

He sent	a telegram	to	the president.
He sent	the president		a telegram.
He gave	a lecture	to	the class.
He gave	the class		a lecture.
He bought	a present	for	his wife.
He bought	his wife		a present.

Or in Sloane (Line 36):

. . . grant	a refund	to	him . . .
. . . grant	him		a refund . . .

But the shorter way is better only *when* it is, and you mustn't eliminate the preposition *unless* it is. For example, you surely prefer the left-side versions of:

The timekeepers give the cards directly *to* the Control Clerk, who files them.	The timekeepers directly give the Control Clerk, who files them, the cards.
List the tube data on Form N-400 and send it *to* the Production Supervisor immediately.	List the tube data on Form N-400 and send the Production Supervisor it immediately.
The sewing and knitting co-op sells products *to* Sears-Roebuck as well as local stores.	The sewing and knitting co-op sells Sears-Roebuck as well as local stores products.

31. "If" First

You can eliminate "if" from either of two kinds of clauses by just beginning the clause with its verb, or, if the verb is in two words, with its "auxiliary" part:

- clauses expressing conditions contrary to fact. (When such a clause contains an auxiliary verb, it's always "had" if the clause is past-tense, "were" if it's present or "future.")

If I *had been* there [says I wasn't; this is what makes it contrary to fact], I'd have kept him from jumping.	*Had* I *been* there, I'd have kept him from jumping.
If I *were* to do it [says—or at least pretends to—that I won't] I'd do it differently.	*Were* I to do it, I'd do it differently.
If mosquitoes *were eating* me [says they aren't], I'd go indoors.	*Were* mosquitoes *eating* me, I'd go indoors.

- a clause containing the auxiliary verb "should":

If you *should decide* to go ahead with this project . .	*Should* you *decide* to go ahead with this project . . .

But first: This agent does *not* apply to any *other* kind of "if" clause—for example, it doesn't to

If I'm pale [I may or may not be], it's because I'm ill.

I asked him if he was going [he may or may not have been].

(Incidentally, the verb after "if" should generally be subjunctive only if the condition *is* contrary to fact. "If he were going, he didn't tell me," and "I asked him if he were going," are pretentious vulgarisms—not merely pompous and obtrusive, but *wrong!*)

And while you *may* eliminate the "if" from *any* contrary-to-fact clause, I urge that you *usually* do only when the verb is

past-tense (had I been there, I'd have kept him from jumping),
"future"-tense (were I to do it, I'd do it differently), or
passive-voice (were I being eaten by mosquitoes, I'd go indoors).

In the present tense, you may prefer either way when your verb is "were," or, though not passive, begins with "were":

If I were king, you'd be queen.	Were I king, you'd be queen.
If mosquitoes were eating me, I'd go indoors.	Were mosquitoes eating me, I'd go indoors.

The complication here is that, except in the passive, a present-tense "if"-

less construction—even one that begins with "were"—has an unfortunate "literary" sound, so some readers may suspect you provided it not chiefly to save them a word, but to show off. So you'd better provide it only very selectively.

And you'd better *never* eliminate the "if"—at least during this century—from a present-tense clause that would then begin with any *other* verb. A sentence like

Ruled I this country, you'd be in jail.

is perfectly "correct," and may some day jar no one—but would jar almost any reader today.

But Sloane's contrary-to-fact construction (Line 42) involves a past-tense verb:

. . . *if* it *had* not *been* for the presence . . .	. . . *had* it not *been* for the presence . . .

He gives us no examples of the other type.

32. Name First

Sometimes when a title could just as well—or better—precede a name, we let the name come first, and then sometimes an extra "a," "an" or "the"—plus, sometimes, a word like "Mr." or "Dr."—results. For example, Sloane should have said:

7-8: . . . collusion between Plant Manager R.W. Smith and the cashier . . .

56-58: . . . the records indicate that Assistant Plant Manager J. J. Blake, who was formerly . . .

And more important than the word reduction: The people in 7-8 are now clearly two. As Sloane listed them, they might have been three.

Sometimes this kind of change saves only a comma or two. But it's generally desirable even then, because the construction is typically a little *smoother* with the title first:

Ray Sawyer, Sales Manager, says these shoes are his top sellers.	Sales Manager Ray Sawyer says these shoes are his top sellers.

Sometimes you can treat as a title something that really isn't:

Arnold Palmer, the golf star	golf star Arnold Palmer
John Jones, a businessman	businessman John Jones

But sometimes, and especially when the title is rather long, it can't comfortably come first, and then don't force it. For example, you surely prefer the left-side versions of:

John Jones, the vice-president for advertising and sales promotion	Vice-President for Advertising and Sales Promotion John Jones.

Mary Smith, the four-time club champion and twice runner-up	Four-time club champion and twice runner-up Mary Smith

33. Preposition First

This reflects the schoolmarms' "rule" that every preposition must physically precede its object—or, as they usually put it, in such a way as to pull out from under it even the flimsy foundation they *can* rest it on when they say it "properly"—that you just "mustn't end a sentence with a preposition." Far from being merely whimsical, this "rule" reflects a profound *mis*understanding.

That is:

It's "based" on the fact that "preposition" comes from two Latin roots: "prae," meaning "before," and "positum," meaning "placed." Therefore, say the schoolmarms—when they say it "properly"—every preposition must be "placed before" its object.

Well, "prae" and "positum" do mean "before" and "placed." But the pre-Christian Roman who first put them together couldn't possibly have meant thereby to prescribe how one might or might not use this kind of word; he can have meant only to *describe its grammatical function*. And grammatically—provided only the construction it appears in makes any sense at all—every preposition *does* precede its object, regardless of which comes first physically . . . even when the object is "understood," and so doesn't appear at all. Even Latin prepositions didn't have to physically precede their objects; for example, "pax vobiscum" translates literally as "peace youwith." And if English prepositions had to, we'd have to give up all such compound words as "therein," "whereby," "hereafter."

So all you need worry about, in relation to a preposition, is whether you've so placed it and its object that your *message* comes through most clearly and easily. And when the object is a relative pronoun, the smooth, easy way may also be the short way, because with the preposition at the end, the pronoun can often be "understood."

Sloane three times sacrificed communication to this schoolmarmish notion of "correctness":

3-4:	the account	in which	these funds are held
	the account		these funds are held in
8-9:	the procedure	in which	they have been engaging
	the procedure		they have been engaging in
48-49:	anything	for which	anyone can justifiably censure him
	anything		anyone can justifiably censure him for

34. "The" First

This is really two distinct constructions, with nothing in common except that each begins with a "the" you can eliminate by rearranging the other words.

1. What you can identify as

1 2 3
the/ordinal number/thing

you can sometimes identity equally well as just

1 2
thing (generally with its first letter capitalized)/cardinal number.

For example:

the third line on the sixth page	Page 6, Line 3
the seventh round	Round 7
the twelfth chapter	Chapter 12

or in Sloane (55-56):

the First World War	World War I

Sometimes the "number" is a letter or letters:

the "C" Horizon	Horizon "C"
the A-K group	Group A-K

But don't change such constructions automatically or unthinkingly. For example, the right-side versions following also may sound normal some day, but they'd jar today:

This is the third time that I've warned you.	This is Time 3 that I've warned you.
John is the second boy from the right.	John is Boy 2 from the right.

2. You can identify a date as well in two words as in four.

For example (54):

the 12th of October	October 12

Sometimes something like "beginning" or "end" substitutes for the number:

the end of October	October 31
the end of the year	December 31
the beginning of the year	January 1

When you needn't name the month—for example, if you can say just "the 12th"—the "-th," "-st" "or "-d" after the number is fine. But I urge that you ditch it when you do need to name the month. It will rarely hurt—but can *never* do any *good.*

For Practice

Two possible "corrections" below are decidedly marginal, and one of them is only temporary. (You'll see all but two of these sentences again in relation to other agents.)

1. COR increases, if they had been passed, could well have been the springboard for other regions that would have resulted in further increases.
2. In essence, the summary indicated that the product was recommended for introduction in practically all of the markets in which the survey was conducted.
3. In summary, I recommend the following:
   1) We place a trial order for both plants with Stilley for 7/16" seven-ply laminated oak drawer stock and, subject to approval by all, that change authorization be put in for costing purposes . . .
4. In the first unit you'll listen to and work with Mr. Burger to build basic writing skills, analyze examples of how not to write and ask questions about your own writing problems.
5. It would be premature also because the market in which WA-1 will compete is changing rapidly and by 1971, the earliest commercial distribution can be achieved, significant changes could invalidate present expansion planning.
6. On Thursday, November 2, I met with Frank Giles, ACE packaging consultant, and Dave Knowles and Pym Wharton, both representing Resnick Paper Box.
7. Since subfreezing temperatures can damage most adhesives–and since carriers are not liable for frozen goods unless we can prove conclusively they were involved–from now on please allow sufficient lead time for suppliers to take proper precautions.
8. The Joplin code, unique numbers, would be satisfactory if equipment were not subject to movement between locations.
9. The program should be presented on the front page or on the second newsfront in a 6" x 9" space.
10. This reduction in quality would be of greater concern if the receivables were separated from the Arnold organization.
11. Without a proven superior product, our most likely potential customers are those with which Ajax now has, or could establish, favorable trade relations.

The Answers

The failures to use indirect objects were in 3 ("Stilley") and 7 ("suppliers"); the if's first in 1, 8 and 10 (the last two are the marginal ones); the name first in 6; the prepositions first in 2 ("in which"), 5 ("in which") and 11 ("with which"); the the's first in 4 ("the first unit") and 9 ("the front page").

1. [The*] COR increases, had they been passed, could well have been the springboard for other regions that would have resulted in further increases.
2. In essence, the summary indicated that the product was recommended for introduction in practically all of the markets the survey was conducted in.
3. In summary, I recommend the following:
   1) We give Stilley a trial order for both plants for 7/16" seven-ply laminated oak drawer stock and, subject to approval by all, that [a*] change authorization be put in for costing purposes . . .
4. In Unit 1 you'll listen to and work with Mr. Burger to build basic writing skills, analyze examples of how not to write and ask questions about your own writing problems.
5. It would be premature also because the market WA-1 will compete in is changing rapidly, and by 1971, the earliest [year*] commercial distribution can be achieved, significant changes could invalidate present expansion planning.
6. On Thursday, November 2, I met with ACE Packaging Consultant Frank Giles, and Dave Knowles and Pym Wharton, both representing Resnick Paper Box.
7. Since subfreezing temperatures can damage most adhesives—and since carriers are not liable for frozen goods unless we can prove conclusively they were involved—from now on please allow suppliers sufficient lead time to take proper precautions.
8. The Joplin code, unique numbers, would be satisfactory were equipment not subject to movement between locations.
9. The program should be presented on Page 1 or on the second newsfront in a 6" x 9" space.
10. This reduction in quality would be of greater concern were the receivables separated from the Arnold organization.
11. Without a proven superior product, our most likely potential customers are just† those Ajax now has, or could establish, favorable trade relations with.

---

*Inserted to relieve terseness (see Page 8).

†Inserted to eliminate arrogation.

Chapter 6

THE FIRST MISCELLANEOUS INEFFICIENCY

17. The Unnecessarily Difficult Verb

One can convey more messages, more precisely, in fewer syllables in English than in any other language, and one of the reasons is our wealth of verb forms. But we too often choose an impressive, conformist form—that is, an unnecessarily difficult one—over the one that would have communicated best. Sloane chose eleven such wrong forms in 889 words, and he's well within the "normal" range for this agent.

Obviously, we can also choose too simple a form—but we seldom do. Sloane didn't even once.

This agent appears in many forms, but especially often in the five I'll discuss below. It rarely hurts much in any one appearance—but for most writers its *total* effect is considerable.

The Unnecessarily Difficult "Contemporary" Tense

English offers options even within each tense. For example, within the present we have what I'd like us to call the

characteristic present: I enjoy April, he drinks too much, they eat pork;
actual present: I am enjoying April, he is drinking too much, they are eating pork;
intensive or emphatic present: I do enjoy April, he does drink too much, they do eat pork.

All are fine forms, and always the one to use is just whichever tells your story best.

But Sloane's actual present "is being taken," 25, and actual perfect "have been engaging," 9, *don't* tell his story best. Change them to "is taken," "have engaged."

Sloane didn't pointlessly use any intensive forms, but the authors of these sentences did:

Do you *have** reason to believe . . . ?	*Have* you reason to believe . . . ?
You *did send* this order, but . . .	You *sent* this order, but . . .

*Some would consider this a fourth type: the "interrogative" present. But all *we* need care about is that in this appearance it's pointlessly long and difficult.

Substitution of Other Tenses for the Simple Past

We especially often substitute the perfect tense—"have" or "has" plus a past participle, like "has done," "have created"—for the simple past.

To understand how the two differ, pretend that at 11:05 a.m. today I bought a hat, and at 2:05 p.m. I want to report that I did.

If I choose to identify when-I-bought-it as a *moment*, I must use the past tense:

I bought a hat at 11:05 a.m. today.
I bought a hat three hours ago.

But if I choose to say only that I bought it within a *period*, my tense depends on *how I identify* the period. If I so identify it that it

- includes the present, I must use the perfect:

I have bought a hat today,
I have bought a hat since I saw you.

- doesn't include the present, I must use the past:

I bought a hat this morning.
I bought a hat before lunch.

Now you *should* use the perfect when you want to say, in effect, "This is where we are now," or stress that an action, though past, has present relevance; so "has achieved," 27, and "has requested," 35, are good perfects. And the change to the past is usually so easy, and the "saving" so obvious, that from now on you'll need to guard against *over*eliminating the perfect.

But till now, I'm convinced, you've used it virtually every time you should have, and often besides when you shouldn't. Change "has done," 38, to "did"; "has been," 60, to "was."

(When I specify neither the moment at *nor* the period during which something happened, I imply that you need to know only that it *has* happened, some time since time began. And since the period "some time since time began" includes the present, I must use the perfect; this explains—for example—"has been," 6.

(But you *may* identify your period as past, and thereby justify past-tense verbs, *before* you tell what happened—for example, by titling a report "May Activities" and dating it June 1.)

Much less often we pointlessly substitute the imperfect—"was" or "were" plus a present participle, like "was doing," "were eating"—for the past. Sloane *sort* of did this in 40 and 49; as first steps change "was obtaining" to "obtained," "was acting" to "acted."

But both these actions relate so importantly to the present that they really call for the perfect. So let's go to the perfect: "has obtained," "has acted."

Still less often we pointlessly substitute a past perfect—"had" plus a past participle, like "had known," "had been"—for a past. Sloane doesn't illustrate this; "had been deducted," 43, is maybe debatable, but I'd defend it. (I'll explain the proper use of this tense in the Glossary.) But the author of this sentence did:

> It was in the light of this experience that Prendigast *had made* the observation quoted above.

Typically, the past perfect there was grammatically correct—but so would the past have been. And the past would have told the story at least as well.

Substitution of Other Tenses for the Present

We should look for excuses to use present-tense verbs; besides being our simplest, they're generally also our most interesting, forceful and—where we can use them at all—relevant. Yet we routinely substitute three other tenses for them.

THE PERFECT: You may use this to report not only a past action, but also one that's still going on. And you *should* use it, in the latter case, when the point is that it *has been* going on. For example, the author of this sentence was annoyed, and wanted his readers to know it; a major project was stalled because they couldn't agree on one detail:

> The decision we *have been trying* to reach involves only a few hundred dollars.

But "has been credited," 33, and "have not been," 68, can't be so justified. Substitute "is credited," "are not."

THE PAST: This substitution rarely costs words, but it's a major agent of *weakness*.

For example, "indicated," 3. Surely Sloane was *not* trying to suggest here that the audit, gee whiz, was just ancient history anyway, so if it ever turned out that he'd goofed, maybe Dawson wouldn't beat him so hard. But it sounds as if this *might* have been his purpose, whereas "indicates"—at least in contrast—sounds fearless, authoritative and intended above all else to communicate. And last week's audit—or scientific experiment—*can* still indicate today, just as Walter Johnson's 416 victories still *show* what a great pitcher he was, the 1948 election results still *prove* pollsters can err, and Shakespeare still *says* "The quality of mercy is not strained."

And unless he had a special reason not to—which I'd bet he didn't—Sloane, in 5, should have said the account "is" in balance, not "was." True, several days had passed since he'd audited it. But

- it *almost* surely was, and
- anyway, the present wouldn't really have guaranteed it any more than the past did. It would merely have said Sloane had no reason to believe it *wasn't*, and wasn't afraid to say so.

THE FUTURE: This is the most common tense substitution, in all kinds of reports. For example: From an engineer's report:

Cold air, introduced at a low level, *will stratify* near the floor.

From a letter from an automobile-company junior executive to one of his company's distributors:

We *will agree* that a customer should not be made to suffer for an error in billing procedure.

And in Sloane, 70:

. . . by which it *will be* equally possible . . .

Change "will be" to "is."

Pointless Use of Infinitive Clauses

A verb's infinitives are various of its forms that begin with "to": "to eat," "to be eating," "to have been eaten" and so forth. And you should virtually *never* eliminate one unless you can replace it with *a predicate verb in the indicative mood*: "eats," "is eating," "was eaten" or the like.

But when you can *so* replace one you virtually always should: not only to save a word, but also–and more importantly–to *simplify* your construction. (More on this in the section on hypercomplexity.)

In 47-48, make Sloane read:

. . . does not consider *he has done* anything . . .

The Practice of Pretending to Pretend

When an airline stewardess says "We would like to thank you for flying with us," she isn't really pretending she can't; she's just pretending to pretend. Because of course she can, and she knows you know it, and knows that you know that *she* knows it.

We often thus inject extra verbs and "auxiliary" verbs–like "can," "could," "may," "might"–that we must hope our readers will disregard, because if they don't they'll misunderstand us.

In 71, for example, surely Sloane meant "*is* so minded."

* * *

Once in a great while shifting to a simpler verb *costs* a word. The cost is typically well worth while; I think *each* change improves this sentence:

But it *would be* [conditional] unfortunate *were* this *done* [subjunctive] at the expense of ongoing projects the FWCC has an interest in.	But it *will be* [simple future] unfortunate *if* this *is done* [indicative] at the expense of ongoing projects the FWCC has an interest in.

For Practice

Obviously, you could more easily spot the unnecessarily difficult verbs below if you could see the reports they appeared in—and still more easily if you could consult with their authors. Still:

1. Assuming average delivery distances are 300 miles longer from one plant compared to two, the freight cost disadvantage would be .7-.8c/bd. ft., which does not offset the f.o.b. plant price advantage.
2. Although this policy may benefit the Arnold operation, it would tend to lessen the quality of the receivables portfolio.
3. Because of differences in health requirements, the "Tridil" formulation as it is known in the U.S. has been altered somewhat to comply with foreign regulations.
4. During this period they have a cash shortage problem and have obtained bank loans in past years to pay supplier invoices.
5. I wish to make the additional recommendation that a capital expenditure be considered for a high-pressure corrosion tester on the Du Pont design.
6. If we require all subsidiaries to comply with the same fiscal year, the parent company should prepare to provide extra help.
7. In accord with our telephone conversation of November 10, I am sending you herewith copies of reports summarizing the results of consumer panel tests initially designed to assess the merits of an experimental bed pillow being developed in Pioneering Research.
8. It should be noted that this cost is in addition to the cost of insurance, since this has been accounted for in the calculation of the net present values.
9. Regardless of the "EXCELLENT" rating, there were two (2) areas which need immediate attention.
10. The circumstances in question appeared to have been correctly managed at first but deteriorated somewhere in process.
11. There are instances in which an established supplier will receive reorders without rebid or testing of prices from other sources.
12. These samples were coded, and special instructions were given to the panel about how the taste tests were to be conducted.
13. This occurence [*sic*—and let's *not* correct it] is very unusual as many of the complaints came from customers who have claimed to be users of this product for twenty years or more.
14. Without a proven superior product, our most likely potential customers are just those Ajax now has, or could establish, favorable trade relations with.

The Answers

1. would be.
2. would tend to lessen.
3. has been altered.
4. have obtained.
5. wish to make.
6. should prepare to divide.
7. am sending.
8. has been accounted (for).
9. were.
10. appeared.
11. will receive.
12. were to be conducted.
13. have claimed. ["To be users" represents something more hurtful than just an unnecessarily difficult verb; we'll fix it later.]
14. could establish.

The sentences with this agent eliminated:

1. Assuming average delivery distances are 300 miles longer from one plant compared to two, the freight cost disadvantage *is* .7-.8c/bd. ft., which does not offset the f.o.b. plant price advantage.
2. Although this policy may benefit the Arnold operation, it *lessens* the quality of the receivables portfolio.
3. Because of differences in health requirements, the "Tridil" formulation as it is known in the U.S. *is altered* somewhat to comply with foreign regulations.
4. During this period they have a cash shortage problem and *obtained* bank loans in past years to pay supplier invoices.
5. I *make* the additional recommendation that a capital expenditure be considered for a high-pressure corrosion tester on the Du Pont design.
6. If we require all subsidiaries to comply with the same fiscal year, the parent company *should provide* extra help.

7. In accord with our telephone conversation of November 10, I *send* you herewith copies of reports summarizing the results of consumer panel tests initially designed to assess the merits of an experimental bed pillow being developed in Pioneering Research. [Yes, "send you herewith" sounds odd–but you'll see later that the change *is* in the right *direction.*]
8. It should be noted that this cost is in addition to the cost of insurance, since this *is accounted* for in the calculation of the net present values.
9. Regardless of the "EXCELLENT" rating, there *are* two (2) areas which need immediate attention.
10. The circumstances in question *appear* to have been correctly managed at first, but the handling* deteriorated somewhere in process.
11. There are instances in which an established supplier *receives* reorders without rebid or testing of prices from other sources.
12. These samples were coded, and special instructions were given to the panel about how the taste tests *should be conducted.*
13. This occurence is very unusual as many of the complaints came from customers who *claimed* to be users of this product for twenty years or more.
14. Without a proven superior product, our most likely potential customers are just those Ajax now has, or *can establish,* favorable trade relations with.

*Inserted to make the sentence say what the author meant.

Chapter 7

THE WRONG-POINT-OF-VIEW FAMILY AND ONE OF ITS MEMBERS

A wrong-point-of-view construction is one that, even if it conveys its message "accurately"—and it may not—so conveys it that its *relevance and significance* come through less clearly than they should.

The major criterion in relation to this family is *not* mere number of words. For example, "Jones got $1,000 from Smith" is a word longer than "Smith gave Jones $1,000"—but probably, nevertheless, the *right* way to report the transaction in a report chiefly about *Jones.*

But we far more often take a wrong longer way than a wrong shorter one, and often take the longer when two ways differ, effectively, only in length. (As, for example, if we were reporting the Smith-Jones transaction in a report chiefly about Robinson.) So over all, all members of this family are agents of wordiness.

26. The Name Substitute

In most of its appearances this consists simply of pointlessly—or for insufficient reason—substituting a longer, more obtrusive "name substitute" for a shorter, less obtrusive name, of either a person or a thing.

The most common insufficient reason is just to avoid repeating a sound.

Now repetition of obtrusive sounds—except where, for some special reason, it achieves a *desirable* effect—is an important factor in the disease of monotony. And names are unquestionably obtrusive.

But:

- You can almost always find a *good* way to avoid it.
- When you can't, a mere "elegant variation" inevitably injects diseases *worse* than the one it mitigates: almost always artificiality, usually pretentiousness, often wordiness, and always at least a *little* ambiguity. (If you call something "the machine" in one sentence, "the equipment" in the next and "the apparatus" in the next, a reader may wonder how many things you're talking about.)

Sloane, I think, gives us thirteen name substitutes. This is extraordinary; you probably won't find half as many in 888 words of your own. (Though I'm sure you'll find enough to see why this agent's "important.") For example: Since in each case he was talking about a person, not a job, "the cashier" and "the plant manager" are name substitutes for "Wright" and "Smith" in

8, 35, 37, 38, 41, 46, 47 and 50-51.

(And now we can further improve 7-8 by transposing the names: ". . . collusion between Wright and Plant Manager R. W. Smith.")

On the other hand, "the cashier" represents the *right* point of view in 21 and 22. Here Sloane was describing a *procedure*, and the name of the man who just happened to be the current Exville cashier would have been irrelevant and distracting.

"The latter," 36, is also name-substitute for "Wright." True, "Wright" obtrudes unpleasantly in "has consistently requested Wright that Wright grant him." But by eliminating the name substitutes we begin to cure the sentence of artificiality and pretentiousness as well as wordiness, and we'll later find a *good* way to eliminate the monotony.

"This year," 54, is name-substitute for "1957." And "shortly after World War I," 55-56, is for some year, and surely Sloane knew which. Let's guess 1919 and change it.

Since we don't know whom Sloane worked for or his ground rules, we can't be quite sure about "this company," 14 and 55. It's *not* name-substitute if his shortest, simplest alternative was longer and/or *more* obtrusive—say Ajax-Consolidated Glazed Doughnut, Dill Pickle & Horseradish Manufacturing Company, Inc.

But I think this is so unlikely that I'd like us to pretend we know whom he worked for: that it *was* Ajax-Consolidated Glazed Doughnut, Dill Pickle & Horseradish Manufacturing Company, Inc. Because if it was, wouldn't you bet he could have called it—at least in this internal report—just "Ajax"?

Substitute "Ajax" both times.

In its less common form, this agent represents refusal to repeat words other than names:

We are hard put to it to produce such evidence and may reply that such a demand is unreasonable as the results are intangible. Yet this is not entirely so unless one classifies such things as recognition by foreign governments, the formation of lasting friendships and maintenance of lively correspondence *under this heading.*	We are hard put to it to produce such evidence and may reply that such a demand is unreasonable as the results are intangible. Yet this is not entirely so unless one classifies such things as recognition by foreign governments, the formation of lasting friendships and maintenance of lively correspondence *as intangible.*

The picture of the Plains Indian riding a horse is so deeply implanted in most people's minds that most can hardly picture these people walking. But the fact is that *these animals* were unknown on this continent until the Spaniards brought them here.

The picture of the Plains Indian riding a horse is so deeply implanted in most people's minds that most can hardly picture these people walking. But the fact is that *horses* were unknown on this continent until the Spaniards brought them here.

For Practice

You can't know, in one case below, *what* name was substituted for. No matter; just tab the substitute.

1. If we require all subsidiaries to comply with the same fiscal year, the parent company should provide extra help.
2. In recent months about fifty to seventy-five complaints concerning the extreme bitter taste in TEJAVA were reported to the Quality Control Laboratory. This occurence is very unusual as many of the complaints came from customers who claimed to be users of this product for twenty years or more.
3. RECOMMENDATIONS: . . .
   2. Continue co-operation at exposure levels up to $20M-$50M with strict prompt payment.
   3. Continue efforts to get support, making this mandatory when yarn availability situation eases or exposure levels increase above limits set in No. 2
4. The creditors were advised by Davis that Charles had borrowed $536,000 from the corporation over a period of 33 years and lost the money gambling . . . Davis and his client were then excused so the creditors could discuss the situation in private.
5. The problem is slightly more complex for WY TONIC Prenatal in Peru since this market has been supplied ex Passaic with WY TONIC Prenatal granulations containing cobalt and in the future no such granulations with cobalt can be shipped from the United States.
6. We need your 1968 scale requirements by October 19 so we can enter our purchase order for the Ohaus scale, which we must buy in a minimum quantity of 200 to get the present low cost. Because the equipment RSWs cannot practically store all 200 scales, we will ask the supplier to ship 100 when the order is received and 100 six months later.

The Answers

1. the parent company.
2. this product.
3. limits set in No. 2.
4. his client.
5. this market.
6. the supplier.

The sentences with this agent eliminated:

1. If we require all subsidiaries to comply with the same fiscal year, *Ajax* should provide extra help.
2. In recent months about fifty to seventy-five complaints concerning the extreme bitter taste in TEJAVA were reported to the Quality Control Laboratory. This occurence is very unusual as many of the complaints came from customers who claimed to be users of *TEJAVA* for twenty years or more.
3. RECOMMENDATIONS: . . .
   2. Continue co-operation at exposure levels up to $20M-50M with strict prompt payment.
   3. Continue efforts to get support, making this mandatory when yarn availability situation eases or exposure levels increase above *$20M-50M.*
4. The creditors were advised by Davis that Charles had borrowed $536,000 from the corporation over a period of 33 years and lost the money gambling . . . Davis and *Charles* were then excused so the creditors could discuss the situation in private.
5. The problem is slightly more complex for WY TONIC Prenatal in Peru since *Peru* has been supplied ex Passaic with WY TONIC Prenatal granulations containing cobalt and in the future no such granulations with cobalt can be shipped from the United States.
6. We need your 1968 scale requirements by October 19 so we can enter our purchase order for the Ohaus scale, which we must buy in a minimum quantity of 200 to get the present low cost. Because the equipment RSWs cannot practically store all 200 scales, we will ask *Ohaus* to ship 100 when the order is received and 100 six months later.

Chapter 8

THREE MORE MISCELLANEOUS INEFFICIENCIES

9. Failure to Use the (Best Possible) Second-Time Word or Phrase

A second-time word or phrase—in our private vocabulary—is one that means nothing or virtually nothing in a vacuum, but that in a "second-time spot" conveys clearly a meaning that had to be conveyed first—in either the same report or its context—by some more obtrusive word or phrase.

So, for example, every pronoun is a second-time word. For example, you've no idea who "he" is, in a vacuum. But it's perfectly clear in Line 49 of Sloane.

Other often useful second-time words include the

adjectives (as opposed to the pronouns) "this," "these," "that," "those";

adjectives "such" and "so";

adverbs "here," "there," "then";

article "the";

verb "do." (In a bridegroom's "I do," "do" means "take this woman for my lawful wedded wife.")

As to pronouns particularly, the "rule" that says they may refer only to preceding nouns—like the one that "forbids" you to end sentences with prepositions—derives strictly from the *name* of this part of speech. Disregard it; good writers—including many whom our teachers held up as examples—have disregarded it for centuries.

But whatever you intend *any* second-time expression to refer to, the reference *must be clear*, at least beyond a reasonable doubt. For example, the "it" in 53; I'm convinced I know now what it means, but for a long time I thought it meant something much different. So whatever it means, I've misunderstood it at least part of the time. (We'll change it later.)

But some second-time expression virtually *must* be best when

- you have to use *something*, and
- the reference *is* clear.

And while it doesn't in Sloane—being one of a few he's remarkably light on—this agent shows up in most reports three to four times per hundred words.

Despite which, it lengthens few reports more than about 3%, so it isn't a top agent of *wordiness*. (It often costs no words, and seldom—except in collaboration with some other agent—more than one or two at a time.) It ranks so high chiefly because it's a major agent of

artificiality and pretentiousness, because instead of a second-time word or phrase we're likely to use an artificial, and often pretentious, elegant variation, and

monotony, because

- the offensiveness of a repetition varies with the *obtrusiveness of the sound repeated*, and
- *any* proper second-time substitute—even "him" for "the dog," "her" for "the cat," "it" for "the table"—is *much* less obtrusive than its alternative.

So of these fixes, those that don't save words improve Sloane as unquestionably as those that do:

1-2:	the Exville	this
10:	the matter	it
13:	the writer	me
17:	Smith's	his
18:	Mr. Smith	he
19:	Smith	he
23-24:	whenever the (individual accounts indicate that) an employee	whose (individual account indicates that) he
30:	this payroll	it
35:	Smith	he
39:	Mr. Smith's	the
62:	Mr. Blake	he

The change in 1-2 is just for demonstration purposes. Later we'll reinsert "Exville" to replace three words.

"The matter," 10, and "the writer" were elegant variations of—*not* proper second-time substitutes for—"the procedure," 8-9, and "N. B. Sloane" in the "from" line. As to the first: Artificiality impedes communication much worse than monotony does, so Sloane should rather have repeated "the procedure" than just "varied" it—but clearly he needed to do neither. And as to "me": If you've been persuaded one should never use "I," "me," "my," I'll try later to change your mind. But Sloane does use them; note Line 53.

And 22-25 now says clearly that the people who got the bonds were those who'd saved the money—which Sloane surely meant, but didn't say.

Second-time *phrases*—we can regard a phrase as just any two or more words conveying a single idea—include such combinations as "do this," "do so," "this procedure," "like this." (Or "the latter" or "this company"

—when they're *less* obtrusive than what they replace.) Each is likely to include at least one standard second-time *word*. We miss far fewer chances to use these than we do to use second-time *words*; Sloane missed only two:

37-38:	acceding to the request	doing so
42:	accede to the request	do this

But while Sloane doesn't show it, failure to use a second-time *phrase* does sometimes cost a lot of words. For example, just "we do this" would have perfectly replaced the sixteen words italicized below:

To: All Engineers

In order for the laboratory to render more efficient service in prototype evaluation and especially in vibration testing, it would be appreciated if all engineers would purchase the male portion of multiple pin connectors when obtaining parts for their prototype black boxes.

It is recognized that in most cases the customer will supply his own mating part; however, due to the myriad configurations of connectors available, and also due to the long lead time required, valuable time will be saved if *mating parts of connectors are made a consideration and purchased along with the original prototype parts.*

Three of the constructions we replaced above *were* second-time: "this payroll" for "the bimonthly payroll," and "accede(-ing) to the request" for "grant(-ing) him a refund of this $100 before the actual date of the payday for that period."

But they weren't *best possible* second-time constructions.

18. Club-Member Phrases

These are the long-winded substitutes for simple English words and phrases that "every" writer uses for no apparent reason except that "every" writer does—as if he believed he had to to prove himself a member in good standing of some sort of writers' "club." Some appear especially often in particular fields, but most show up about equally frequently in all fields.

They mustn't be confused with jargon. Most jargon expressions—and *all* the *good* ones—are coined within particular environments to convey special meanings that would otherwise require *more* words; and any such you should feel perfectly free to use to anyone who shares it with you.

(But *never* to anyone who may *not* share it with you. If he doesn't, only at best will he just not understand it; at worst it will mean to him something quite different than you intended it to.)

Club-member phrases, on the other hand, you should never use.

A "typical" club-member phrase has two secondary characteristics:

- However often you see it on paper, you rarely or never *hear* it.

- It's unmistakably more "elegant" than its spoken-language equivalent.

But even where these exist, they're *just* secondary; the one feature that characterizes *every* club-member phrase is just that it conveys through more words an idea that would have been conveyed better through fewer.

Sloane gives us twelve examples. He may have invented "a sufficient purchase price"; I can't recall ever seeing it anywhere else. (But it's no less club-member on that account.) All the others are "standard":

18:	that time	then
24-25:	a sufficient purchase price	enough money
25:	the present time	now
30:	as soon as	when
39:	and therefore	so
49:	inasmuch as	since
55:	in the employ of	with
61:	has provided (himself) with	has given (himself)
62:	the same	this
66:	the following	these
67:	the above named	these
73:	prior to	before

"As soon as" exemplifies especially well the phrase that's only sometimes club-member; it isn't where a writer means it. But most writers often use it, as Sloane did, where all they really mean is just "when."

Six club-member phrases—"the following," "yours truly" (and its variants), "compared to" (or "as compared to," or "compared with"), "prior to," "in addition to" and "inasmuch as"—appear far more often than any others.

"The following" is club-member any time "this," "these" or "the" would have done the job—which means in about 99% of its appearances.

But the farther it is from what it refers to, the less likely it is to be replaceable. For example, it wasn't replaceable—and so wasn't club-member—in:

> The following data are the fruit of an extremely careful search and analysis, and I want to thank J. L. Faucett of Sales, C. D. Harper of Research, and Paul Hook and M. J. Dow of Abbott & Fowler Company for helping me to prepare them: . . .

"Yours truly" and its variants really say nothing at all, and letters need *not* end with "complimentary closes"; all you need at the foot of a letter is your signature. But if you're not ready yet to go all the way—and this is the first situation we've come to where the first W applies—at least "sincerely" and "cordially" say nothing in *one* word each.

"Prior" alone is a fine adjective, and "compare" is a fine verb, and just "in addition" can *sometimes* be justified. (And when it can't, as in 56, it represents something other than a club-member phrase.)

But I can't recall even one good "prior *to*," "compared *to*" or "in addition *to*."

"In addition to" is usually best replaced by "besides."

"Compared to" needs continually to be removed from three kinds of constructions, but from only two of them as club-member. (In the third it involves verb mutilation, which we'll get to later.)

- When it appears with a comparative adjective—or one that should have been comparative—you can almost automatically replace it with "than":

Durability of this product is *extremely high compared to* that of its predecessor.	Durability of this product is *much higher than* that of its predecessor.

- In other constructions it typically means just "versus" or "against":

  Table 1 lists the properties of XN-3 *compared to* those of XN-1.

"Inasmuch as" is club-member only when it can be replaced perfectly by "since" or "because"—*not* when it means "because *and to the extent that*," as in "Inasmuch as ye have done this to the least of my children . . . " But except in the Bible, I can't recall *ever* seeing it where it *wasn't* club-member.

Also club-member is the longer, more obtrusive "correct" name for something your reader would have recognized as easily by a shorter, easier "nickname," usually an abbreviation. Almost every field has some such; for example:

electronic data processing	EDP
estimated time of arrival	ETA
extrasensory perception	ESP
General Motors Acceptance Corporation	GMAC
intelligence quotient	IQ
North Atlantic Treaty Organization	NATO
pounds per square inch	psi
research and development	R&D
return on investment	ROI
revolutions per minute	rpm

Incidentally, I urge that abbreviations that are to be read as abbreviated—for example, you'd read "rpm" as "r-p-m," not "revolutions per minute"—be spelled without periods.

And while you *should* use the "correct" name if it would be *easier* for your reader, you can sometimes "define" an abbreviation early in a report and use it thereafter as a second-time word:

> Attached is the new procedure for submitting Emergency Work Requests (EWR's) . . . Do not submit an EWR unless the proposed work is really of an emergency nature.

(But you shouldn't define it *unless* you need to.)

And talking about second-time words: For "Ajax," 55, now substitute "us." (Which is second-time in Sloane's and Dawson's *context*.)

35. Failure to Use Summary Words and Phrases

Some words and phrases "summarize" others just—or just about—by definition. Like "children" ("boys and girls"), "parents" ("fathers and mothers"), "cattle" ("cows, bulls, steers and oxen"), "the officers of this company" ("the president of this company, the executive vice-president, the financial vice-president, the treasurer, the chief counsel, etc.").

But one that doesn't summarize by definition *may* summarize *in context*. For example, surely no dictionary will ever define the adjective "joint" as meaning, among other things, "Du Pont/Excelso/Paragon." But it perfectly replaced all those words in:

> The writer also recommends that we immediately allocate $2,000 for a Du Pont/Excelso/Paragon advertising campaign.

We miss relatively few chances to so summarize—chiefly because we don't get many.

But surely "pay" perfectly summarizes "wages and salaries" in 3.

For Practice

Just for so long as you spot every *failure* to use a second-time word, don't mind if you sometimes guess wrong on *which* one to substitute.

1. After meeting with Onley and/or Bender on several occasions we have reached the following conclusions:
2. Alicia Skin Tone Cream has been distributed in both the domestic and international markets for the past 4½ years.
3. Although the convenience features of the Hitachi are not critical, they increase the information output of the instrument in a given period of time.
4. Assuming average delivery distances are 300 miles longer from one plant compared to two, the freight cost disadvantage is .7-.8c/bd. ft., which does not offset the f.o.b. plant price advantage.
5. But for all future visits of this nature I would like each of you to prepare a program of instructions in all phases of World-Wide's operations, policies and procedures you are concerned with.
6. For example, if we assume a sales price of $50,000 and a 15%/year cost of capital, it would cost us $3,000 per year to retain the drag line. It should be noted that this cost is in addition to the cost of insurance, since this is accounted for in the calculation of the net present values.

7. If we require all subsidiaries to comply with the same fiscal year, Ajax should provide extra help.
8. Because the equipment RSWs cannot practically store all 200 scales, we will ask Ohaus to ship 100 when the purchase order is received and 100 six months later. Ohaus has honored this type of an arrangement in the past.
9. In a company where 7.1% of its jobs fall in the unskilled category, and in North Carolina and South Carolina, where the ratio of unskilled jobs is 6.2%, it is apparent that the bulk of the better job opportunities call for a background and training in the technical aspects of our operations.
10. In recent months about fifty to seventy-five complaints concerning the extreme bitter taste in TEJAVA were reported to the Quality Control Laboratory. This occurence is very unusual as many of the complaints came from customers who claimed to be users of TEJAVA for twenty years or more . . . Twenty-five samples from among the retained files were selected at random. These samples were coded, and special instructions were given to the panel about how the taste tests should be conducted.
11. Regardless of the "EXCELLENT" rating, there are two (2) areas which need immediate attention.
12. The present laboratory surfacing based on polyester glass would require a substantial investment in low-pressure pressing equipment. This investment cannot be justified because . . .
13. The problem is slightly more complex for WY TONIC Prenatal in Peru since Peru has been supplied ex Passaic with WY TONIC Prenatal granulations containing cobalt and in the future no such granulations with cobalt can be shipped from the United States.
14. The tax for the second five-year period is 50% of the normal 45% rate, or 22.5%.
15. Without a proven superior product, our most likely potential customers are just those Ajax now has, or can establish, favorable trade relations with.
16. The creditors were advised by Davis that Charles had borrowed $536,000 from the corporation over a period of 33 years and lost the money gambling.

The Answers

The failures to use best possible second-time words and phrases:

5. World-Wide's.
6. this cost.
8. Ohaus [second sentence].
10. this "occurence," these samples.
12. this investment.
13. the United States.
15. Ajax.
16. the money.

The club-member phrases:

1. on several occasions, the following.
3. in a given period.
4. compared to.
6. in addition to, is accounted for.
7. comply with.
9. the bulk, call for, job opportunities.
11. regardless of.
14. 50% [takes up less space than "half," but besides being much harder to conceptualize is four syllables as opposed to one, and therefore takes *longer* to *read.*]

The failure to use a summary word was in 2 ("both the domestic and international").

1. After meeting with Onley and/or Bender *several times* we have reached *these* conclusions:
2. Alicia Skin Tone Cream has been distributed in *all* markets for the past 4½ years.
3. Although the convenience features of the Hitachi are not critical, they increase the information output of the instrument *per unit* of time.
4. Assuming average delivery distances are 300 miles longer from one plant *than from* two, the freight cost disadvantage is .7-.8c/bd. ft., which does not offset the f.o.b. plant price advantage. ["Than" alone replaces "compared to"; the original compared not distances and distances, but distances and *plants.*]
5. But for all future visits of this nature I would like each of you to prepare a program of instructions in all phases of *our* operations, policies and procedures you are concerned with.
6. For example, if we assume a sales price of $50,000 and a 15%/year cost of capital, it would cost us $3,000 per year to retain the drag line. It should be noted that *this* is *besides* the cost of insurance, since this *is included* in the calculation of the net present values.
7. If we require all subsidiaries to *use* the same fiscal year, Ajax should provide extra help.
8. Because the equipment RSWs cannot practically store all 200 scales, we will ask Ohaus to ship 100 when the purchase order is received and 100 six months later. *They* have honored this type of an arrangement in the past.

9. In a company where only* 7.1% of its jobs fall in the unskilled category, and in North Carolina and South Carolina, where the ratio of unskilled jobs is 6.2%, it is apparent that *most* of the better *jobs require* a background and training in the technical aspects of our operations.
10. In recent months about fifty to seventy-five complaints concerning the extreme bitter taste in TEJAVA were reported to the Quality Control Laboratory. *This* is very unusual as many of the complaints came from customers who claimed to be users of TEJAVA for twenty years or more . . . Twenty-five samples from among the retained files were selected at random. *They* were coded, and special instructions were given to the panel about how the taste tests should be conducted.
11. *Despite* the "EXCELLENT" rating, there are two (2) areas which need immediate attention.
12. The present laboratory surfacing based on polyester glass would require a substantial investment in low-pressure pressing equipment. *This* cannot be justified because . . .
13. The problem is slightly more complex for WY TONIC Prenatal in Peru since Peru has been supplied ex Passaic with WY TONIC Prenatal granulations containing cobalt and in the future no such granulations with cobalt can be shipped from *this country.*
14. The tax for the second five-year period is *half* of the normal 45% rate, or 22.5%.
15. Without a proven superior product, our most likely potential customers are just those *we* now have, or can establish, favorable trade relations with.
16. The creditors were advised by Davis that Charles had borrowed $536,000 from the corporation over a period of 33 years and lost *it* gambling.

---

*Inserted to provide an emphasis that the author really wanted.

Chapter 9

THREE MORE WRONG-POINT-OF-VIEW AGENTS

36. The (Usually) Long-Winded Affirmative

Every so often—maybe once every twenty thousand words—your typical writer tries to convey through affirmative words a story whose significant aspect is negative: He says, for example, that someone stayed too long at a party when the important thing is he didn't get home on time, or that someone did something when the important thing is he didn't do something else. And usually—as in Sloane, 10—the practice costs words:

each of them fails to see	neither of them sees

20. The (Usually) Long-Winded Negative

Fairly frequently, on the other hand—though not nearly as frequently as Sloane—your typical writer

- tries to convey through *negative* words a story whose significant aspect is *affirmative,* or
- pointlessly takes the longer of two negative ways—for example, says "not any" instead of "no" or "none."

The practice costs relatively few words; typically, Sloane's twelve examples cost only sixteen words, or 1.33 each. This agent's importance is chiefly in relation to *weakness*, of which it's the third most important agent. For example, these changes, by themselves, won't make Sloane sound *really* forceful and self-confident—but they'll have been an important factor when he finally does:

9-10:	not a very common one	a relatively uncommon one
18-19:	has not purchased any bonds	has purchased no bonds
28-29:	has never purchased any bonds	has purchased no bonds
39:	not really any money	really no money
41:	would not have been able	would have been unable
42:	had it not been	except
45:	not a proper procedure	an improper procedure
47-48:	does not consider he has done anything	considers he has done nothing
51:	does not feel that there have been any	feels that there have been no

58-59:	not utilized this procedure as frequently as	utilized this procedure less frequently than
65:	not much	little
68:	not within	outside

The new "relatively," 9, is meaningless. But it will serve later to remind us of Sloane's "very."

Not surprisingly, the twelve examples included three "not any's," plus a "never any" and a "not anything," which are essentially the same thing. This is the most common long-winded-negative construction.

16. The Wrong Number

This appears chiefly in two forms.

Lying With Numbers

"The kids went to the store for an ice-cream cone" could be a true statement. Plural kids *can* go to the store for one cone, which then, presumably, either

- they'll take turns licking, or
- the biggest and toughest will eat while the others stand by and drool.

So if the kids really went to get *cones*, it's a lie.

Yet that's the meaning it would usually be intended to convey.

Sloane provided three such wrong numbers. Had the procedure really been as he described it in 30-32, there'd have been no Sloane Report, because "Ajax" would have gone broke years before, because *no* company can afford to credit *each* employee with *all* employees' deductions; the deductions were posted to "*the* individual *employees' accounts*." And Smith was getting not "advances" every period (40-41), but "an advance"; while Blake (61-62) had taken "advances" through this means.

None of these misstatements fooled us, any more than the one about the ice-cream cone would have. In fact, you probably translated them without even realizing you'd had to. And if you thus lie to your readers, you probably don't often fool them.

You need to stop anyway. For at least four reasons:

- However often you get away with them, any such wrong number *may* fool a reader.
- However easy the translation—even when he doesn't even realize he's had to translate—the job costs him *some* energy. And no reader's energy is unlimited—so as a result of having to translate a wrong number he may misunderstand something else in a report.
- While few readers will think *much* less of you for such wrong numbers, *none* will think *better* of you for them.

- Above all else, the practice reflects an attitude: a willingness to depend on a reader's ability to extract one's message *despite* one's words rather than take the trouble to find the words that will really convey it. And so long as anyone's willing to do this, he'll *never* write *well.*

In this form, as Sloane shows, this agent sometimes "saves" words. No matter; you must root it out regardless.

Sloane is surprisingly light on it.

The Pointless Representative Singular

A representative singular—this is another of our private terms—is a construction through which you convey about just one, or each, member of a group a message you really *mean* to convey about *all* its members, so to really understand it, your reader must project from the one to the all.

Far from being always pointless, the construction is often a good way to show one-to-one relationships, or stress that a message applies to each member without exception. Therefore these singulars, from reports turned in for in-company writing courses, were not pluralized, though obviously they could have been:

> I propose to send *each prospect a sample* of each.
>
> *The* left-over *portion* of *every* split *package* must be rewrapped, relabeled and put back in the warehouse.
>
> *Any operator who violates* this rule *makes himself* subject to immediate discharge.

Actually, representative singulars—even when they're pointless—typically hurt very little *per appearance.* But each does slightly lengthen and fog the message it appears in, and many writers provide them in great profusion, and their effect cumulates; so over all, this agent *is* important.

Two of Sloane's sentences contained several examples:

22-26: It then becomes the duty of the cashier to purchase *a bond* for *any* individual *employee* whose individual *account indicates* that *he has* accrued enough money for *one.*	It then becomes the duty of the cashier to purchase *bonds* for individual *employees* whose individual *accounts indicate* that *they have* accrued enough money for *bonds.*
70-74: There is a loophole here by which it is equally possible for *any* additional plant *manager* who *is* so minded to perhaps also follow the Smith procedure, thereby also obtaining *an* improper *advance* on *his salary* before the *day* on which *it* actually *becomes* due.	There is a loophole here by which it is equally possible for additional plant *managers* who *are* so minded to perhaps also follow the Smith procedure, thereby also obtaining improper *advances* on *their salaries* before the *days* on which *they* actually *become* due.

(Yes, "the days on which" is horrible.

(But so was "the day on which," and at least the plural says what Sloane meant. So while we've still a long way to go with this sentence, the change really does improve it—slightly.)

For Practice

That the long-winded affirmative below really is one will become clear after we've eliminated some other agents, but don't hate yourself if you miss it at this stage.

Another sentence contains, in one phrase, a wrong number *and* a failure to use a second-time word.

1. Assuming average delivery distances are 300 miles longer from one plant than from two, the freight cost disadvantage is .7-.8c/bd. ft., which does not offset the f.o.b. plant price advantage.
2. Absecon Point does not accept our recommended procedures for handling off-spec G-3783.
3. Because of differences in health requirements, the "Tridil" formulation as it is known in the U.S. is altered somewhat to comply with foreign regulations. As the formulations are changed, a different suffix is added to the "Tridil" name.
4. But some investigators reject them and results may be biased because the lists of side effects may be incomplete.
5. I gained an appreciation of the importance of an appraisal in an employee's development.
6. In summary, I recommend the following:
   1) We give Stilley a trial order for both plants for 7/16" seven-ply laminated oak drawer stock and, subject to approval by all, that a change authorization be put in for costing purposes . . .
7. Previously the Laboratory examined competitive products and sent the completed report to Wilmington for approval prior to distribution.
8. Some meetings were not well organized and the problems were repeated but in general I gained a lot from the meetings.
9. The disadvantages are increased handling cost (.33c/lb. to .995c/lb.), increased freight costs, necessity of breaking down pallets for small orders at warehouses (majority of sales are to small-quantity customers), and the distributor's need for mechanized equipment (lift truck) for removal from delivery trucks.
10. We need your 1968 scale requirements by October 19 so we can enter our purchase order for the Ohaus scale, which we must buy in a minimum quantity of 200 to get the present low cost.

The Answers

The long-winded affirmative was in 4 ("may be incomplete"). The long-winded negatives were in 2 ("does not accept") and 8 ("not well organized"). The wrong numbers were in:

1. distances are.
3. the formulations are.
5. an appraisal, an employee's.
6. both plants.
7. the completed report.
9. the distributor's, lift truck.
10. the Ohaus scale.

1. Assuming average delivery *distance is* 300 miles longer from one plant than from two, the freight cost disadvantage is .7-.8c/bd. ft., which does not offset the f.o.b. plant price advantage. ["Does not offset" *is* negative, and shouldn't be, but—as you'll see later—another agent is involved here.]
2. Absecon Point *has rejected* our recommended procedures for handling off-spec G-3783.
3. Because of differences in health requirements, the "Tridil" formulation as it is known in the U.S. is altered somewhat to comply with foreign regulations. As *it is* changed, a different suffix is added to the "Tridil" name.
4. But some investigators reject them and results may be biased because the lists of side effects may *not* be *complete*.
5. I gained an appreciation of the importance of *appraisals* in *employees'* development.
6. In summary, I recommend the following:
   1) We give Stilley a trial order for *each plant* for 7/16" seven-ply laminated oak drawer stock and, subject to approval by all, that a change authorization be put in for costing purposes.
7. Previously the Laboratory examined competitive products and sent completed *reports* to Wilmington for approval prior to distribution. [Yes, "prior to" is club-member—but we can replace it more easily later than now.]
8. Some meetings were poorly organized and the problems were repeated but in general I gained a lot from the meetings.
9. The disadvantages are increased handling cost (.33c/lb. to .995c/lb.), increased freight cost*, the† necessity of breaking down pallets for small orders at warehouses (the† majority of sales are to small-quantity customers), and *distributors'* need for mechanized equipment (lift *trucks*) for removal from delivery trucks.
10. We need your 1968 scale requirements by October 19 so we can enter our purchase order for the Ohaus *scales*, which we must buy in a minimum quantity of 200 to get the present low cost.

* * *

Time for a fresh worksheet.

---

*Singularized to eliminate inconsistency.

†Inserted to relieve terseness.

SLOANE REPORT - Stage 2

September 9, 1957

To : H. B. Dawson

From : N. B. Sloane

Subject : Audit of Payroll Deduction Funds, Exville Plant

The audit last week of the records of those employees at this
plant who have deductions for U. S. Savings Bonds withheld from their
pay indicates that the account these funds are held in at the First
National Bank-- the account R. J. Wright, Cashier-- is in balance with
5 the individual account cards of the employees' deductions. However,
there has been a mishandling of the funds which represents what might
be considered collusion between Wright and Plant Manager R. W. Smith,
although both of them advise that, while the procedure they have engaged
in is admittedly a relatively uncommon one, neither of them sees how
10 his own actions in it can be considered in any way improper or otherwise
deserving of censure. Smith has authorized payroll deductions for savings bonds since July 1, 1950, at which time Miss Platt informed me that
it was decided by Ajax to undertake a concentrated buy-savings-bonds
campaign for the purpose of convincing all of our employees to sign up
15 to purchase bonds under the payroll deduction plan. Upon examination of
Mr.Smith's deduction card it was indicated that although deductions from
his pay check have continued to be made since then, he has purchased no
bonds. He is on a bimonthly payroll that is made up here at the main
office. As you know, the total of all of the deductions on every payroll
20 is forwarded to the cashier on every payday in order to be deposited by
him in this account. It then becomes the duty of the cashier to purchase
bonds for individual employees whose individual accounts indicate that
they have accrued enough money for bonds. As of now the plan is taken
advantage of by nearly 1,000 of our employees, 997 to be exact, therefore
25 it has clearly achieved a considerable degree of success.

As was mentioned in the above paragraph, however, Smith has
purchased no bonds. The bimonthly payroll is written very early in the
payroll period, and when it is written the bond deductions which are
listed on it are posted to the individual employees' accounts. There-
30 fore, very early in the month in each payroll period, Smith's bond
deduction card is credited with his regular $100 deduction. However,

upon investigation of his individual deduction card it was ascertained that he has consistently requested of Wright that Wright grant him a refund of this $100 before the actual date of the payday for that period,
35 Wright always doing so. This means that whenever Wright did this there was really no money in the bank for the refund, so Smith, the plant manager, has actually obtained an advance in every single payroll period. Wright, of course, would have been unable to do this except for the presence in the account R. J. Wright, Cashier, of funds that had been
40 deducted on earlier payrolls from the pay of the other employees.

Feeling that this is an improper procedure, it has been brought to the attention of Smith and also to the attention of Wright. Mr. Wright, the cashier, says that he considers he has done nothing anyone can justifiably censure him for since he has merely acted pursuant to
45 the instructions to give Mr. Smith the refund that he has regularly received from Smith. Mr. Smith says that he feels that there have been no violations of the company's rules and/or policies and for this reason I have apprised him that I would include it in my audit report. Mr. Wright will be 65 years of age on October 12 of 1957 and has been with
50 us since 1919. In addition there is the further complication that the records indicate that Assistant Plant Manager J. J. Blake, who was formerly at our Chicago, Ill., plant, while he has utilized this procedure less frequently than Smith, on one or two occassions during the past several months, when for some reason or another he was financially embar-
55 assed, he has in effect likewise given himself payroll advances through this means. He, too, is on the bimonthly payroll that is made up here at the main office, whereas all of the other employees who have bond deductions withheld from their pay are on a weekly payroll that is made at the plant. There is little doubt in my mind that you will agree with
60 these two conclusions:

1. That the actions of these personnel in this matter are outside the intended results desired to be achieved by the ''Buy U. S. Savings Bonds'' campaign, and that
2. There is a loophole here by which it is equally possible for
65 additional plant managers who are so minded to perhaps also follow the Smith procedure, thereby also obtaining improper advances on their salaries before the days on which they actually become due.

Chapter 10

THE WRONG-WAYS-TO-MODIFY FAMILY AND THREE OF ITS MEMBERS

"Modify," in English grammar, means "describe, limit or identify," and modifiers are words, phrases and clauses that modify other words, phrases and clauses. English has two general types: The function of our

adjective types is to modify "substantives": nouns, pronouns, noun phrases and—rarely—noun clauses;

adverb types is to modify verbs, adjectives, adverbs, all phrases except noun phrases, all clauses except the few noun clauses best modified adjectivally, and complete sentences.

(You may use either type to modify a gerund, which I'll define later.)

Each general type includes various specific kinds of words and constructions. In this chapter we'll be concerned only with simple adverbs and three adjective types: adjectives, possessive nouns and "nonce adjectives."

"Nonce adjectives"—this is still another of our private terms—are nouns used as adjectives "for the nonce": that is, for (more or less) special occasions, as in "*company* policy," "*classroom* procedure," "*city* street," "*kitchen* sink." You shouldn't use one where a "pure" adjective would tell your story. But often the "pure" one you need just doesn't exist, and then a noun-used-as-an-adjective may communicate beautifully, and if it does it's perfectly "correct."

37. Failure to Use the Possessive

Once in a great while you may provide an unnecessary word by using a nonce adjective instead of a possessive noun:

66: the Smith   Smith's

38. Overuse of the Possessive

Once in a great while you may provide an unnecessary word by using a possessive noun instead of an adjective or nonce adjective:

47: the company's   company

And sometimes, while just as many words, a construction just "reads better" with a nonce adjective:

Azco's salesmen are known throughout the industry for their judgment and expertise.	*Azco* salesmen are known throughout the industry for their judgment and expertise.

24. The Misattached Modifier

In 29, surely "individual" conveys exactly the adjective idea Sloane wanted to convey.

But surely he wanted to convey it about "accounts," not "employees."

But "employees" sneaked in. And instead of removing it, he made it possessive, and made *it* modify "accounts."

Now clearly, the idea of "individual" does fairly well seep through to "accounts." And this isn't extraordinary—especially since "employees" and "accounts" here are

- side by side, and
- both nouns (so "individual" needn't be twisted into an adverb).

But even at best, modification by seepage is a *little* less sharp, a *little* less clear and a *little* harder for readers than direct modification. Cross out "employees'."

When as a result of being misattached an adjective idea must be expressed through an adverb-type modifier, or an adverbial idea through an adjective type, the modification may be *much* less clear. As in these left-side sentences; each was intended to convey just the simple message to its right:

His ability to cut through to the nub of things is *remarkably* well developed. ["Remarkably," an adverb, modifies the adverb "well," which modifies the participle "developed," which—finally—modifies "ability."]	He has a *remarkable* ability to cut through to the nub of things.
I am sure you will find he will listen to you *sympathetically.* ["Sympathetically" modifies "listen," which it must seep through to "he."]	I am sure you will find him *sympathetic.*

Sloane's example, though less spectacular, still needs to be fixed:

66: . . . thereby also obtaining *improper* advances on their salaries.	. . . thereby also *improperly* obtaining advances on their salaries.

For Practice

One phrase below contains a misattached modifier *and* a wrong number.

1. A separate project will be supplied to provide this protection for the Belle Works adipic-acid unit.

2. Control recently compiled 2,000 lowest rates from newspapers' rate cards.
3. Existing samples are impressive in their uniform pile height and drape.
4. However, the pharmacy plays an important role as the place where purchases are made, and we should know what factors influence purchases here.
5. I gained an appreciation of the importance of appraisals in employees' development.
6. I make the additional recommendation that a capital expenditure be considered for a high-pressure corrosion tester on the Du Pont design.
7. I think we should omit the bottom 25% of the population, because "Tridil C" potential there is small.
8. Some are unlikely to ever be cleared.
9. The denim of 50/50 420 nylon/cotton should provide a high level of durability which would be lower than that of the combination denim of 80/20-50/50 "Dacron"/cotton but noticeably superior to that of 50/50 polyester/cotton.
10. They have honored this type of an arrangement in the past.
11. This would be a management training program for the latter, and give us a trained pool of sales-management manpower.
12. Assuming average delivery distance is 300 miles longer from one plant than from two, the freight cost disadvantage is .7-.8c/bd. ft., which does not offset the f.o.b. plant price advantage.

The Answers

The failures to use the possessive were in 1 ("the Belle Works") and 6 ("the Du Pont"). The overuses of the possessive were in 2 ("newspapers' ") and 5 ("employees' "). The misattached modifiers were in:

3. impressive [an adjective modifying "samples" instead of an adverb modifying "uniform"].
4. important [modified "role" instead of "pharmacy"]; here [an adverb modifying "influence" instead of an adjective modifying "purchases"].
7. there [an adverb modifying "is" instead of a possessive pronoun modifying " 'Tridil C' potential"].
8. unlikely [an adjective modifying "some" instead of an adverb modifying "be cleared"].
9. high [modified "level" instead of "durability"].
10. this [modified "type" instead of "arrangement(s)"].
11. trained [modified "pool" instead of "sales-management manpower"].
12. not [an adverb modifying "offset" instead of an adjective modifying "which"].

The sentences with these agents eliminated:

1. A separate project will be supplied to provide this protection for *Belle Works'* adipic-acid unit.
2. Control recently compiled 2,000 lowest rates from *newspaper* rate cards.
3. Pile height and drape of existing samples are *impressively* uniform.
4. However, the pharmacy is important as the place where purchases are made, and we should know what factors influence *these* purchases.
5. I gained an appreciation of the importance of appraisals in *employee* development.
6. I make the additional recommendation that a capital expenditure be considered for a high-pressure corrosion tester on *Du Pont's* design.
7. I think we should omit the bottom 25% of the population, because *its* "Tridil C" potential is small.
8. Some will *probably* never be cleared. [So this also contained a long-winded affirmative.]
9. The denim of 50/50 420 nylon/cotton should provide *good* durability which would be lower than that of the combination denim of 80/20-50/50 "Dacron"/cotton but noticeably superior to that of 50/50 polyester/cotton.
10. They have honored *such* arrangements in the past.

11. This would be a management training program for the latter, and give us a pool of *trained* sales-management manpower.
12. Assuming average delivery distance is 300 miles longer from one plant than from two, the freight cost disadvantage is .7-.8c/bd. ft., which is *less* than the f.o.b. plant price advantage.

Chapter 11

THE FIRST TWO MEMBERS OF THE WRONG-KIND-OF-WORD FAMILY

28. The Wrong Form of the "Each"-Type Word

One group of English words—among others "each," "all," "most," "half," "both," "some" and every cardinal number—share a remarkable characteristic: Each may serve as a substantive or an adjective, and some may serve also as adverbs.

Now any time there's a *best* way to convey a message that includes an "each"-type word, that's how to convey it, however many words it requires.

But you should take a longer way *only* if it tells your story best.

And when in the substantive form an "each"-type word must be *modified by a prepositional phrase* (like "of the children," in the example following):

- The substantive way is always longer than the adverbial*:

  Each [pronoun] of the children had an ice-cream cone.

  The children had an ice-cream cone each [adverb].
- The adverbial way is always at least as long as—and sometimes longer than—the adjective:

  Each [adjective] child had an ice-cream cone.

But now let's put the last into a kind of context:

The children went to the zoo. Each child had an ice-cream cone.

"Child" is now superfluous.

So when the substantive way *doesn't* require a prepositional phrase, it's the shortest of all.

Sloane is lighter than most on this agent. He used three substantives where he should have used adjectives:

14:	all of our employees	all employees
24:	1,000 of our employees	1,000 employees
57:	all of the other employees	all other employees

*Unless the preposition is "understood," as in "all (of) the children," in which case it may be just equally long.

And one substantive that, just to prove that we can, let's first change to an adverb:

8: both of them they both

But with the last we can take the last step, crossing out "they" and returning to the substantive "both."

("The total of all of the deductions," 19, also looks like an example of this agent, and we *could* change it to "the total of all deductions." But really it represents other agents; we'll change it differently later.)

An adjective with its modificand "understood" may also be a wrong "each"-type word. Here, for example, you "understand" "possibility" after "economical":

> The most economical of these possibilities will then be investigated further.

Had this sentence's context been different, one perhaps couldn't have killed "of these"; this, too, is a kind of change you mustn't make automatically or unthinkingly. But in its actual context, "of these" contributed nothing, and its author was happy to kill it.

21. Modifier Mutilation

This is the practice of trying to convey essentially modifying ideas–ideas that are significant *in* that they limit, describe or identify–through nouns and (rarely) verbs, which we'll call their "containers." And a mutilated modifier typically modifies much less well even than one that's been misattached, because in English, nouns and verbs essentially *can't* modify*.

The noun that *most* often contains a mutilated modifier is "number," which I see used in report after report to convey such adjective ideas as "many," "several," "some":

A number of employees have loans outstanding with foreign subsidiaries.	*Several* employees have loans outstanding with foreign subsidiaries.
The Playhouse manager tells us the number of nights the facility is used.	The Playhouse manager tells us how *many* nights the facility is used.
It is admitted that a number of customers may take unfair advantage of the plan, but most can be expected to treat us fairly.	It is admitted that a *few* customers may take unfair advantage of the plan, but most can be expected to treat us fairly.

*Except nouns used as nonce adjectives and verbs in their participial forms, which I'll explain in Chapter 15; you do *not* mutilate a modifier when you convey an adjective idea through one of these.

But we also routinely mutilate adjectives into such nouns as "height," "weight," "length," "breadth," "width," "depth," "size," "age," "quantity," "quality":

As a result they tend to denigrate the *quality* of our service.	As a result they often say our service isn't *good* enough.
We urge that you be careful about the *quantity* of naphtha you use.	We urge that you be careful about how *much* naphtha you use.
Another disadvantage is the *height* of the ceiling.	Also, the ceiling is too *high*.
Bill, the Home Office is complaining about the *length* of our reports . . .	Bill, the Home Office is complaining that our reports are too *long* . . .
The *age, weight* and *size* of this equipment make it unsuitable for our purposes.	This equipment is too *old,* too *big* and too *heavy* for us.

(The last three show why this agent is also one of ambiguity: You might have thought they meant the ceiling was too *low*, the reports too *short*, the equipment too *new*, too *small*, too *light*.)

Also common containers are all nouns ending in "-ty" (especially "-bility" and "-vity"), "-ence" (and its variants) and "-ness":

From this point you may move ahead in a *variety* of ways.	From this point you may move ahead in *various* ways.
Bill, the Home Office is complaining about the length of our reports. Please tell your people to strive for greater *brevity*.	Bill, the Home Office is complaining that our reports are too long. Please tell your people to try to keep them *shorter*.
His *intelligence* is beyond question, but he has occasionally manifested a certain *stubbornness* which, I feel, tends to disqualify him from consideration.	He is unquestionably *intelligent,* but he can be terribly *stubborn*, and this, I feel, tends to disqualify him from consideration.

But virtually any noun *may* contain a mutilated adjective:

Enthusiasm ran high as more than 200 employees attended the first annual company picnic on Saturday, August 1.	More than 200 *enthusiastic* employees attended the first annual company picnic on Saturday, August 1.
Machine B is unanimously recommended on the bases of both its *performance* and its *price.*	Machine B is unanimously recommended; it is both more *efficient* and less *expensive.*

And in Sloane, 25:

. . . therefore it has clearly achieved a considerable degree of *success.*	. . . therefore it has clearly been quite *successful.*

We mutilate adverbs less often than we do adjectives—but we do mutilate them:

Obviously, the *rate* at which you advance in this company will depend on a number of factors.	Obviously, how *quickly* you advance in this company will depend on several factors.
He has carried out several difficult assignments for us, and never yet known *failure.*	He has carried out several difficult assignments for us, and all *successfully.* [So the original contained also a long-winded negative.]
Just a few minor adjustments will greatly improve its *efficiency.*	With just a few minor adjustments it will operate much more *efficiently.*

But since your noun or verb contains a mutilated modifier only if you've used it to convey a modifying *idea*, before you can really eliminate this agent you'll have to have trained yourself to identify your ideas *as* noun, verb or modifying.

And first, you've probably never even realized till now that you could do this, much less that you should, so you've had absolutely no practice doing it (your teachers, if anything, had you distinguish among kinds of *words*, not kinds of ideas). And second: No one can really show you how to do it: You must train yourself.

But if you keep trying, suddenly you'll find that you can.

And it's a skill well worth developing.

This agent, too, you need to eliminate equally where it costs words and where it doesn't.

Sloane is remarkably light on it. Its "normal" incidence is 0.5 to 1.0 appearances per hundred words.

For Practice

6 contains also a wrong number.

1. Assuming average delivery distance is 300 miles longer from one plant than from two, the freight cost disadvantage is .7-.8c/bd. ft., which is less than the f.o.b. price advantage.
2. But for all future visits of this nature I would like each of you to prepare a program of instructions in all phases of our operations, policies and procedures you are concerned with.
3. Central Engineering Department will prepare a definite cost estimate, which requires accuracy to be within ±10%.
4. Continue efforts to get support, making this mandatory when yarn availability situation eases or exposure levels increase above $20M-$50M.
5. During this period they have a cash shortage problem and obtained bank loans in past years to pay supplier invoices.

6. In essence, the summary indicated that the product was recommended for introduction in practically all of the markets the survey was conducted in.
7. In recent months about fifty to seventy-five complaints concerning the extreme bitter taste in TEJAVA were reported to the Quality Control Laboratory. This is very unusual as many of the complaints came from customers who claimed to be users of TEJAVA for twenty years or more.
8. The disadvantages are increased handling cost (.33c/lb. to .995c/lb.), increased freight cost, the necessity of breaking down pallets for small orders at warehouses (the majority of sales are to small-quantity customers), and distributors' need for mechanized equipment (lift trucks) for removal from delivery trucks.
9. The principal reason for increased advertising costs was the spending for space, radio, literature and mailings (primarily for "Astor" and "Topquality"), which amount to $150,000 in 1967, an increase of $100,000 over 1966.

The Answers

All the wrong "each"-type words were modified substantives; they should have been, in turn, an adverb, an adjective and an unmodified substantive:

2. each. 6. all. 7. many.

The mutilated modifiers had all been twisted into nouns.

1. disadvantage. 4. availability. 8. majority.
3. accuracy. 5. shortage. 9. increase.

1. Assuming average delivery distance is 300 miles longer from one plant than from two, the freight cost is .7-.8c/bd. ft. *more*, which is less than the f.o.b. plant price advantage.
2. But for all future visits of this nature I would like you *each* to prepare a program of instructions in all phases of our operations, policies and procedures you are concerned with.
3. Central Engineering Department will prepare a definite cost estimate, which requires us to be *accurate* within ±10%.
4. Continue efforts to get support, making this mandatory when more yarn becomes *available* or exposure levels increase above $20M-$50M.
5. During this period they are *short* of cash and obtained bank loans in past years to pay supplier invoices.
6. In essence the summary indicated that the product was recommended for introduction in practically *every market* the survey was conducted in.
7. In recent months about fifty to seventy-five complaints concerning the extreme bitter taste in TEJAVA were reported to the Quality Control Laboratory. This is very unusual as *many* came from customers who claimed to be users of TEJAVA for twenty years or more.
8. The disadvantages are increased handling cost (.33c/lb. to .995c/lb.), increased freight cost, the necessity of breaking down pallets for small orders at warehouses (*most* sales are to small-quantity customers), and distributors' need for mechanized equipment (lift trucks) for removal from delivery trucks.
9. The principal reason for increased advertising costs was the spending for space, radio, literature and mailings (primarily for "Astor" and "Topquality"), which amount to $150,000 in 1967, *up* $100,000 from 1966.

Chapter 12

THE SHEER SUPERFLUITIES

Each of the five members of this group—besides its other effects—is in the top seven agents of wordiness. If you're in the "normal" range, they've provided 60% to 75% of your superfluous words.

5. The Zero Word

When you edit yourself, you need to regard each of your words as essential, optional or zero.

An essential word is one that—in your judgment—you can't tell a story without.

An optional word is one that your judgment tells you you don't *need* to provide, but that, if you provide it, at least *may* somehow benefit your reader (and/or you, by promoting the likelihood that he'll react as you want him to).

A zero word is one that *at best says nothing*—at least, nothing you want to say—and at worst hurts in some positive way. For example, by making an otherwise true statement false, by inaccurately limiting the scope of a sentence, by producing a grammatical error.

For example, this sentence:

> We must not permit ourselves to lose out on this valuable business, even if it turns out that we must replace all of their present machines in order to satisfy them.

"Valuable" was optional; the author had to decide whether to save it or kill it. (He saved it.)

But of the other thirty, twelve said nothing; the author meant simply:

> We must not lose this valuable business, even if we must replace all their present machines to satisfy them.

Sloane is unusually heavy on this agent; he runs more than 9% zero words. But if you're about average, you've run 6% to 7%.

Let's first eliminate from Sloane those that require little or no discussion. Those asterisked are "standard," meaning they occur and recur, as zero words, in "everyone's" copy.

1: *those.

One of the eight or ten *most* common zero words.

6: represents what.

10: in any way.

Zero because—I'm convinced—Sloane didn't *want* to emphasize this point.

17: check.

Makes an otherwise true statement false.

21: *then.

Another especially common zero word, especially in "if-then" constructions:

If you go, *then* I will.

If $x = 3$, *then* $2x = 6$.

If you were twins, *then* I'd hate you both.

23: *as of [move "now" to between "is" and "taken"].

26: was.

30: in the month.

Also makes an otherwise true story false.

34: the actual date of the, for that period.

42: *also.

Does not echo "and"; it just says nothing.

47: *and [in "and/or"].

"And/or" is fine when you mean either or both. But Sloane didn't.

54: or another.

54: for some reason.

55: he.

A subject without a predicate. (The subject of "has given" is "Assistant Plant Manager J. J. Blake," in 51.)

64: *equally.

65: who are so minded.

Inaccurately limits the scope of the statement: The loophole exists—potentially—for *all* plant managers. True, only those "so minded" will try to crawl through it—but that's not what the sentence says.

67: the days on which.

67: *actually.

Not always zero, and neither is "really"; for example, "actually" isn't in 36-37 or "really" in 35. But both are *often* zero.

As to the others:

RELATIVELY, 9 (change "a" to "an"); IN EFFECT, 55, PERHAPS, 65, and NOT VERY (which we replaced with "relatively") all exemplify the "hedge" word or phrase. And you *should* hedge any time you've good reason to.

But not only do most writers often hedge unnecessarily; many hedge almost automatically, even where they don't really want to. In fact, I think Sloane, had he thought of it, would rather *not* have hedged in these cases.

TO BE MADE, 17, isn't standardly zero, but "to be," alone, is. Especially after verbs like "seem," "prove," "appear":

> They seemed *to be* happy.
> The last attempt proved *to be* successful.
> These appear *to have been* freshly laundered.

UP, 18 and 56, is one of a group with "down," "over," "out," "in"; each is often part of a biphrasal (two-word) verb. None is always zero in this role; some accountants even deny "up" is in Sloane. And "stand up," for example, is great—when you mean something like "stop slouching and stand *erect*."

But whether or not "up" is in Sloane—and *most* of my accountant friends say it is, and Sloane didn't provide it in 58-59 ("payroll that is made at the plant")—all these words are often zero. For example: If I decide to rise from a chair, I can stand in no direction *but* up; if I tire of standing, I can sit in no direction *but* down; to pick something off the floor I can lean in no direction *but* over.

OF, 19 (between "all" and "the deductions"); OF, 33; IN, 37; ON, 49, and OF, 49 (in front of "1957"; surround "1957" with commas), are all prepositions, and any preposition is zero where it can be "understood." And you can *usually* understand

- "of"
  - after "all" (even a properly substantive "all," as in Line 19 or the phrase "all of us boys");
  - in front of the name of a year (as in 49), and
  - in such constructions as

    John Brown *of* Goshen, New York [where you can replace it with a comma] or

    John Doe, president, and Richard Roe, vice-president, *of* Doe-Roe, Inc.;
- "on" in front of
  - the name of a day ("I'll arrive on Friday," "On Tuesday my suit will be ready") or
  - a date, except at the beginning of a clause. And sometimes it's zero even at the beginning of a clause. And few clauses should begin with dates anyway; "On July 13 I'm going to the ball game" would in most contexts reflect a major agent of disorganization. (Which I'll name in the section on disorganization.)

ALL, 19, another very common zero word, does not echo "total" here; it just says nothing.

IN ORDER, 20, in "in order for," "in order that" and "in order to," comes closer than any other English word or phrase to being always zero. In the last 7½ years I've seen only six cases where it wasn't–and in each of those the whole construction was bad for other reasons.

INDIVIDUAL, 22 (third word) and 32, and SINGLE, 37, are a group with "particular" and "specific." By all means use one of these when it

- clarifies what you need to clarify, or
- emphasizes what you want to emphasize.

But all four are standardly zero just about as frequently as they are in Sloane: in 50% of their appearances. (Sloane gave Dawson five "individuals," one "single," no "particulars" and no "specifics," but that hardly matters.)

NOW, 23, is *not* zero, even with a present-tense verb, when you want to stress the difference between now and some other time. But as I see it, it's zero more often than not.

HOWEVER, 26; THIS MEANS THAT, 35; and FOR THIS REASON, 47, all exemplify the "transition," or "bridge," word or phrase, and good bridges can help readers greatly. But it's not true, as many seem to believe, that the more bridges the better; you should *not* provide one over perfectly dry land or, more importantly, over a 6-inch-wide puddle. In the latter case it may actually *trip* a reader, because if he decides you couldn't have provided it just to help him cross the puddle, he may figure out some *other* function for it–and thereby get an entirely different message than you intended him to.

This has probably never been illustrated better than by Sloane and me. The sentence is the one now in 46-48:

> Mr. Smith says that he feels that there have been no violations of company rules or policies and *for this reason* I have apprised him that I would include it in my audit report.

What Sloane meant to convey through "I have apprised . . . "–I'm now convinced–was that he'd properly notified Smith that he'd report the *practice*. (And now change "it" to "the practice.")

But for a long time I thought "it" meant something like "how he feels."

Partly, of course, this was because Sloane had misused a second-time word. But *mostly* it was because he'd said "for this reason," and far from realizing it was zero, I "understood" it, and interpreted the rest of the sentence in its light.

Dawson, presumably, came to this report better equipped than I, so maybe he didn't get trapped.

But I wouldn't bet he didn't.

AND, after "policies" in 47 (replace it with a period), and WHEREAS, 57 (change the comma preceding it to a semicolon), exemplify the zero connective, the most pernicious of all zero words. Because it hooks together in one tougher construction what should have been two easier ones, and is therefore a major agent of hypercomplexity.

THE, 40, and in front of "instructions" in 45, is rarely zero except in three situations, yet it's most writers' most common zero word. How Sloane managed to provide only two zero "the's" I'll never understand.

It's especially often zero in front of plural nouns, as both times in Sloane.

But it's also often zero in front of

- proper nouns:

  In our dealings with *the* Smith Corporation we have found . . .

  A marked deterioration of energy is observed below the top of *the* "C" Horizon.

- nouns denoting general rather than specific things, or continuing activities rather than specific events:

  In purchasing *the* equipment for this project it is important that due consideration be given to its resale value.

  The construction of this building is two months behind schedule.

But it's the second we've come to of the four constructions you must guard against *over*eliminating. (The first, may I remind you, was the perfect tense.) If you kill every "the" in your copy that's genuinely zero, you'll kill a great many and improve your copy every time. But if you *over*kill it, you'll be terse rather than concise, and readers will look for excuses to lay your reports down unread. It's significant, for example, that forty "the's" are *not* zero in Sloane, including nine in front of plural nouns and the one preceding the proper noun "First National Bank" in 3-4.

The subordinating conjunction THAT (12, 22, 43, 46, 46 and 48) is the third of the constructions you must guard against overeliminating. But for most writers, it trails only "the" in number of zero appearances, and only "in order" in ratio of zero appearances to nonzero.

Its function is to signal that a clause is coming, so readers won't incorrectly assign the clause's role in the sentence to some other word or phrase. And sometimes this signal helps greatly; for example, it would have helped in:

I believe the junior senator from Pennsylvania, one of the great statesmen of our time, whom I have admired for many years and who, I trust, will continue to adorn the Senate for many years to come, is an authority on this subject.

Unless you're quite unusual, you had to read that at least twice to understand it. The reason: You unconsciously parsed it as you read it—as you do every sentence—and by the time you'd gone about seven words you'd identified it to yourself as one of the very common type in which a transitive verb ("believe") is followed by a noun object ("senator"): The author, you decided, was saying he believed the senator. So when "is" suddenly appeared, six words from the end, you had no place to put it in your mental diagram, and your first reaction was that either you or the author had somehow goofed.

Finally, I'm sure, you did figure it out.

But a "that" after "believe" would have saved you that trouble: You'd have known immediately that the object of "believe" was a clause rather than an individual noun, and understood the sentence the first time.

(You see, you know a lot more grammar than you think you do.)

And the sentence exemplifies a quite common type. It has two characteristics:

1. The subject of the subordinate clause is a noun that you might reasonably assume is *itself* the object of the main-clause verb.
2. The subordinate-clause verb takes long enough to arrive so that you've *time* to thus misconstrue it. ("Is" was the fiftieth syllable after "believe"; sometimes just four or five syllables justify a "that.")

The sentence in 1-5 is also of this type: You could reasonably expect "account" to be itself the object of "indicates," and without the "that," twenty-three syllables would have separated "indicates" and "is."

(But note: Characteristic 1, alone, generally does *not* justify a "that." For example, you've no trouble with just "I believe the senator is an authority on this subject," or "Last week's audit indicates the account is in balance.")

Also, you may need a "that" to eliminate ambiguity when some kind of adverbial modifier intervenes between your main-clause verb and the subject of your subordinate clause:

With an adverb: He said *previously* canned apricots would be acceptable.

Did he say it previously, or about previously canned apricots?

With an adverbial phrase: He remembered *in Chicago* I'd worn red suspenders.

Is that where he remembered it, or where I'd worn them?

With an adverbial clause: He said *when he was 23* he wanted to marry a movie star.

Is that when he said it, or when he wanted to marry her?

With "only" (which is special because sometimes you can't tell whether it's an adverb or an adjective): I said *only* I was going to the movies.

Is that all I said, or did I intend to go alone?

(But sometimes you can eliminate the ambiguity by just *moving the modifier*—for example, "When he was 23 he said he wanted to marry a movie star.")

Some other, less common constructions also typically require "that's." And often you'll need to insert one just because your judgment tells you to.

But it's not surprising that the subordinating "that" has already proved zero in six of its seventeen appearances in Sloane*, and it's zero also in several other spots where I want to save it for a while.

"1," 61, and "2," 64, exemplify the zero numbers, which clutter report after report after report.

Such numbers are sometimes *not* zero. Rather, first, you should *always* numerate where numbers will facilitate later reference, by yourself or your reader—so that, for example, you can later refer to something as "Point 2," or someone can phone someone and say "Now about this Item 4 on Page 7 . . . " And often, besides, they're a good way to

- show an order of importance, ascending or descending;
- show a sequence or chronology, or
- stress that a list contains exactly—or at least—a certain number of items. For example: "The two disadvantages are more than outweighed by the seven advantages"—whereafter you number the advantages to stress that they're seven.

But you mustn't numerate without *some* good reason. And when you've good reason to separate, but none to numerate, some other device—and there are many—*must* be better than numeration.

The one I find most often useful is called by various names, of which I prefer "the dots"; you've seen them often in these pages. To make one in typed copy, you type a lower-case "o," which—after you've removed the page from the machine—you fill in, reasonably carefully, with a sharp, soft black pencil.

I mean both words in "reasonably carefully." I'd not entrust the job to a 6-year-old. On the other hand, you don't need a micrometer or calipers; if you're just reasonably careful, few readers—except those who themselves use dots,who won't care—will even realize the filling *has* been penciled in.

(But don't use a hard pencil, or a dull one, or pen and ink.)

---

*The "that" in 18, 39, 45, 56 and 58 is an entirely different word—a relative pronoun that just happens to be spelled the same way.

Now some, having just discovered the dots, overuse them. You must especially resist the temptation to use them where you *should numerate*.

But where you should use them, you should for at least three reasons:

LEAST IMPORTANT: They "dress up" a report. Whereas numbers—especially since each must be followed by a period, or surrounded by parentheses, or both—at best don't dress it up, and at worst make it less attractive.

MORE IMPORTANT: They lighten your reader's burden; he notices and understands them, but needn't—in fact, can't—read them. (Maybe he won't read your numbers, either—but by providing them, you suggest he should.)

MOST IMPORTANT: They can't be misunderstood, and zero numbers can be. That is: Any time you numerate merely because you've separated, your reader may decide you had some other reason—that you did want to show a sequence, order of importance or the like. Which if he does, of course, he'll get a different message than you intended him to.

Or sometimes the best device is some sort of "read-in," like "least important," "more important," "most important," above. (Which you needn't capitalize, but, I think, generally should.)

Or you may just begin each item with its key word or phrase, like "adjective types," "adverb types," on Page 49.

(In either case above you generally best use a "hanging indent"—that is, in each item you indent every line *except* the first.)

And finally, when you've no reason to do anything else you can use the simplest device of all: Just list the items down the middle of your page. As in:

The equipment we must dispose of includes:

six erasers
two slightly worn waste-paper baskets
half a ream of yellow paper
twelve pencils
etc.

Let's give Sloane dots in 61 and 64.

2. (Pointlessly) Saying What Goes Without Saying

Unlike your zero word, your goes-without-saying word or phrase says something—but something that your reader either

- already knows, or
- couldn't help but deduce from *other* things you've said, are saying or are about to say.

Sometimes you *should* say something you can be pretty sure your reader knows or could figure out. You should, for example, when

- you want to emphasize it—and believe that the best way *is* by saying it.

  But this applies only quite seldom, because if something really goes without saying you can *usually* best emphasize it by *not* saying it. Because you then, in effect, make your reader say it to himself, and most readers are much more impressed by what they "figure out for themselves" than they are by what writers tell them.

- you thereby save your reader some trouble.

  This applies fairly often. For example, suppose you've said the three parts of a three-part project cost $12,345.67, $23,456.78 and $34,567.89; surely anyone you write to can add those three numbers—correctly—himself. But most readers are lazy; if such a total is relevant, most would greatly prefer that you provide it.

  But you can easily be too helpful, and thereby insult a reader. Imagine, for example, how its reader must have reacted to this sentence:

  > There are 27 people interested in Phase I of this seminar, and two interested in Phase II, so altogether 29 people are interested.

- you need your reader to think of it *at a particular point*, and however clearly it *should* go without saying, unless you say it he just *may not happen to think of it* at that point.

  And this applies *very* often, in report after report. For example, the sentence now in 19-21: Clearly Sloane thought Dawson was familiar with this part of the procedure; this is why the "as you know." But had Sloane not said it, Dawson just might not have thought of it at that point.

  Incidentally, I think you *should* say something like "of course," "obviously," "as you know" when you say something you think your reader knows or could figure out. Readers, typically, are also thin-skinned; given an excuse to infer that you think they're stupid, they typically will infer it, and resent you.

But *most* goes-without-sayings clutter our copy for no reason except that we *just don't think to get rid of them.* And so often do we fail to that this agent produces *far* more superfluous words than any other.

For example: Temporarily retaining many others that also involve other agents, surely we can now remove from Sloane:

0: Subject.

> Had this been printed on Sloane's page, probably Dawson wouldn't even have noticed it, much less read it. But Sloane, per his typist, typed it, and thereby implied Dawson *should* read it. This was an imposition.
>
> Having removed it, we must of course center the rest of the line—and I'd also capitalize it.

2, 62: U.S.

5: of the employees' deductions.

8-9: they have engaged in.

9: of them.

10: in it.

"It" was our second-time substitute for "the matter," which was Sloane's "elegant variation" of "the procedure," now in 8. Clearly, here's another good way to avoid repeating sounds.

13, 62: buy.

14: all.

21: in this account.

23: for bonds.

25: clearly.

26: in the above paragraph.

28: bond.

28-29: which are listed on it.

43-44: he considers he has done nothing anyone can justifiably censure him for since.

When a cashier says he's just followed his boss's instructions, what else can he mean?

48: audit.

49: 1957.

One of the six standard goes-without-sayings: the name of the year. And not only may the name of the current year go without saying: If your day or date is less than twelve months away, in either direction, so may the name of next year or last. (Though of course it becomes less and less likely to as you approach either end of the 24-month period.) For example: From a letter written by a college student's mother and dated July 1 (the year doesn't matter):

> We haven't seen him since Labor Day, and now he says he won't be home till Easter.

On the other hand, sometimes even the current year doesn't go without saying. Fine: When your judgment says provide it, provide it.

52: Ill.

Another standard goes-without-saying: the name of the state or country.

Some state and national names virtually always go without saying. Like Illinois after Chicago, Michigan after Detroit, Japan after Tokyo.

Others sometimes do and sometimes don't—the key factor, usually, being not the locality's size or importance, but context. Generally, for example, you'd better add

"Iowa" after "New Sharon"—but you could hardly need to if your reader lived in Oskaloosa, just a few miles down the road. And in different contexts, *different* state and national names may be clear after such local names as Portland, Charleston, Wilmington; for example:

If your context is	*"Wilmington," alone, virtually must mean the one in*
Du Pont,	Delaware;
Jewel Box Stores,	North Carolina;
Quaker education,	Ohio.

Still, every case is unique. So consider each in the light of your judgment, and provide state names, too, where it tells you to.

55: payroll.

There are other kinds of advances—but none Sloane could have meant here.

60: two.

61: in this matter.

"Mr." (16, 42, 45, 46 and 48) is undoubtedly—though *very* slowly—becoming archaic, at least in writing; and personally, I'll be glad to be rid of it. As a "title of respect"—unless one uses it only for *selected* adult males, which virtually no one does—it's zero. So all it says, almost any time you see it, is that the person whose name it precedes *is* an adult male—which almost always would have been perfectly clear without it.

But as of today many writers still shudder at the thought of dropping it, and if that's how you feel, you can always retain it on any of three grounds:

- In your context it doesn't go without saying. (As, for example, if your context is a women's college.)
- Your ground rules require it.
- The first W: You *just don't want to drop it.*

But all Sloane's "Mr.'s" do go without saying, and his ground rules apparently don't require it, and in view of the way he often *doesn't* use it, he can't cite the first W. Kill it all five times.

Two other groups of words go without saying just about often enough so we can consider them "standard":

"a.m." and "p.m.," and

possessive nouns and pronouns, and proper nouns used as nonce adjectives:

Your management wishes to remind all front-line *Azco* supervision that they have been chosen by *Azco's* management on the basis of *their* presumed loyalty as well as *their* ability.

In computing *one's* travel expenses, please hereafter exclude . . .

. . . it would be appreciated if all engineers would purchase the male portion of multiple pin connectors when obtaining parts for *their* prototype black boxes. [Note the wrong number in "portion."]

But the goes-without-saying words that take up the *most* wasted space in English prose are those like "company," "corporation," "department," "division," "office," as they appear in proper names.

Many such names also include zero "the's":

In our dealings with *the* General Motors *Corporation* we have found that . . .

Needless to say, I have checked this with *the* Legal *Department.*

Many also include other goes-without-saying words:

Recruiters will be here today from *the* Metropolitan Life *Insurance Company, the* Ford *Motor Company,* and Jones & Laughlin *Steel Corporation.*

E. I. du Pont *de Nemours & Company, Inc.,* has its main offices in Wilmington, Delaware.

But if your reader would recognize a company or organization as readily by an even shorter and easier "nickname," its official name even without the zero and goes-without-saying components is pointlessly long and obtrusive—which makes it, by our definition, a club-member phrase. Within Du Pont, for example, "the Organic Chemicals Department" should generally be reduced not just to "Organic Chemicals," but to "Orchem." Similarly, "Columbia Broadcasting," even without "System," would ordinarily be club-member for "CBS," "International Business Machines" for "IBM," "General Electric" for "GE."

The objection I often hear to thus shortening a name—"But that's the *official* name"—is rarely valid. Just so long as you give him only nicknames he *understands*, your typical reader won't care if you *never* use an "official" name.

7. The Irrelevancy

An irrelevancy is anything a writer should have killed for the reason that it just couldn't, in any way, even to the slightest degree, have benefited his readers or promoted the likelihood that they'd react as he wanted them to.

Now a point is relevant or irrelevant only within a particular report; and every decision about relevance is a judgment decision; and to make a *valid* judgment decision about any report one must know exactly what message it's intended to convey, and why—and the only one who can really know these things is its author. So I may be wrong about every one of the words and phrases I'm about to kill as irrelevant in Sloane.

But I'd bet that if we could now make Sloane think about them, he'd agree about at least most of them. And not because I think he'd have changed his mind about any, but because, I think, it would be the first time he *had* thought about them.

The point is: Very few irrelevancies reflect errors of judgment; the great bulk clutter our copy simply because we *just don't think to question ourselves about them*. The moment you begin to just continually ask yourself "Is this point relevant or isn't it?"—even if more often than most you answer it *wrong*—this agent, for you, will become one of the least important of the thirty-nine.

All right; I think Sloane just didn't question himself about (among many other such that I don't want to kill yet, because they also illustrate other agents):

13: concentrated.

> This is a wrong word; technically, at least, you can't start a concentrated anything, but can concentrate it only after it's in existence. Sloane meant some other word.
>
> But that doesn't matter. Because *nothing* he could have meant here was relevant to the *loophole*.

20-21: by him.

24-25: therefore it has been quite successful.

> Would have been relevant in a report reviewing the history of the program, or the career of the man who ran it—but not in this report.

51-52: who was formerly at our Chicago plant.

> Conceivably—as some have suggested—Sloane included this to suggest maybe they should look at the Chicago operation too. But I don't believe this: I think the only reason it appears here is that he just happened to remember it at this point, and it leaked out of his mind onto the paper, and he never thought to mop it up.

54-55: when he was financially embarrassed [with "embarrassed" misspelled].

> All Dawson could have cared about was *that* Blake did this—not why or when.

10. The Trivium

A trivium is something you couldn't have killed as irrelevant—usually because you could never have *quite* made up your mind that it was—but that, even if it did somehow relate to your subject, just wasn't worth the words that it cost—you and your reader—to convey it.

Sloane, I think, gives us only two examples, which is somewhat amazing. Further, each is just one word, and this agent averages more superfluous words per appearance than any other. (In which respect, incidentally, the irrelevancy ranks second.)

Except in this respect, though, they illustrate the agent beautifully.

First, the "1" after "July" in 12. It is not surely irrelevant; for example, Dawson might have been glad to have it if, after reading this report, he decided to go to the files.

But first, I doubt this happened; and second, if it helped it surely didn't help much. So, inexpensive though it is, I think it's uneconomical, and want to kill it.

Second, "July" in 12. This, too, might have helped; and if it did, it probably did more than the "1" could have.

But I'd guess it didn't help either; and if it did, even it didn't help much; and besides, it's more "expensive" than "1." Kill it, too.

22. Pointless Attribution

Attribution is just the act of attributing—of explicitly telling your reader where a fact or idea came from. And often you've good reason to attribute; and any time you have, you'd better.

But you should attribute something *only* if

(1) there's at least a reasonable possibility that your reader won't be able to *see for himself* where it came from; and

(2) the attribution protects or benefits at least one of four parties:

yourself—as when you must relay an idea or alleged fact that you aren't sure is sound or accurate, and don't want to be held personally responsible for;

your source—when by not attributing you'd be stealing his credit;

your reader—when he can best understand or evaluate it in the light of where it came from, or when—as *often* happens—the important thing isn't even whether it's true, but just that someone in particular has *said* it;

your subject—as when his good name or reputation is at stake, especially if your reader knows your source isn't completely objective or reliable.

Which means that really this agent is always a special kind of goes-without-saying or a special kind of irrelevancy. But it's so common that we need to look at it individually anyway, and so might as well give it its own name and spot on the list.

The irrelevant type is by far the less common. Sloane gives us just one; kill "Miss Platt informed me" in 12.

Of his others, first kill the simple attribution to a person—"says he"—in

46. (Really the attribution is in "Smith says," but if we killed that we'd have to change "he" to "Smith.") This leaves "Smith feels there have been no violations of company rules or policies," which Sloane can have learned *only* from Smith.

On the other hand, the attribution in 43 is *not* pointless; Sloane's whole purpose here was to tell Dawson what Wright *said*. (Because if one cashier could consider this a valid excuse for mishandling funds, so might others.) And without the "says he" Sloane *wouldn't* obviously have been quoting Wright.

Next kill the simple attribution to the records—"the records indicate that"—in 50-51. This is something Sloane *must* have checked against the records. (And he *doesn't* say he *got* it from the records—and it wouldn't matter if he did.)

In three cases Sloane attributes doubly: to the records, and to his own audit of the records. Let's look first at:

15-16: Upon examination of Smith's deduction card it was indicated that . . .

32-33: Upon investigation of his deduction card it was ascertained that . . .

We *could* reduce these to single attributions:

Smith's deduction card indicates that . . .

His deduction card reveals . . .

But I think that in each case both halves are pointless; I want to change these sentences to:

Although deductions from his pay have continued since then, he has purchased no bonds.

However, he has consistently requested Wright that Wright grant him a refund of this $100 before payday, Wright always doing so.

(Writers often *should* attribute to themselves: to their own surveys, analyses, opinions. But such attributions *can* be as pointless as any others.)

Sloane also attributes doubly in 1-3: "The *audit* last week of the *records* . . . indicates that." But this one we must rewrite to fix (which means it's atypical of not only this agent, but also the whole family), and the sentence contains also other mistakes that I want to save. So I've rewritten it to eliminate *only* the attribution; as thus "corrected," it's the first two sentences in Stage 3.

Attributions to no one in particular are especially often pointless:

One might say that this vendor has not been as co-operative as he had been before Mr. Wallace's unfortunate death.

For Practice

You almost certainly won't spot all the sheer superfluities in 6 and 12; the only reason *I* know what they are is that I could check with their authors. (You're especially unlikely to spot one zero phrase in 6; it's zero only because its author didn't mean it.)

The sentences contain relatively few examples of Agents 7 and 10; this is because these are so hard to spot out of context. And for the same reason, don't hate yourself if you miss any that they do contain. And of those you do spot, you absolutely won't be able to know which are 7 and which are 10, so I'll lump the two together in the "Answers" section.

1. After a careful blend study, a 70% "Dacron" Type 65/30% wool blend was chosen for knits because of best performance and aesthetics.
2. Alicia Skin Tone Cream has been distributed in all markets for the past 4½ years.
3. Assuming average plant delivery distance is 300 miles longer from one plant than from two, the freight cost is .7-.8c/bd. ft. more, which is less than the f.o.b. plant price advantage.
4. Based on this sampling, there is a potential membership of some 1,200 people from the Department's 1,300 employees.
5. Because of differences in health requirements, the "Tridil" formulation as it is known in the U.S. is altered somewhat to comply with foreign regulations. As it is changed, a different suffix is added to the "Tridil" name.
6. CUSTOMER IDENTIFICATION NUMBERS (ID)

   Definition: A precise and concise method for identifying a specific customer, needed because of the many different combinations of "Sold To" and "Ship To" names and addresses used in ordering our products and because of the specific instructions and specifications applicable to each combination.
7. But for all future visits of this nature I would like you each to prepare a program of instructions in all phases of our operations, policies and procedures you are concerned with.
8. Central Engineering Department will prepare a definite cost estimate, which requires us to be accurate within ±10%.
9. FLOORING TEST INSTALLATION – BESTFLOOR®

   February 7 and 8 we installed a ¾" green entrance at William A. Foster's residence, 112 W. Ashbury Drive, Ashbury. About 30 square feet of 25/32" oak flooring and threshold were replaced with 16" x 16" BESTFLOOR tile.
10. For example, if we assume a sales price of $50,000 and a 15%/year cost of capital, it would cost us $3,000 per year to retain the drag line.
11. I believe that the co-operation we are receiving from Dr. Alexander on Vizaid Ophthalmic deserves that serious consideration be given to purchasing a quantity of his book, but that we must first assure ourselves it is in the best interest of our future eye-area promotion.
12. In a company where only 7.1% of its jobs fall in the unskilled category, and in North Carolina and South Carolina, where the ratio of unskilled jobs is 6.2%, it is apparent that most of the better

jobs require a background and training in the technical aspects of our operations.

13. In accord with our telephone conversation of November 10, I send you herewith copies of reports summarizing the results of consumer panel tests initially designed to assess the merits of an experimental bed pillow being developed in Pioneering Research.
14. In essence, the summary indicated that the product was recommended for introduction in practically every market the survey was conducted in.
15. In recent months about fifty to seventy-five complaints concerning the extreme bitter taste in TEJAVA were reported to the Quality Control Laboratory. This is very unusual as many came from customers who claimed to be users of TEJAVA for twenty years or more. Immediately I set up a taste panel in an effort to determine whether there was any basis for this recent surge of complaints. Twenty-five samples from among the retained files were selected at random. They were coded, and special instructions were given to the panel about how the taste tests should be conducted.
16. In summary, I recommend the following:
    1) We give Stilley a trial order for each plant for 7/16" seven-ply laminated oak drawer stock and, subject to approval by all, that a change authorization be put in for costing purposes.
    2) A man be placed in Trim R&G for up to 90 days who will work directly with me to ensure that we do the best possible job in utilizing our cutting lengths to the best advantage.
17. On Thursday, November 2, I met with ACE Packaging Consultant Frank Giles, and Dave Knowles and Pym Wharton, both representing Resnick Paper Box.
18. RECOMMENDATIONS: . . .
    2. Continue co-operation at exposure levels up to $20M-50M with strict prompt payment.
    3. Continue efforts to get support, making this mandatory when more yarn becomes available or exposure levels increase above $20M-50M.
19. Since subfreezing temperatures can damage most adhesives—and since carriers are not liable for frozen goods unless we can prove conclusively they were involved—from now on please allow suppliers sufficient lead time to take proper precautions.
20. Some meetings were poorly organized and the problems were repeated but in general I gained a lot from the meetings.
21. The circumstances in question appear to have been correctly managed at first, but the handling deteriorated somewhere in process.
22. The creditors were advised by Davis that Charles had borrowed $536,000 from the corporation over a period of 33 years and lost it gambling.
23. The denim of 50/50 420 nylon/cotton should provide good

durability which would be lower than that of the combination denim of 80/20-50/50 "Dacron"/cotton but noticeably superior to that of 50/50 polyester/cotton.

24. The tax for the second five-year period is half of the normal 45% rate, or 22.5%.
25. There are instances in which an established supplier receives reorders without rebid or testing of prices from other sources.
26. This is an apt description, too, of the problem that we face in Wilmington.
27. We need your 1968 scale requirements by October 19 so we can enter our purchase order for the Ohaus scales, which we must buy in a minimum quantity of 200 to get the present low cost. Because the equipment RSWs cannot practically store all 200 scales, we will ask Ohaus to ship 100 when the order is received and 100 six months later.
28. Without a proven superior product, our most likely potential customers are just those we now have, or can establish, favorable trade relations with.
29. Absecon Point has rejected our recommended procedures for handling off-spec G-3783.
30. The "Dacron" Type 65 is offered in 3-denier staple and tow.

The Answers

The zero words:

2. the past.
3. the [before "freight cost"].
4. some.
6. and [between "precise" and "concise"]; specific [before "customer"]; because of [before "the specific instructions"; this is the one the author just didn't mean].
8. ±.
10. a [before "cost of capital"]; per [replaceable by a slash].
11. that [after "I believe" and before "we must first assure ourselves"].
12. its; and [after "category"]; where; a [before "background"].
14. that.
15. about; the [before "extreme bitter taste" and before "Quality Control Laboratory"]; among; to [before "the panel"].
16. 1, 2; and [after "drawer stock"; this author was offering *three* recommendations]; that [before "a change authorization" and after "to ensure"]; directly.
17. on.
18. at exposure levels; $20M [both times].

19. conclusively.
20. the [before "problems"].
21. somewhere.
22. a period of.
23. the [first word].
24. of.
26. that.
27. all; and [after "the order is received"; replaceable by a comma].
28. potential; trade.
29. handling.
30. the.

The goes-without-sayings:

1. blend [fourth word]; for knits.
3. plant.
5. "Tridil"; to the "Tridil" name.
6. precise; concise; different.
7. all.
8. Department.
9. about; tile.
11. first; future.
13. you.
15. in an effort; taste [before "tests should be conducted"].
16. subject to approval by all.
17. both.
20. from the meetings.
23. the combination denim of.
24. 45%.
25. prices from.
27. scale [fifth word]; purchase.

The irrelevancies and trivia:

5. because of differences in health requirements; somewhat.
9. 7 and 8; William A. Foster's residence.
13. initially designed.
15. this is very unusual (as); immediately; special.

The pointless attributions were in 11 ("I believe") and 14 ("the survey indicated").

1. After a careful study, a 70% "Dacron" Type 65/30% wool blend was chosen because of best performance and aesthetics.
2. Alicia Skin Tone Cream has been distributed in all markets for 4½ years.
3. Assuming average delivery distance is 300 miles longer from one plant than from two, freight cost is .7-.8c/bd. ft. more, which is less than the f.o.b. plant price advantage.

4. Based on this sampling, there is a potential membership of 1,200 people from the Department's 1,300 employees.
5. The formulation as it is known in the U.S. is altered to comply with foreign regulations. As it is changed, a different suffix is added.
6. CUSTOMER IDENTIFICATION NUMBERS (ID)

   Definition: A numerical* method for identifying

   - a customer, needed because of the many combinations of "Sold To" and "Ship To" names and addresses used in ordering our products, and
   - the specific instructions and specifications applicable to each combination.

   [Clearly, this was—and still is—very badly organized. But we'll fix that later.]
7. But for future visits of this nature I would like you each to prepare a program of instructions in all phases of our operations, policies and procedures you are concerned with.
8. Central Engineering will prepare a definite cost estimate, which requires us to be accurate within 10%.
9. FLOORING TEST INSTALLATION—BESTFLOOR®

   In February we installed a 3/4" green entrance at 112 W. Ashbury Drive, Ashbury. 30 square feet of 25/32" oak flooring and threshold were replaced with 16" x 16" BESTFLOOR.
10. For example, if we assume a sales price of $50,000 and 15%/year cost of capital, it would cost us $3,000/year to retain the drag line.
11. The co-operation we are receiving from Dr. Alexander on Vizaid Ophthalmic deserves that serious consideration be given to purchasing a quantity of his book, but we must assure ourselves it is in the best interest of our eye-area promotion.
12. In a company where only 7.1% of jobs fall in the unskilled category—in North Carolina and South Carolina the ratio of unskilled jobs is 6.2%—it is apparent that most of the better jobs require background and training in the technical aspects of our operations.
13. In accord with our telephone conversation November 10, I send herewith copies of reports summarizing the results of consumer panel tests assessing the merits of an experimental bed pillow being developed in Pioneering Research.
14. In essence, the product was recommended for introduction in practically every market the survey was conducted in.
15. In recent months fifty to seventy-five complaints concerning extreme bitter taste in TEJAVA were reported to Quality Control Laboratory. Many came from customers who claimed to be users of TEJAVA for twenty years or more. I set up a taste panel to determine whether there was any basis for this recent surge of

---

*Inserted to eliminate arrogation (see Page 8).

complaints. Twenty-five samples from the retained files were selected at random. They were coded, and instructions were given the panel about how the tests should be conducted.

16. In summary, I recommended the following:
    - We give Stilley a trial order for each plant for 7/16" seven-ply laminated oak drawer stock.
    - A change authorization be put in for costing purposes.
    - A man be placed in Trim R&G for up to 90 days who will work with me to ensure we do the best possible job in utilizing our cutting lengths to the best advantage.
17. Thursday, November 2, I met with ACE Packaging Consultant Frank Giles, and Dave Knowles and Pym Wharton representing Resnick Paper Box.
18. RECOMMENDATIONS: . . .
    2. Continue co-operation up to $50M with strict prompt payment.
    3. Continue efforts to get support, making this mandatory when more yarn becomes available or exposure levels increase above $50M.
19. Since subfreezing temperatures can damage most adhesives—and since carriers are not liable for frozen goods unless we can prove they were involved—from now on please allow suppliers sufficient lead time to take proper precautions.
20. Some meetings were poorly organized and problems were repeated, but in general I gained a lot.
21. The circumstances in question appear to have been correctly managed at first, but the handling deteriorated in process.
22. The creditors were advised by Davis that Charles had borrowed $536,000 from the corporation over 33 years and lost it gambling.
23. Denim of 50/50 420 nylon/cotton should provide good durability which would be lower than that of 80/20-50/50 "Dacron"/cotton but noticeably superior to that of 50/50 polyester/cotton.
24. The tax for the second five-year period is half the normal rate, or 22.5%.
25. There are instances in which an established supplier receives reorders without rebid or testing of other sources.
26. This is an apt description, too, of the problem we face in Wilmington.
27. We need your 1968 requirements by October 19 so we can enter our order for the Ohaus scales, which we must buy in a minimum quantity of 200 to get the present low cost. Because the equipment RSWs cannot practically store 200 scales, we will ask Ohaus to ship 100 when the order is received, 100 six months later.
28. Without a proven superior product, our most likely customers are just those we now have, or can establish, favorable relations with.
29. Absecon Point has rejected our recommended procedures for off-spec G-3783.
30. "Dacron" Type 65 is offered in 3-denier staple and tow.

SLOANE REPORT - Stage 3

September 9, 1957

To : H. B. Dawson

From : N. B. Sloane

AUDIT OF PAYROLL DEDUCTION FUNDS, EXVILLE PLANT

Deductions we have withheld for Savings Bonds from the pay of employees at this plant are held in an account at the First National Bank-- the account R. J. Wright, Cashier. This account is in balance with the individual account cards. However, there has been a mishandling
5 of the funds which might be considered collusion between Wright and Plant Manager R. W. Smith, although both advise that, while the procedure is admittedly an uncommon one, neither sees how his own actions can be considered improper or otherwise deserving of censure. Smith has authorized payroll deductions for savings bonds since 1950, at which time it
10 was decided by Ajax to undertake a savings-bonds campaign for the purpose of convincing employees to sign up to purchase bonds under the payroll deduction plan. Although deductions from his pay have continued since then, he has purchased no bonds. He is on a bimonthly payroll that is made here at the main office. As you know, the total of the deductions
15 on every payroll is forwarded to the cashier on every payday to be deposited. It becomes the duty of the cashier to purchase bonds for employees whose individual accounts indicate they have accrued enough money. The plan is taken advantage of by nearly 1,000 employees, 997 to be exact.

20 As mentioned, Smith has purchased no bonds. The bimonthly payroll is written very early in the payroll period, and when it is written the deductions are posted to the individual accounts. Therefore, very early in each payroll period, Smith's bond deduction card is credited with his regular $100 deduction. However, he has consistently
25 requested Wright that Wright grant him a refund of this $100 before payday, Wright always doing so. Whenever Wright did this there was really no money in the bank for the refund, so Smith, the plant manager, has actually obtained an advance every payroll period. Wright, of course, would have been unable to do this except for the presence in the
30 account R. J. Wright, Cashier, of funds that had been deducted on earlier payrolls from the pay of other employees.

Feeling that this is an improper procedure, it has been brought to the attention of Smith and to the attention of Wright. Wright, the cashier, says he has merely acted pursuant to instructions to give Smith the refund that he has regularly received from Smith. Smith feels there have been no violations of company rules or policies. I have apprised him I would include the practice in my report. Wright will be 65 years of age October 12 and has been with us since 1919. In addition there is the further complication that Assistant Plant Manager J. J. Blake, while he has utilized this procedure less frequently than Smith, on one or two occassions during the past several months has likewise given himself advances through this means. He, too, is on the bimonthly payroll that is made here at the main office; all other employees who have bond deductions withheld from their pay are on a weekly payroll that is made at the plant. There is little doubt in my mind that you will agree with these conclusions:

- That the actions of these personnel are outside the intended results desired to be achieved by the Savings Bonds campaign, and that
- There is a loophole here by which it is possible for additional plant managers to also follow Smith's procedure, thereby also improperly obtaining advances on their salaries before they become due.

Chapter 13

THE REPETITIVE AGENTS

These are the ones that produce the superfluous words that are superfluous because the messages they convey are conveyed too *often.*

25, 11 and 23 are essentially just special cases of 19.

19. Simple Pointless Repetition

This is *only* the two practices following. The first is by far the more common, but Sloane is unusually heavy on it.

Pointless Repetition of Modifying or Identifying Words

This is the practice of pointlessly reproviding—almost always via (1) a modifying word or phrase or (2) a noun or noun phrase "in apposition"—a description, limitation or identification that *still clearly applies from the last time it was provided.*

(But note "pointlessly." When you've *reason* to repeat, by all means do.)

To eliminate it, you just cross out the word or phrase that reconveys the message. For example:

Because Sloane, quite properly,	*we can kill*
associated "payroll" and "deductions" in the subject line (where, in effect, they modify each other),	"payroll" in 9, and either "payroll" or "deduction"—and I'd rather kill "deduction"—in 11-12.
modified "bonds" with "savings" in 1,	"savings" in 9, 10 and 48.
modified "cards" with "individual account" in 4,	"bond deduction"—patently a paraphrase of "individual account"—in 23.
modified "period" with "payroll" in 21,	"payroll" in 23 and 28.
identified Smith as the plant manager in 6,	"the plant manager" in 27.
named the account in 3,	"R. J. Wright, Cashier," in 30.
identified Wright as the cashier in 3,	"the cashier" in 33-34.
defined Smith's instructions to Wright in 25-26 (as "that Wright grant him a refund, etc."),	"to give Smith the refund" in 34-35.

modified "bimonthly payroll" with "that is made here at the main office" in 13-14,	"that is made here at the main office" in 43.
modified "withheld" with "from the pay of employees" in 1-2,	"from their pay" in 44.
modified "deductions" with "we have withheld, etc.," in 1-2,	"withheld" in 44.
modified "campaign" with "bonds" in 10,	"bonds" in 48.

Again we've fixed Sloane's grammar—that is, made him say what he meant—by crossing out words: Until we killed "to give Smith the refund" he said in 33-35 that Wright had regularly been getting a *refund* from Smith. (True, we "understood" him—but only because we see so many such constructions that we've *had* to learn how to cope with them.)

And now we can kill two more goes-without-sayings in 29-30: "in the account," and then "presence of." (So really we had here a nine-word goes-without-saying that *included* a pointless repetition.)

Sloane showed how a word may be pointlessly repeated from a subject line; one may also be so repeated from a subhead:

Acetate Sales

June *acetate* sales were 55.5M pounds, versus 49.1M in May.

Sometimes to eliminate this agent you change the modifer to a noun and eliminate the repetition of the modified word:

The Russian people want to strengthen the bond between our countries, say three American teachers who visited Moscow schools last spring . . . The *American teachers* were overwhelmed by their welcome at the schools.	The Russian people want to strengthen the bond between our countries, say three American teachers who visited Moscow schools last spring . . . The *Americans* were overwhelmed by their welcome at the schools.

When you disguise a repetition by paraphrasing, as Sloane did with "individual account" and "bond deduction," it's of course harder to spot; and the paraphrase may be quite severe, involving even drastic changes in parts of speech:

Due to its greater efficiency, the proposal has the following advantages: . . .

2. *Because the operation is more efficient*, two men are freed for other work.

But with a little practice you'll see through most such disguises quite easily.

Sloane's one example of this type differs from most in that the way to fix it is to kill the repeated statement the first time it appears: Retaining "Smith has purchased no bonds," 20, kill "he has purchased no bonds," 13. (Whereupon "although," 12, and "as mentioned," 20, become zero. But we do need a "bridge" in 20: Insert "but" to replace "as mentioned.")

Otherwise it's an excellent example.

25. The Bangbang Paraphrase

This is the practice of saying the same thing twice, but in different words, in more or less the same breath. For example:

"in addition," 38, and "further," 39;
"likewise," 41, and "through this means," 42;
"intended," 47, and "desired to be achieved," 48.

Retaining in each case a construction we'll eliminate later, kill "further," "likewise," "intended."

11. Fractional Anticipation

When you fractionally anticipate you say something more than once, but less than twice. That is:

First you say it, but not quite—for example, not quite precisely enough, or in insufficient detail.

Then you either

(1) say it inadequately again, filling in all the gaps you left the first time but leaving unsaid *some* of what you said the first time, or

(2) say it *as you should have said it in the first place.*

It's easily fixed. In Case

1, you just complete either statement and kill the other;

2, you either

- just kill the first, or
- kill the first and bring the second up to replace it.

If you've been writing "topic sentences"—the kind that, we learned in school, we were supposed to prefix to every paragraph to "state its topic" —probably many have just fractionally anticipated what followed them. For example, from three very dissimilar reports:

1. Susceptibility studies and field surveys indicate that dogs serve as hosts to certain arboviruses. They apparently maintain Western and St. Louis encephalitic viruses incidentally to the basic avian and culicine transmission cycle.
2. This chart is on a different scale. It reproduces the information in Charts 2 and 3 but on a scale in which 1948 is taken as the base year.

3. Reed does not do this. His formal statement of objectives tells us he intends only to improve the design of gas-enclosed speakers.

In 1, neither sentence quite told the story: "Serve as hosts to certain arboviruses" conveyed only inadequately the message "maintain Western and St. Louis encephalitic viruses, etc.," and the second sentence didn't mention the studies or surveys. In each of the others, on the other hand, the second sentence—except that a second-time word needed to be replaced—did tell the story.

Fixed, each paragraph became a single sentence:

1. Susceptibility studies and field surveys indicate that dogs maintain Western and St. Louis encephalitic viruses incidentally to the basic avian and culicine transmission cycle.
2. This chart reproduces the information in Charts 2 and 3, but on a scale in which 1948 is taken as the base year.
3. (But) Reed's formal statement of objectives tells us he intends only to improve the design of gas-enclosed speakers.

But—as Sloane is about to show us—you *can* fractionally anticipate *without* topic sentences.

To fix his easier cases, we just kill the left-side words and phrases following (including those in parentheses); each just conveys inaccurately or incompletely the message that's then conveyed *properly* by the phrase to its right:

8:	improper (or otherwise)	deserving of censure
10:	bonds	for the purpose of convincing employees to sign up to purchase bonds under the payroll plan
14:	here	at the main office
40:	(while he has utilized this procedure) less frequently than Smith	on one or two occasions

In two cases he tells the story inadequately each time:

2-3: First he doesn't name the account, then he doesn't locate it.

Make the sentence read "Deductions we have withheld for Savings Bonds from the pay of employees at this plant are held in *the account R. J. Wright, Cashier, at the First National Bank.*"

8-9: Smith has authorized not just deductions, but $100 deductions. And this Sloane doesn't tell us till 23-24—where he doesn't say Smith authorized them.

Insert "$100" before "deductions" in 9, and kill "his regular" and "deduction" in 24.

But one case requires much more muscular activity than this agent usually does; to fix it we must kill twenty-four words, then insert twelve:

7-8: "Neither sees how his own actions can be considered deserving of censure" turns out to mean—but hardly even *begins* to say—"Wright says he has merely acted pursuant to instructions that he has regularly received from Smith" and "Smith feels there have been no violations of company rules or policies" (33-36).

Change the comma after "Smith," 6, to a period, and kill the rest of the sentence (through "censure," 8). Then change 33-37 to:

> . . . to the attention of Wright. *Although both advise that the procedure is admittedly an uncommon one*, Wright says he has merely acted pursuant to instructions that he has regularly received from Smith, *and* Smith feels there have been no violations of company rules or policies. I have apprised *them* I would include the practice in my report. [Surely Sloane "apprised" both men!]

This agent can be pretty hard to spot, especially in your own copy, and most especially when you've just begun to look for it.

But if you keep trying, you *will* begin to spot it regularly after a while.

23. Repetition Plus

But sometimes the less precise, less detailed way is the *right* way; unless your reader can somehow *benefit* from getting something precisely or in detail, you just pointlessly increase his burden by providing it that way. And you repeat-plus when you say something once as you should, and once *too* precisely or elaborately.

(Or, as a variant, when you say it once from the right point of view, once from a wrong one.)

I think Sloane repeated-plus three times:

	I want to kill		*as repetition plus of*
18-19:	997 to be exact	18:	nearly 1,000.
22-24:	therefore, very early in each period, Smith's card is credited with $100 [then change "he," 24, to "Smith," and "this," 25, to "his"]	8-9:	Smith has authorized $100 deductions for bonds since 1950 [and]
		20-22:	The bimonthly payroll is written very early in the payroll period, and when it is written the deductions are posted to the individual accounts.
52-53:	before they become due	52:	advances.

As to "997" versus "nearly 1,000": Besides being much harder to conceptualize—and it doesn't matter that Dawson is presumably an accountant; it's harder for *anyone*—"997" even takes longer to read. So all it would save is space, and while space is worth something—the shorter a report, the more likely one is to *start* reading it—the saving here is trivial, and the "precision," I think, totally pointless.

But if we disagree about this—or, for that matter, about any other construction that I think represents this agent or Agent 11—it doesn't matter. Because neither of *us* can really *know* about *any* of them. Because—as in relation to the irrelevancy—to *know* which of these agents a case involves you must know just how precisely and completely the story *should* have been told; and to know this you must know exactly what its author wanted to say, and exactly why; and the only one who can really know these things is its author.

But you always know what *you* want to say, and why. So whichever way you decide to fix such a case in your copy—provided only you do really decide, as opposed to, say, flipping a coin—will be the *right* way.

Sometimes a repetition plus precedes what it "repeats"—in which case you must still kill it:

> The Program Office will have resident representatives *at our Andover plant, our Haverstraw plant and Ideal's Orlando plant—in other words*, at every major producing facility—and through them provide industrial direction to the line manufacturing organization.
>
> Generally, your paper is overloaded with jargon, like "multiform," "vertical integration," "impractical utilization of lumber species." You need to *get rid of the jargon and* express your ideas so a lay reader can understand them.

But:

Sometimes you *should* say it both ways. For example:

The left-side sentences following are from reports turned in for in-company writing courses; when they were analyzed, some saw possible fractional anticipation in all three, others possible repetition plus in 2 and 3. And each *might* have been rewritten as on its right:

1. Since we must vacate the Scott Street warehouse by April 1, I request you let us deviate from established procedure and sell the surplus equipment stored there as follows:	1. Since we must vacate the Scott Street warehouse by April 1, I request you let us sell the surplus equipment stored there as follows:
2. The improved product remains flexible at low temperatures (to -40°F) and resists high-temperature (400°F) aging.	2. The improved product remains flexible at -40°F and resists aging at 400°F. [or] The improved product remains flexible at low temperatures and resists high-temperature aging.

3. The products were identified as A and B. Both were prepared like present production material (blended, citrus-flavored, dull-finished tablets).	3. The products were identified as A and B. Both were prepared as blended, citrus-flavored, orange-colored, dull-finished tablets. [or] The products were identified as A and B. Both were prepared like present production material.

But the author of 1 felt that unless he pointed out that he *knew* he was proposing to "deviate from established procedure," his boss might turn him down simply because he was. And both the others were writing to multiple readers; in

Case 2, some readers needed to know the exact temperatures, while others wouldn't have recognized that—for these purposes— -40°F and 400°F *were* "low" and "high";

Case 3, some readers needed to be told that "present production material" *was* "blended, citrus-flavored, orange-colored, dull-finished tablets."

So none of them was changed.

Incidentally, you can most often justify this kind of "repetition" when you *are* writing to multiple readers.

For Practice

Where you think you see fractional anticipation or repetition plus, count yourself right if the construction turns out to have contained either.

1. Advertising costs were $206,000, or 10.7% of sales, in 1966, as compared with $84,000, or 6.3% of sales, in 1958. The principal reason for increased advertising costs was the spending for space, radio, literature and mailings (primarily for "Astor" and "Topquality"), which amount to $150,000 in 1967, up $100,000 from 1966.
2. After a careful study, a 70% "Dacron" Type 65/30% wool blend was chosen because of best performance and aesthetics . . . "Dacron" Type 65 is offered in 3-denier staple and tow.
3. Although this policy may benefit the Arnold operation, it lessens the quality of the receivables portfolio. This reduction in quality would be of greater concern were the receivables separated from the Arnold organization.
4. But some investigators reject them and results may be biased because the lists of side effects may not be complete.
5. Definition: A numerical method for identifying . . . the specific instructions and specifications applicable to each combination.
6. Despite the "EXCELLENT" rating, there are two (2) areas which need immediate attention.

7. In a company where only 7.1% of jobs fall in the unskilled category—in North Carolina and South Carolina the ratio of unskilled jobs is 6.2%—it is apparent that most of the better jobs require background and training in the technical aspects of our operations.
8. In recent months fifty to seventy-five complaints concerning extreme bitter taste in TEJAVA were reported to Quality Control Laboratory . . . I set up a taste panel to determine whether there was any basis for this recent surge of complaints. Twenty-five samples from the retained files were selected at random. They were coded, and instructions were given the panel about how the tests should be conducted. The twenty-five samples included the three batches that were claimed to be very bitter.
9. Recently we encountered a sensitive situation as a result of assisting one customer in relieving his inventories. The circumstances in question appear to have been correctly managed at first, but the handling deteriorated in process.
10. The disadvantages are increased handling cost (.33c/lb. to .995c/lb.), increased freight cost, the necessity of breaking down pallets for small orders at warehouses (most sales are to small-quantity customers), and distributors' need for mechanized equipment (lift trucks) for removal from delivery trucks.
11. The problem is slightly more complex for WY TONIC Prenatal in Peru since Peru has been supplied ex Passaic with WY TONIC Prenatal granulations containing cobalt and in the future no such granulations with cobalt can be shipped from this country.
12. Thursday, November 2, I met with ACE Packaging Consultant Frank Giles, and Dave Knowles and Pym Wharton representing Resnick Paper Box.

The Answers

The pointless repetitions:

1. advertising.
2. "Dacron."
6. (2).
8. recent surge of, twenty-five.
11. Prenatal.

The repetitions plus:

3. in quality [repeated "this," before "reduction"—and now the second-time phrase "this reduction" can be replaced by the second-time *word* "this"].
4. results may be biased because [conveyed from a less meaningful point of view the message then reconveyed as "the list of side effects may not be complete"].
9. in question [repeated "the," before "circumstances"].
11. with cobalt [repeated "such," before "granulations"].

The fractional anticipations:

10. mechanized equipment [lift trucks].
12. Thursday [November 2].

The bangbang paraphrases:

5. instructions and specifications.
7. background and training.

The sentences with these agents eliminated:

1. Advertising costs were $206,000, or 10.7% of sales, in 1966, as compared with $84,000, or 6.3% of sales, in 1958. The principal reason for the increased costs was the spending for space, radio, literature and mailings (primarily for "Astor" and "Topquality"), which amount to $150,000 in 1967, up $100,000 from 1966.
2. After a careful study, a 70% "Dacron" Type 65/30% wool blend was chosen because of best performance and aesthetics. Type 65 is offered in 3-denier staple and tow.
3. Although this policy may benefit the Arnold operation, it lessens the quality of the receivables portfolio. This would be of greater concern were the receivables separated from the Arnold organization.
4. But some investigators reject them and the lists of side effects may not be complete.
5. Definition: A numerical method for identifying . . . the specific instructions applicable to each combination.
6. Despite the "EXCELLENT" rating, there are two areas which need immediate attention.

7. In a company where only 7.1% of jobs fall in the unskilled category—in North Carolina and South Carolina the ratio of unskilled jobs is 6.2%—it is apparent that most of the better jobs require background in the technical aspects of our operations.
8. In recent months fifty to seventy-five complaints concerning extreme bitter taste in TEJAVA were reported to Quality Control Laboratory . . . I set up a taste panel to determine whether there was any basis for these complaints. Twenty-five samples from the retained files were selected at random. They were coded, and instructions were given the panel about how the tests should be conducted. The samples included the three batches that were claimed to be very bitter.
9. Recently we encountered a sensitive situation as a result of assisting one customer in relieving his inventories. The circumstances appear to have been correctly managed at first, but the handling deteriorated in process.
10. The disadvantages are increased handling cost (.33c/lb. to .995c/lb.), increased freight cost, the necessity of breaking down pallets for small orders at warehouses (most sales are to small-quantity customers), and distributors' need for lift trucks for removal from delivery trucks.
11. The problem is slightly more complex for WY TONIC Prenatal in Peru since Peru has been supplied ex Passaic with WY TONIC granulations containing cobalt and in the future no such granulations can be shipped from this country.
12. I met November 2 with ACE Packaging Consultant Frank Giles, and Dave Knowles and Pym Wharton representing Resnick Paper Box.

Chapter 14

STARTING THE DISREGARD-OF-USABLE-COMMON-ELEMENTS FAMILY

A disregarded common element is a word, phrase or idea that appears more than once in a report:

- in different contexts or associations,
- on both sides of a colon,
- on both sides of a "linking" verb (like "be," "seem," "appear"), or
- in an "appositive" construction:

> This is due to the fact that apples are cheaper. ["That apples are cheaper" is a noun clause in apposition to "the fact," and *is* "the fact."]
>
> In the event that you disagree . . . ["That you disagree" is appositive to, and *is*, "the event."]

You "use" one when, without reducing your message, you eliminate one or more of its appearances. (For example, by changing the example sentences to "This is because apples are cheaper," "If you disagree . . . ") But a *usable* common element, for us, isn't just one you *can* use (because if you tried hard enough, and were willing to write some monstrous sentences, you probably *could* use *every* one); it's one you'd *improve* a report by using. (For example: While the two above would probably be indefensible in any context, some appositive constructions are fine.)

Any kind of word or phrase may be part of an unused common element. In fact, the separate references may involve two or more different kinds.

While sometimes some members of this family seem to resemble the repetitive agents, they really reflect an entirely different phenomenon.

12 and 13 are just special cases of 3. We'll attack only 3 and 12 in this chapter.

3. Simple Disregard of Usable Common Elements

The sentences

> Mary is blond.
> Mary is pretty.
> Mary wants to be an actress.

contain *two* unused common elements; "Mary is," common to only the first two, and "Mary," common to all three.

To use "Mary is" we combine only the first two—for example, into:

Mary is blond and pretty.

Then to use "Mary," we combine all three—for example, into:

Pretty, blond Mary wants to be an actress.

And now eight words convey all the *facts* that, with the common elements disregarded, required twelve.

But often you need to convey not only facts, but also overtones, implications, emphases. And even when this isn't the case: Often, to use a common element, you'd have to sacrifice some simplicity. (This shows even in relation to Mary: While no normal reader would find the one sentence really *tough*, it's unquestionably tough*er* than any of the three.) So every possible use of a common element requires a judgment decision: If what you'd gain by using it seems more valuable than what it'd cost, you use it; if not, you don't.

And for this agent rather especially you must apply your judgment in the light of the four W's, and especially the WHAT and TO WHOM. The easier your message, and the more intelligent, better educated, more experienced and sophisticated your reader, the better you can afford to sacrifice some simplicity; the tougher your message, and the less well equipped your reader, the less well you can afford to.

But almost regardless of what you personally have been writing about, or to whom, I'd bet that over the past *n* years *you* have failed to use *countless* common elements that were *unquestionably* "usable." In fact, this agent—among its other effects—has almost certainly produced more of your superfluous words than any other except the goes-without-saying.

A common element is of course easiest to spot when it's called by the same name every time. For example:

"every," twice in 15. Kill it the second time.

"Wright," twice in 25; replace "that Wright" with "to." This makes Wright in effect—though not technically—simultaneously the object of "requested" and the subject of "to grant."

But now recall, please, that Sloane didn't say "Wright that Wright"; we substituted the "Wright's" for "the cashier" and "the latter," which we called name substitutes. Clearly, use of common elements is another good way to avoid repeating sounds.

"to the attention of," 33; kill it the second time.

And this illustrates something the "Mary" sentences didn't: Sometimes you *simplify* a construction by using a common element.

the subordinating "that," 47 and 49; kill it in 49.

Then kill it also in 47, as zero; and then kill the zero "and" in 49, changing the comma after "campaign" to a period. The "and" was another instance (see Page 65) of the connective that hooks together in one tougher construction what should have been two easier ones, and is therefore a major agent of hypercomplexity. Its effect here was somewhat mitigated by the typographical breakdown, but clearly, it wasn't *completely* eliminated.

But since we mostly paraphrase our common elements in particular ways, you can soon train yourself to spot even most of those that you haven't called each by the same name every time.

The most common paraphrase is a second-time word or phrase, and of course every second-time substitute is a common element–though, of course, not necessarily a usable one–with what it refers to. In Sloane, for example:

16-17: the noun "employees," the pronouns "whose" and "they."

While three references are too many, I think we do need two; rewrite as ". . . for *employees who* have accrued enough money."

Which shows how Agents 2 and 3 sometimes collaborate: We can use the common element because "the accounts indicate" goes without saying.

30: the noun "funds," the pronoun "that."

Kill "for the," 29, and "that," 30, and insert a new "that"–a subordinating conjunction, an entirely different word–between "except" and "funds."

32: the pronoun "this," the noun "procedure."

Rewrite as "Feeling that this procedure is improper . . ." (The new "this" is an adjective.)

32: the noun "procedure," the pronoun "it."

Rewrite as "This improper procedure has been brought to the attention of Smith and Wright." And this time *not* because "feeling that" goes without saying; rather because–among other reasons–I think Sloane *didn't* just "feel" this. Rather I think that if we could ask him he'd say he *knew* it.

Further, "feeling" was a participle, and the subject of the original sentence was "it," meaning the procedure, and a participle at the beginning of a sentence–for *communicative* reasons–must modify the subject of its sentence; so the original–though, again, we "understood" it–said the *procedure* felt the procedure was improper. I'm sure I know what happened: Sloane, when he wrote "feeling that," expected–though surely not consciously–to complete the sentence with something like "*I* have brought it to the attention of Smith and Wright," which at least would have attributed the feeling to a modificand that could feel. But when it came time to do this, he found himself not quite able to produce the "I"–auditors, like chemists, engineers and people in your field, are taught that they "aren't supposed to"–so he slid into the passive. And never thought to go back and change the first phrase.

This kind of construction is far too common. It's the product of two practices, which we'll look at individually under Agents 1 and 4; while neither is *always* bad, and while even in combination they *may* say what a writer means, most writers often use one or both where—even if they've used them "correctly"—other constructions would have told their stories much better.

33: (in "Although both advise that the procedure is admittedly an uncommon one"): the noun "procedure," the pronoun "one."

Kill "an" and "one." And then replace "the procedure" with "it."

"The following," whether or not it's club-member—or, if you've replaced it, whatever you've replaced it with—is also always a common element with what it refers to. And far more often than not you can just kill it, and often one or more other words with it. For example:

"These conclusions," 46—originally "the following conclusions"—and the conclusions themselves in 47-53.

Kill "with these conclusions." And then you may, if you like, insert a "that" before "agree"—but me, I wouldn't.

Often the best way to use common elements is by tabulating. For example, the information in

John is 18 years old and 6 feet tall and weighs 190 pounds. Peter, 17, is 6 feet tall and weighs 195. Richard, also 17, is 5:10 and weighs 165. Andrew, 18, is 5:10 and weighs 175.

comes through much more easily, and in far fewer words, as:

	Age	*Height*	*Weight*
Peter	17	6:0	195
John	18	6:0	190
Andrew	18	5:10	175
Richard	17	5:10	165

Essentially, in fact, the reason for tabulating is always *to* use common elements, and usually the best test of a table is just: Does it, or doesn't it, use common elements effectively? If it does, you can bet it's a good one; whereas if you can still see a lot of unused common elements scattered through it, it's at least *somewhat* likely that you either put it together badly, or shouldn't have tabulated in the first place.

You've been especially disregarding common elements if your writing is "choppier" than most. Because that means you've been stringing together too many short, simple sentences—which you virtually *can't* do if you use your common elements intelligently.

12. Zigzagging

You've zigzagged when your separate references to your common element are far enough apart so that to "use" it—or replace it in one of its appearances with a second-time word or phrase, which *sometimes* is all you can do—you must reorganize, at least slightly. So this agent is also one of disorganization.

Sloane gives us several examples. I want to point now to just
"bimonthly payroll," 13, 20-21 and 42-43;
"Smith has purchased no bonds," 20, and the paraphrase "Smith has consistently requested Wright to grant him a refund of this $100 before payday," 24-26;
"Wright did this," 26, and "Wright . . . do this," 29-30.

It would be uneconomical to point out all the steps by which these are combined, but each *is* combined in Stage 4. In which, as a result of the reorganization, a couple of words that we killed in Stage 3 will have had to be reinserted—but the *net* saving will be appreciable.

For Practice

One of these sentences contains also several irrelevancies.

1. Recently we encountered a sensitive situation as a result of assisting one customer in relieving his inventories. The circumstances appear to have been correctly managed at first, but the handling deteriorated in process.
2. Advertising costs were $206,000, or 10.7% of sales, in 1966, as compared with $84,000, or 6.3% of sales, in 1958.
3. Although the convenience features of the Hitachi are not critical, they increase the information output of the instrument per unit of time.
4. Based on this sampling, there is a potential membership of 1,200 people from the Department's 1,300 employees.
5. Definition: A numerical method for identifying
   - a customer, needed because of the many combinations of "Sold To" and "Ship To" names and addresses used in ordering our products, and
   - the specific instructions applicable to each combination.
6. However, the pharmacy is important as the place where purchases are made, and we should know what factors influence these purchases.
7. In a company where only 7.1% of jobs fall in the unskilled category—in North Carolina and South Carolina the ratio of unskilled jobs is 6.2%—it is apparent that most of the better jobs require background in the technical aspects of our operations.
8. In February we installed a 3/4" green entrance at 112 W. Ashbury Drive, Ashbury. 30 square feet of 25/32" oak flooring and threshold were replaced with 16" x 16" BESTFLOOR.
9. In recent months fifty to seventy-five complaints concerning extreme bitter taste in TEJAVA were reported to Quality Control Laboratory. Many came from customers who claimed to be users

of TEJAVA for twenty years or more. I set up a taste panel to determine whether there was any basis for these complaints. Twenty-five samples from the retained files were selected at random. They were coded, and instructions were given the panel about how the tests should be conducted. The samples included the three batches that were claimed to be very bitter.

10. In summary, I recommend the following:
    - We give Stilley a trial order for each plant for 7/16" seven-ply laminated oak drawer stock.
    - A change authorization be put in for costing purposes.
    - A man be placed in Trim R&G for up to 90 days who will work with me to ensure we do the best possible job in utilizing our cutting lengths to the best advantage.
11. Since subfreezing temperatures can damage most adhesives–and since carriers are not liable for frozen goods unless we can prove they were involved–from now on please allow suppliers sufficient lead time to take proper precautions.
12. The advantages of the proposal are shorter unloading and loading time and neater warehouse stacking. The disadvantages are increased handling cost (.33c/lb. to .995c/lb.), increased freight cost, the necessity of breaking down pallets for small orders at warehouses (most sales are to small-quantity customers), and distributors' need for lift trucks for removal from delivery trucks.
13. The formulation as it is known in the U.S. is altered to comply with foreign regulations. As it is changed, a different suffix is added.
14. The problem is slightly more complex for WY TONIC Prenatal in Peru since Peru has been supplied ex Passaic with WY TONIC granulations containing cobalt and in the future no such granulations can be shipped from this country.
15. We need your 1968 requirements by October 19 so we can enter our order for the Ohaus scales, which we must buy in a minimum quantity of 200 to get the present low cost. Because the equipment RSWs cannot practically store 200 scales, we will ask Ohaus to ship 100 when the order is received, 100 six months later.
16. After meeting with Onley and/or Bender several times we have reached these conclusions:

The Answers

Some of the unused, and usable, common elements (we'll expose others as we eliminate other agents):

1. situation, which, circumstances [three references]; to have been managed, handling.
2. of sales, of sales.
3. of the Hitachi, of the instrument.
4. people, employees.
6. the pharmacy, the place.
7. company, where; ratio, %; Carolina, Carolina; the unskilled category, unskilled jobs.
8. installed, replaced.
9. were reported, came.
10. the recommendations [first called "the following," then listed].
11. since, since.
12. lb., lb.; the advantages [first *called* advantages, then listed]; the disadvantages [ditto]; increased, increased.
13. altered, changed.
14. WY TONIC, WY TONIC.
15. scales, which, scales [three references].
16. Onley and/or Bender, we ["we" *includes* Onley and Bender].

The zigzags:

5. combinations, combination.
9. samples, samples.

The irrelevancies were the ideas expressed through "encountered," "sensitive" and "result" in 1.

1. A recent situation in which we assisted one customer in relieving his inventories appears to have been correctly managed at first, but not all the way through.
2. Advertising costs were $206,000, or 10.7% of sales, in 1966, as compared with $84,000, or 6.3%, in 1958.
3. Although the convenience features are not critical, they increase the information output of the Hitachi per unit of time.
4. Based on this sampling, there is a potential membership of 1,200 of the Department's 1,300 employees.
5. Definition: A numerical method for identifying a customer and his instructions, needed because of the many combinations of "Sold To" and "Ship To" names and addresses used in ordering our products. ["Specific" would now be zero before "instructions."]
6. However, the pharmacy is where purchases are made, and we should know what factors influence these purchases.

7. Since in our company only 7.1% of jobs fall in the unskilled category–in the Carolinas, only 6.2%–it is apparent that most of the better jobs require background in the technical aspects of our operations.
8. In February we replaced 30 square feet of 25/32" oak flooring and threshold with 3/4" green 16" x 16" BESTFLOOR at the entrance to 112 W. Ashbury Drive, Ashbury.
9. In recent months fifty to seventy-five complaints concerning extreme bitter taste in TEJAVA were reported to Quality Control Laboratory, many from customers who claimed to be users of TEJAVA for twenty years or more. I set up a taste panel to determine whether there was any basis for these complaints. Twenty-five samples were selected at random from retained files of the three batches that were claimed to be very bitter. They were coded, and instructions were given the panel about how the tests should be conducted.
10. In summary, I recommend: . . .
11. Since subfreezing temperatures can damage most adhesives–and carriers are not liable for frozen goods unless we can prove they were involved–from now on please allow suppliers sufficient lead time to take proper precautions.
12. The proposal would result in shorter unloading and loading time and neater warehouse stacking, but also in
    - increased handling cost (.33c to .995c/lb.) and freight cost;
    - the necessity of breaking down pallets for small orders at warehouses (most sales are to small-quantity customers), and
    - distributors' need for lift trucks for removal from delivery trucks.
13. The formulation as it is known in the U.S. is altered to comply with foreign regulations; each time it is, a different suffix is added.
14. The problem is slightly more complex in Peru since Peru has been supplied ex Passaic with WY TONIC Prenatal granulations containing cobalt and in the future no such granulations can be shipped from this country.
15. We need your 1968 requirements by October 19 so we can enter our order for the Ohaus scales; we must buy at least 200 to get the present low cost. Because the equipment RSWs cannot practically store 200, we will ask Ohaus to ship 100 when the order is received, 100 six months later. [The prepositional phrase "in a minimum quantity," which modified "must buy," was misattached; its replacement, "at least," modifies "200."]
16. Onley, Bender and I have reached these conclusions:

SLOANE REPORT - Stage 4

September 9, 1957

To : H. B. Dawson

From : N. B. Sloane

AUDIT OF PAYROLL DEDUCTION FUNDS, EXVILLE PLANT

Deductions we have withheld for Savings Bonds from the pay of
employees at this plant are held in the account R. J. Wright, Cashier,
at the First National Bank. This account is in balance with the individual account cards. However, there has been a mishandling of the
5 funds which might be considered collusion between Wright and Plant Manager R. W. Smith.

Smith has authorized $100 deductions for bonds since 1950, at
which time it was decided by Ajax to undertake a campaign for the purpose
of convincing employees to sign up to purchase bonds under the payroll
10 plan. He and Assistant Plant Manager J. J. Blake are on a bimonthly
payroll that is made at the main office; all other employees who have
bond deductions are on a weekly payroll that is made at the plant. The
bimonthly payroll is written very early in the payroll period, and when
it is written the deductions are posted to the individual accounts; as
15 you know, the total of the deductions on every payroll is forwarded to
the cashier on payday to be deposited. It becomes the duty of the cash-
ier to purchase bonds for employees who have accrued enough money. The
plan is taken advantage of by nearly 1,000 employees.

But Smith has consistently requested Wright to grant him a
20 refund of his $100 before payday, and Wright has always done so, out of
funds that had been deducted on earlier payrolls from the pay of other
employees, so Smith has actually obtained an advance every payroll
period. In addition there is the complication that Blake, on one or two
occassions during the past several months, has given himself advances
25 through this means.

This improper procedure has been brought to the attention of
Smith and Wright. Although both advise that it is admittedly uncommon,
Wright says he has merely acted pursuant to instructions that he has
regularly received from Smith, and Smith feels there have been no vio-
30 lations of company rules or policies. I have apprised them I would
include the practice in my report. Wright will be 65 years of age Octo-

ber 12 and has been with us since 1919. There is little doubt in my mind that you will agree:

- The actions of these personnel are outside the results desired

35 to be achieved by the campaign.

- There is a loophole here by which it is possible for additional plant managers to also follow Smith's procedure, thereby also improperly obtaining advances on their salaries.

But now "so Smith has actually obtained an advance every payroll period," 22-23, is exposed as just repetition plus of what precedes it. Kill it.

Chapter 15

ANOTHER WRONG-POINT-OF-VIEW AGENT

8. The (Just Generally) Wrong Point of View

This is the one that produces any wrong-point-of-view construction except one of the specific kinds produced by other members of its family—for example, the wrong number or the long-winded negative.

Sometimes you need to shift a point of view only slightly to correct it. As in this excerpt from a geophysical report:

Below the unconformity the beds are tilted much more steeply.	Below the unconformity the tilt is much steeper.

But sometimes you need to shift 180 degrees:

Even a mild recession would drive this company out of business.	This company needs continuous prosperity to survive.

Sloane, who's surprisingly light on this agent—I'd not have been surprised had he given us six to ten examples—nevertheless illustrates both types:

3-4: This account is in balance with the individual account cards.

True, and not irrelevant or unimportant. But what *really* matters is that:

This account is in balance with the individual *accounts.*

23-25: . . . Blake, on one or two occasions during the past several months, has given himself advances through this means.

"Given" is absurd; what disturbed Sloane was that:

Blake, on one or two occasions during the past several months, has *taken* advances through this means.

It's not surprising that both these changes—plus those in the other examples—saved words. This agent costs words far more often than not.

But to repeat: The word saving is only a bonus; the important thing is that each of these stories is now so told that its *significance* comes through more clearly. Any time you must add words to fix a point of view you'll still be eliminating this agent.

For Practice

You can't possibly fix 5—but maybe you can spot the words that need to come out.

1. But for future visits of this nature I would like you each to prepare a program of instructions in all phases of our operations, policies and procedures you are concerned with.
2. Central Engineering will prepare a definite cost estimate, which requires us to be accurate within 10%.
3. Du Pont's retention periods, now used for these records, range from ten years to permanent; AEC's, from three to ten . . . Most other records can be kept for periods shorter than Du Pont commercial records because . . .
4. During this period they are short of cash and obtained bank loans in past years to pay supplier invoices.
5. Heating cycle results do not give information on actual heat transfer coefficient because the calculated U's reflect the heat of reaction from the exothermic imination.
6. If we require all subsidiaries to use the same fiscal year, Ajax should provide extra help.
7. The creditors were advised by Davis that Charles had borrowed $536,000 from the corporation over 33 years and lost it gambling.
8. The formulation as it is known in the U.S. is altered to comply with foreign regulations; each time it is, a different suffix is added.

The Answers

The words that provided the wrong points of view:

1. I would like you each [an "indicative" construction that should have been "imperative"].
2. which requires us to [the important that was "*we must*"].
3. kept [the important thing was when they could be *destroyed*]; for periods shorter than Du Pont commercial records [the important thing was how many *years*].
4. supplier invoices.
5. do not give information on actual heat transfer coefficient.
6. if we require all subsidiaries to [the "we" was trivial and went without saying].
7. over 33 years.
8. to comply with foreign regulations.

The sentences with their points of view corrected:

1. But for future visits of this nature *please* prepare a program of instructions in all phases of our operations, policies and procedures you are concerned with.
2. Central Engineering will prepare a definite cost estimate, *so we must* be accurate within 10%.
3. Du Pont's retention periods, now used for these records, range from ten years to permanent; AEC's, from three to ten . . . Most other records can be *destroyed/in less than ten years* because . . .
4. During this period they are short of cash and obtained bank loans in past years to pay *suppliers.*
5. Heating cycle results *are too high* because the calculated U's reflect the heat of reaction from the exothermic imination.
6. If *all subsidiaries must* use the same fiscal year, Ajax should provide extra help.
7. The creditors were advised by Davis that Charles had borrowed $536,000 from the corporation *since 1934* and lost it gambling.
8. The formulation as it is known in the U.S. is altered *as foreign regulations require*; each time it is, a different suffix is added.

Chapter 16

THE WRONG-WAY-TO-MODIFY AGENT THAT ALSO INVOLVES DISREGARD OF COMMON ELEMENTS

13. The Pointless Modifying Clause

First: How to modify best is often a relatively minor consideration; often a construction that modifies poorly is your best construction. For example: However you'd thereby improve your modification—and despite the fact that you'd save words—you must *never* eliminate a clause whose verb conveys a "key verb idea." (If you don't understand that now, no matter; you will after a while.)

But there are four "levels of desirability" for adjectival modifiers, three for adverbial. And in this chapter we'll be concerned only with how to modify best.

Of the grammatical terms that relate to this agent, adjective, adverb and possessive noun and pronoun are defined in the Glossary, and "nonce adjective" and infinitive in Chapters 10 and 16. I'll define the others now.

PREPOSITIONS are words like "at," "in," "of," "from," "with," "by," "through"; every preposition begins a PREPOSITIONAL PHRASE, and every prepositional phrase is adjective or adverbial.

These modify nouns, so they're adjective:

> This is a story *by* Shakespeare *about* a couple *of* boys *from* Verona.

These are adverbial; they modify a verb ("started"), an adjective "happy") and an adverb ("where"):

> He started *at* a rapid pace, happy *as* a lark, but wondering where *in* the world he was going.

A verb's PARTICIPLES are the forms in which, though retaining *some* of its "verbness," it's supposed to be used to modify substantives, so it's also partly an adjective. Every verb—except the few called "defective," which we'll disregard—has two.

The *present* participle of *every* verb is itself plus "-ing" (except that final "e's" are usually dropped, as in "creating," and some final letters are doubled, as in "hitting," "slipping," "humming").

The *past* participle of a *regular* verb is the same as its past tense—that is, it's the verb plus "-d" or "-ed." (Again a final letter may be doubled; and a final "y," if it follows a consonant, is changed to "i," as in "fried," "multiplied.")

But the past participle of an *ir*regular verb—and English has many such—may be almost anything: "eaten," "made," "thought," "thrown," "found" and so forth. But even if you've never thought of these as participles, you know and recognize every one of them, so this is nothing to worry about.

For example:

The *sobbing* child stared at the *broken* toy.
Fascinated, the snake watched the fakir.
Smiling, the fakir looked at the snake.
The snake, *fascinated*, watched the fakir.
The fakir, *smiling*, looked at the snake.
You look *frustrated.*

A participle may itself be modified by an adverbial modifier or modifiers:

There you were, jumping *up* and *down* [adverbs] *like a wild man* [prepositional phrase].

As tired *as if he'd run all the way* [adverbial clause], he got there just in time.

And since it's partly a verb, it may take an object or objects:

Changing *the tire*, I reflected on my bad luck.
I heard you playing *the piano.*

And such instances of participles plus we'll call PARTICIPIAL PHRASES.

Similarly, an INFINITIVE PHRASE is an infinitive plus one or more modifiers and/or objects.

Some infinitives and infinitive phrases used adjectivally:

This is a *never-to-be-forgotten* moment.
His story is *not to be believed.*
You're a sight *to behold.*

Some used adverbially (the modificands are "changed," a verb; "good," an adjective, and "enough," an adverb):

To make amends, he changed the tire.
Apples are good *to eat.*
He's tall enough *to play forecourt.*

Infinitives may serve also as pure verbs or substantives, but that's irrelevant here.

An ADJECTIVE PHRASE is an adjective plus one or more modifiers of its own. You'll see one later in this chapter.

A CLAUSE is a group of words containing a subject and a predicate; the subject must be or include at least one substantive (like "boy," below), the predicate must be or include at least one "predicate verb" (like "was going"):

SUBJECT PREDICATE

The boy / was going to the movies.

And it doesn't matter that that's also a sentence; a simple sentence *is* a clause. And it could equally have been part of a sentence, as in "You could see that the boy was going to the movies."

Every modifying clause is adjective or adverbial.

An ADJECTIVE CLAUSE is one that's introduced by a relative pronoun or adjective; it's adjective because it modifies the substantive—which ideally, as in each example following, it follows immediately—that the "relative" word refers to.

Theoretically, the only relative pronouns are:

THAT: This is the house that Jack built.

WHICH: My hat, which I bought yesterday, is in the closet.

WHO: John, who is nearly deaf, never heard us.

WHOM: This is the man whom I spoke to you about.

WHOSE: Is this the child whose dog is missing?

And occasionally such variants as "whoever," "whichever" and the like.

But sometimes a "relative adverb," like "where" or "when," becomes in effect a relative pronoun:

This is the house where I was born.

I met him last Friday, when I was in Duluth.

And sometimes the relative pronoun is understood:

This is the house (that) Jack built.

This is the man (whom) I spoke to you about.

Relative adjectives are relative pronouns used as adjectives:

We used the machine only a week and a half, during which time it broke down twice.

ADVERBIAL CLAUSES are introduced by subordinating conjunctions, like "as," "when," "because," "after"; they modify verbs (like "came," below), adjectives (like "taller") and adverbs (like "quickly"):

He came when I called*.

He was taller than I'd expected.

I came as quickly as I could.

*Most words that can serve as subordinating conjunctions can serve also as other parts of speech; for example, in the sentence a few lines back "when" was a "relative adverb." The difference: There it "referred" to a preceding word, here it doesn't.

Grammatically, any modifier is as good as any other.

But communicatively:

ADJECTIVALLY—disregarding "predicate adjectives," which are irrelevant here—you modify

best with *any* modifier that *precedes* its modificand (which of all types of adjectival modifiers only a clause can never do), provided it does so smoothly and easily;

and when your modifier must follow its modificand,

second best with a prepositional phrase, infinitive or infinitive phrase;

third best with an adjective, adjective phrase, participle or participial phrase.

ADVERBIALLY, you modify

best with an adverb;

second best with a prepositional phrase, infinitive or infinitive phrase.

And adjectivally *or* adverbially, you modify *least* well with a clause.

Now back to Sloane.

Stage 4 contains six modifying clauses whose verbs don't convey key verb ideas.

Not surprisingly, five are adjective; this type is by far the more common. What's a little surprising, though, is that three of the five hurt so relatively little, among other things costing a total of only six words. (The others each cost a lot of words and injected some *real* fog.)

1-2: (that) we have withheld for Savings Bonds from the pay of employees at this plant.

11-12: who have bond deductions.

12: that is made at the plant.

21-22: that had been deducted on earlier payrolls from the pay of other employees.

28-29: that he has regularly received from Smith.

(But not "that is made at the main office," 11; in this one the predicate verb does convey a key verb idea. The difference between it and "that is made at the plant": Where the *weekly* payroll is made matters very little in this report, but where the "bimonthly" payroll is matters greatly. So while we *could* eliminate it, exactly as we're about to eliminate the others, we won't. More on this under Agent 1.)

If nothing else, you can *always* promote an adjective clause to a third-level modifier, almost always a participle or participial phrase. To do this, you just

- kill the relative pronoun (this uses the common element) and
- change the verb to a participle—which about 999 times in a thousand involves just crossing out its "auxiliary" part, like "have" in "have

withheld," "is" in "is made," "had been" in "had been deducted," "has" in "has received."

And sometimes, sort of in passing, you can also kill one or more miscellaneous words.

For example, we can now remove from Sloane:

1. (that) we have

11: who [and change "have" to "having"; this is the one case in a thousand]

12: that is

21: that had been

28: that he has

And this is as far as you *should* go when the idea conveyed by your verb, though not "key," is *somewhat* verblike and important.

But when it's not even *somewhat* verblike or important, or it goes without saying, you need to go farther; otherwise you just replace Agent 13 with Agent 14. (Which we'll attack in the next chapter.) In this case, besides using the common element, you must

- eliminate the verb *completely* and
- extract whatever the clause contains that *should* be conveyed and convey it through *first- and/or second-level* adjectival modifiers:

11-12: . . . employees *with bond deductions* [prepositional phrase].

28: . . . has merely acted pursuant to *Smith's* [possessive noun] *regular* [adjective] instructions.

Later we'll also fix the construction in 1-2 in this more drastic way. (But not the others; I think the ideas conveyed by "made" and "deducted" *are* somewhat verblike and important.)

If its verb is some form of "to be"—and sometimes when it's some other "linking" verb—you can typically eliminate a clause just by crossing out the verb and the relative pronoun.

If what followed the verb was

an adjective or adjective phrase, this leaves a third-level modifier:

> The objective *which is* most important to us right now is to reduce this waste to a more tolerable level. ["Most," "to us" and "right now" all modify the adjective "important"; this is what makes the six words an adjective phrase.]

a substantive—whether a single word or phrase—the substantive becomes appositive to the preceding substantive:

> I spoke to John Owens, *who is* their superintendent for maintenance.

Since Sloane's pointless adjective clauses were relatively so innocuous, let's throw in a few from other reports:

July expectancy is 900M gallons, *which is an increase of 40M gallons over forecast.*	July expectancy is 900M gallons—*40M gallons over forecast.*

To repeat *the* suggestions *that we offered you in our letter of April 11*: Combine 30 parts of . . .

To repeat *our* suggestions *of April 11*: Combine 30 parts of . . .

In two cases input rates were 200,000 pounds/day; in two they were 160,000 pounds. The cases *that had input rates of 160,000 pounds/day* were marginal.

In two cases input rates were 200,000 pounds/day; in two they were 160,000 pounds. The *160,000-pound* cases were marginal.

A pointless *adverbial* clause usually involves disregard of common elements only when the modifying idea is really adjective, and so needs to be conveyed through one or more *adjectival* modifiers:

Continue to study all overhead accounts and make dollar reductions *when any are indicated.* [Common element: "reductions" and the pronoun "any"; the clause modifies the verb "make."]

Continue to study all overhead accounts and make *any indicated* dollar reductions. [The new "any" is an adjective, and "indicated" is a participle modifying "reductions."]

After you have completed it, send this form to A. B. Parker, Industrial Relations. [Common element: "it" and "this form"; the clause modifies "send."]

Send the *completed* form to A. B. Parker, Industrial Relations.

Otherwise it generally involves just inefficient modification or a wrong point of view.

When the Paragon scale is substituted, the selling price is $262.

With the Paragon scale, the selling price is $262.

If no inert gas is present, the pressure should extrapolate to zero at zero B_2H_2.

With no inert gas present, the pressure should extrapolate to zero at zero B_2H_2.

Also, we might violate Texas Air Control Commission regulations *if we used a flare stack here.*

Also, a flare stack here might violate Texas Air Control Commission regulations. [Far from being used as a common element, "we" drops out both times.]

And this is the case with Sloane's example: The clause "when it is written" (13-14)–originally "as soon as this payroll is written"–can be replaced by just one second-time adverb:

12-14: The bimonthly payroll is written very early in the payroll period, and the deductions are *then* posted to the individual accounts.

But "then" is a common element with "very early in the payroll period" (as also, of course, was "when it is written"). So we can now take the sentence one step farther:

> The bimonthly payroll is written—and the deductions are posted to the individual accounts—very early in the payroll period.

But sometimes a common element gets used sort of incidentally:

> The invoice goes to Accounts Receivable, which issues a refund check about three weeks *after the invoice has been received.*

> The invoice goes to Accounts Receivable, which issues a refund check about three weeks *later.*

For Practice

1. Although the convenience features are not critical, they increase the information output of the Hitachi per unit of time.
2. An advisory panel will help us prepare the manual. It will be composed of:
   - Anslinger, Bloomquist, Brill and Canlis, who were on our Law Enforcement Manual panel . . .
3. Denim of 50/50 420 nylon/cotton should provide good durability which would be lower than that of 80/20-50/50 "Dacron"/cotton but noticeably superior to that of 50/50 polyester/cotton.
4. In summary, I recommend: . . .
   - A man be placed in Trim R&G for up to 90 days who will work with me to ensure we do the best possible job in utilizing our cutting lengths to the best advantage.
5. It would be premature also because the market WA-1 will compete in is changing rapidly, and by 1971, the earliest year commercial distribution can be achieved, significant changes could invalidate present expansion planning.
6. The co-operation we are receiving from Dr. Alexander on Vizaid Ophthalmic deserves that serious consideration be given to purchasing a quantity of his book, but we must assure ourselves it is in the best interest of our eye-area promotion.
7. The formulation as it is known in the U.S. is altered as foreign regulations require; each time it is, a different suffix is added.
8. This is an apt description, too, of the problem we face in Wilmington.
9. Twenty-five samples were selected at random from retained files of the three batches that were claimed to be very bitter.

The Answers

1. although the convenience features are not critical.
2. who were on our Law Enforcement Manual panel.
3. which would be lower, etc.
4. who will work with me, etc.
5. (that) WA-1 will compete in.
6. (that) we are receiving from Dr. Alexander, etc.
7. as it is known in the U.S.
8. (that) we face in Wilmington.
9. that were claimed to be very bitter.

1. Although not critical, the convenience features increase the information output of the Hitachi per unit of time.
2. An advisory panel will help us prepare the manual . . . It will be composed of:
   - Anslinger, Bloomquist, Brill and Canlis from our Law Enforcement Manual panel . . .
3. Denim of 50/50 420 nylon/cotton should provide good durability—lower than that of 80/20-50/50 "Dacron"/cotton but noticeably superior to that of 50/50 polyester/cotton.
4. In summary, I recommend: . . .
   - A man be placed in Trim R&G for up to 90 days to work with me to ensure we do the best possible job in utilizing our cutting lengths to the best advantage.
5. It would be premature also because the prospective market for WA-1 is changing rapidly, and by 1971, the earliest year commercial distribution can be achieved, significant changes could invalidate present expansion planning.
6. Dr. Alexander's co-operation on Vizaid Ophthalmic deserves that serious consideration be given to purchasing a quantity of his book, but we must assure ourselves it is in the best interest of our eye-area promotion.
7. The U.S. formulation is altered as foreign regulations require; each time it is, a different suffix is added.
8. This is an apt description, too, of our problem in Wilmington.
9. Twenty-five samples were selected at random from retained files of the three batches alleged to be very bitter.

Chapter 17

THE LAST TWO WRONG-WAY-TO-MODIFY AGENTS

14. The Pointless Third-Level Modifier

Almost always this is just the remnant of an adjective clause whose author should have eliminated it the more drastic way, but who instead—whether or not knowingly—just promoted it to a participle or participial phrase. For example, we'd now have two more in Sloane had we been satisfied to change 11-12 and 28-29 to:

. . . all other employees *having bond deductions* . . .

. . . instructions *regularly received from Smith* . . .

Actually, it's almost too bad you *can* so easily replace a clause with a third-level modifier. Because when you kill the relative word, you eliminate a loud, clear signal that you've modified inefficiently; if you need to go farther, the only remaining objective signal is the participle itself, which to most people signals much less loudly and clearly.

Like an adjective clause, a third-level modifier may be good, also for reasons related to Agent 1; and the "made" and "deducted" phrases *are* good in 12 and 21. But one that's intended only to *modify* needs to be promoted. So in 34-35, now replace "desired to be achieved by the campaign" with just a past participle (preceding its modificand) and a prepositional phrase:

. . . the *desired* results *of the campaign.*

Stage 4 contains also another example of this agent, but we'll save it for a while.

Often you can promote a participial phrase to a prepositional phrase by just crossing out the participle, or the participle and its object:

Broughton, whom I spoke to first, is a consultant *sent* from the main office.

Further investigation disclosed that the trouble apparently originated in the line *bringing the solvent* from Tank 1 . . . The line *coming* from Tank 2 was also investigated, but the investigation revealed it could not have been the source of the trouble.

An example of pointless third-level modification involving an adjective phrase (on Page 111 I went only part way with this sentence):

The objective *most important to us right now* is to reduce this waste to a more tolerable level.

Our most important immediate objective is to reduce this waste to a more tolerable level.

6. Prepositionitis

This, of course—except rarely—is the practice of pointlessly modifying through prepositional phrases instead of first-level modifiers. (What it rarely is you'll see in Chapter 22.) As Sloane suggests—and he's not extraordinarily heavy on it—it's by far the most common of the wrong-way-to-modify agents.

In well over half its appearances the prepositional phrase is adjective and needs just to become a first-level adjectival modifier:

2: employees *at this plant.*

> Sloane, you may recall, said "employees at the Exville plant"; we pretended "the Exville" represented failure to use a second-time word, but I said at the time we'd *really* fix the construction later. All right: First change it back to the original—and then make it "Exville employees."

1-2: *the* pay *of Exville employees*	Exville employees' pay
7: *deductions* for bonds	bond deductions
16-17: *the* duty *of the cashier*	the cashier's duty
21-22: *the* pay *of other employees*	other employees' pay
26-27: *the* attention *of Smith and Wright*	Smith's and Wright's attention
31: years *of age*	years old
34: *the* actions *of these personnel*	these actions
38: advances *on their salaries*	salary advances

(The "the's" that dropped out in front of their modificands weren't zero; they were incidental fruits of prepositionitis.)

Next most often the phrase is adverbial and needs to become an adverb:

7-8: at which time	when
21: on earlier payrolls	earlier
23: in addition	also
24: during the past several months	recently

Fairly often, though, a phrase is adverbial only because it was misattached, and needs to become a first-level *adjectival* modifier. As in 23-25, where Sloane attached "on one or two occasions [misspelled]" and "through this means" to "has taken," though he clearly meant:

> There is also the complication that Blake has taken *one or two such* advances recently.

(When it isn't misattached, "on one or two occasions" should almost any time be the adverbs "once or twice.")

Once in a great while, similarly, an adjective prepositional phrase needs to become an adverb. Sloane gives us no examples.

Since prepositions can often be "understood," you may sometimes have prepositionitis without a preposition. This was the case in the first four words in Stage 1; "the audit last week" was a slightly abbreviated form of "the audit *of* last week," and could have been just "last week's audit."

As Sloane suggests, the preposition most often involved in prepositionitis is "of."

But this agent *may* involve *any* preposition; Sloane showed us also "at," "for," "on," "in," "during," "through." And to list some that he didn't:

a play *by* Shakespeare	a Shakespeare play
a split *between* Russia and China	a Russo-Chinese split
a salary of $10,000 *per* annum	a $10,000 annual salary
the era *before* the Revolution	the pre-Revolutionary era
the period *after* the Revolution	the post-Revolutionary period
a man *with* money	a rich man
a horseman *without* a head	a headless horseman
ears *like* a rabbit's	rabbit ears
everyone *except* the preceding	everyone else

But:

Prepositional phrases, in general, are the fourth of the four constructions you must guard against overeliminating. If ever you eliminate one that's smoother and easier than its shorter alternative, at best you'll be terse rather than concise, and at worst you'll be unclear.

Obviously, some cases will be borderline. For example, if you don't like "Smith's and Wright's attention," about as many agree with you as with me. And many who've been through this report have wanted to change "the desired results of the campaign," 34-35, to "the desired campaign results" or "the campaign's desired results," which *I* don't like. In such a case anyone's judgment is as good as anyone else's, and everyone's right.

But I hope no one will ever want to change 4-6 to:

> However, there has been a funds mishandling which might be considered Wright-Plant Manager R. W. Smith collusion.

Now we can eliminate some more examples of other agents.

First the long participial phrase in 1-2; we've just killed two prepositional phrases within it, but it's still a pointless third-level modifier. (It was originally a *clause*; in Chapter 16 we *promoted* it to a phrase.) Two nonce adjectives and a prepositional phrase replace it perfectly:

Exville payroll deductions *for Savings Bonds* are held in the account R. J. Wright, Cashier, in the First National Bank.

And "for bonds," 7, wasn't only prepositionitis; it also went without saying. And now "bond" does; kill it.

In 31, "years old" goes without saying.

But the whole sentence in 31-32 has been irrelevant from the beginning, and when we killed "years old" we lost our last reason to retain it. If, as some have suggested, Sloane provided it to suggest that Dawson go easy on Wright, he shouldn't have; my accountant-auditor friends say it's almost impossible that Wright *would* have been punished severely. But I don't think he did; I think it just sneaked in, and survived simply because he never questioned himself about it.

For Practice

The reason we can promote one third-level modifier below is that most of the information it conveys is irrelevant. And one case of prepositionitis involves also a misattached modifier.

1. Although not critical, the convenience features increase the information output of the Hitachi per unit of time.
2. But for future visits of this nature please prepare a program of instructions in all phases of our operations, policies and procedures you are concerned with.
3. Davis and Charles were then excused so the creditors could discuss the situation in private.
4. Definition: A numerical method for identifying a customer and his instructions, needed because of the many combinations of "Sold To" and "Ship To" names and addresses used in ordering our products.
5. For example, if we assume a sales price of $50,000 and 15%/year cost of capital, it would cost us $3,000/year to retain the drag line.
6. I met November 2 with ACE Packaging Consultant Frank Giles, and Dave Knowles and Pym Wharton representing Resnick Paper Box.
7. Since in our company only 7.1% of jobs fall in the unskilled category–in the Carolinas, only 6.2%–it is apparent that most of the better jobs require background in the technical aspects of our operation.
8. This would be of greater concern were the receivables separated from the Arnold organization.
9. The problem is slightly more complex in Peru since Peru has been supplied ex Passaic with WY TONIC Prenatal granulations containing cobalt and in the future no such granulations can be shipped from this country.

The Answers

The pointless third-level modifiers:

4. needed because of the many combinations of "Sold To" and "Ship To" names and addresses used in ordering our products.
6. representing Resnick Paper Box.

The pointless prepositional phrases:

1. *of* the Hitachi.
2. *of* this nature.
3. *in* private.
5. *of* $50,000.
7. *in* the unskilled category; *in* the technical aspects *of* our operations.
8. *of* greater concern.
9. *in* the future.

The sentences with these agents eliminated:

1. Although not critical, the convenience features increase *the Hitachi's* information output per unit of time.
2. But for future *such* visits, please prepare a program of instructions in all phases of our operations, policies and procedures you are concerned with.
3. Davis and Charles were then excused so the creditors could discuss the situation *privately.*
4. Definition: A numerical method for identifying a customer and his *shipping* instructions.
5. For example, if we assume a *$50,000* sales price and 15%/year cost of capital, it would cost us $3,000/year to retain the drag line.
6. I met November 2 with ACE Packaging Consultant Frank Giles, and Dave Knowles and Pym Wharton *of Resnick Paper Box.*
7. Since in our company only 7.1% of jobs are *unskilled*—in the Carolinas, only 6.2%—it is apparent that most of the better jobs require *some technical* background. ["Fall" should have been "are" all the time.]
8. This would be *more serious* were the receivables separated from the Arnold organization.
9. The problem is slightly more complex in Peru since Peru has been supplied ex Passaic with WY TONIC Prenatal granulations containing cobalt and such granulations can no longer be shipped from this country. [The misattached modifier was "no," which originally modified "granulations."]

Chapter 18

THE LAST MISCELLANEOUS INEFFICIENCY

15. The Impersonal Introduction

This–still another of our private terms–is a construction that begins with

- a "there" that doesn't mean "in that place," or
- an "it" that refers not to a *preceding* substantive, but to a clause, infinitive or infinitive phrase that will *follow.*

As in "*There* has been a mishandling of the funds," or "*It* becomes the cashier's duty *to purchase bonds for employees who have accrued enough money.*"

(But not in "There is the ashtray; it is full." Because "there," there, does mean "in that place," and "it" refers to the preceding noun "ashtray.")

The construction may begin in the middle of a sentence:

> I have not tried to list all the problems that *there* may be in this area.
>
> This makes *it* more difficult for us *to train the operators properly.*

Every impersonal introduction is one of eight types. Those we'll number 1 through 6 *always* hurt, and every 7 does except one that can be replaced only in one of two particular ways (which I'll identify when I define this type). Your 8's, on the other hand, are fine constructions, and I hope you'll never try to eliminate one.

But 1 and 2 involve also other agents that we haven't reached yet, so in this chapter we'll look at only 3 through 8.

A 7 can begin only with "it," an 8 only with "there." Any of the others may begin with either.

Sloane illustrates only 1 through 5.

TYPE 3: The Type You Can Just Cross Out

Sloane's example is in 23. First move "also" to between "has" and "taken," 24; then cross out "there is the complication that."

TYPE 4: The Long-Winded-Adverb Type

Like "There is little doubt in my mind that," 32-33; all it means can be expressed through one adverb:

You will *surely* agree:

And now I *would* insert a "that" after "agree." (And change the punctuation; you'll see how in Stage 5.)

And "surely"—and such of its (alleged) synonyms as "unquestionably," "certainly," "doubtlessly," "undoubtedly"—are often expressed in this long-winded way. As also—to list just a few—are:

probably	it is probable that it is likely that there is a likelihood that
clearly, obviously	it is clear that it is obvious that there can be no doubt that
significantly	it is significant that
notably	it is noteworthy that
maybe, possibly, perhaps	it is possible that there is a possibility that it may be the case that it may turn out that it is conceivable that

TYPE 5: The Type Involving Disregard of Common Elements (Other Than the Common Element "It" and What It Refers to, Which Is Disregarded in *Every* "It"-Type Impersonal Introduction)

Usually, with this type, the common element is mentioned only twice:

There have been a number of companies who have gone into private carriage because they thought they could save money. [Common element: "companies" and "who." And note the mutilated adjective.]	Several companies have gone into private carriage because they thought they could save money.
I realize there are times when an emotional experience may be more valuable than acquiring factual knowledge. [Common element: "times" and "when an emotional experience . . ."]	I realize that sometimes an emotional experience may be more valuable than acquiring factual knowledge.
If there are any questions or problems, please call them to my personal attention. [Common element: "questions or problems," "them."]	Please call any questions or problems to my personal attention.

But Sloane, in 36-38, mentions his three times: First he calls it "loophole," then "which," then "Smith's procedure."

To eliminate just "which," we redo the sentence as:

This loophole makes it possible for additional plant managers to also follow Smith's procedure, thereby also improperly obtaining salary advances.

But really all he meant was:

> It is possible for additional plant managers to also use this loophole, thereby also improperly obtaining salary advances.

TYPE 6: The Type That Tells Its Story From a Less Than Maximally Meaningful Point of View

This is the only type that sometimes doesn't cost words. Also—except in the relatively rare case where the point of view is *seriously* wrong, as in the first example following—it usually hurts less generally than any of the first five.

But it always does hurt, at least a little. For example:

Also, *it would help* to know the responsibilities of the cost supervisor.	Also, *I need* to know the responsibilities of the cost supervisor.
If #7105 is absorbed, *there will be* about 42 days' excess in the Philadelphia area.	If #7105 is absorbed, *we will have* about 42 days' excess in the Philadelphia area.
The patch stayed in place at 430 rpm, so *there is* no serious problem here.	The patch stayed in place at 430 rpm, so *we have* no serious problem here.
It will take about a week and a half to accumulate a truckload.	*You will need* about a week and a half to accumulate a truckload.

TYPE 7: The Type That Has Nothing *Necessarily* Wrong With It Except That the Impersonal "It" Is Itself an Unused Common Element With What It Refers to

You *should* use this type any time that (1) it has nothing *else* wrong with it, and (2) it's your smoothest and most economical alternative to

- mutilating a verb (I'll illustrate this in Chapter 20) or
- a construction like this, which is tough because the main clause verb—"is"—arrives so late:

  > To study pantheistic philosophy on a day like this, when the birds are singing and the flowers blooming, and you can just FEEL the sunshine beaming gently on the happy smiling faces of people beneath your window, is very difficult.

  An "it" at the beginning—followed immediately by the "is very difficult"—would have been an additional word, but clearly well worth its cost.

But few Type 7's—even of those that have nothing else wrong with them—are the best alternatives to constructions like these. And many have other things *incidentally* wrong with them—involving, for example, such other agents as pointless attribution, the long-winded negative or failure to use second-time words or phrases, to name just a few. For example, the first following involved also a long-winded affirmative:

It will take until October for the whole Bangor work force to complete their third and fourth weeks of vacation. Meanwhile *it* will be difficult to maintain the required production levels.	The whole Bangor work force will not have completed their third and fourth weeks of vacation until October. Meanwhile required production levels will be hard to maintain.
Unless one knows the concepts, terminology and accounts related to our cost-accounting system, *it* is very hard to understand our cost-accounting procedure.	Unless one knows the concepts, terminology and accounts related to our cost-accounting system, our cost-accounting procedure is very hard to understand.

TYPE 8: The "There-Is-a-Tavern-in-the-Town" Construction

What distinguishes this from the other "there" types is that the only way to reduce it without distorting it is to replace "there is" with "exists" or "occurs." ("A tavern is in the town," or "The town has a tavern," does *not* perfectly express "There is a tavern in the town.")

Well, why not so reduce it?

Because while a perfect report contains no superfluous words, it also contains none that are unnecessarily *difficult*; and when you substitute one tougher word for just *two* simpler ones—if all else is equal—what you lose in simplicity exceeds what you gain in efficiency. And while surely no one you write to would find "exists" or "occurs" really *tough*, unquestionably either is tough*er* than either "there" or "is."

This is why, in this book,

I've said	*instead of*
And when you've good reason to separate, but none to numerate, some other device—and *there are* many—must be better than numeration.	And when you've good reason to separate, but none to numerate, some other device—and many *exist*—must be better than numeration.
There are other kinds of advances—but none Sloane could have meant here.	Other kinds of advances *exist*—but none Sloane could have meant here.
. . . *there's* at least a reasonable possibility that your reader won't be able to see for himself where it came from.	. . . at least a reasonable possibility *exists* that your reader won't be able to see for himself where it came from.

More on this in the section on pretentiousness.

For Practice

1. Based on this sampling, there is a potential membership of 1,200 of the Department's 1,300 employees.

2. Despite its "EXCELLENT" rating, there are two areas which need immediate attention.
3. For example, if we assume a $50,000 sales price and 15%/year cost of capital, it would cost us $3,000/year to retain the drag line. It should be noted this is besides the cost of insurance, since this is included in the calculation of the net present values.
4. Since in our company only 7.1% of jobs are unskilled–in the Carolinas, only 6.2%–it is apparent that most of the better jobs require some technical background.
5. Since the rear wheels are out of line even though the gauges show in-spec dimensions along the suspension bar, and since this has been true since the car was new, I wonder if there is a built-in defect that prevents the various shops from obtaining proper alignment.
6. There are instances in which an established supplier receives reorders without rebid or testing of other sources.

The Answers

The Type 3 was in the second sentence in 3; the Type 4, in 4; the Type 5's, in 2, 5 and 6; the Type 6, in 1; and a *good* Type 7 in the first sentence in 3.

1. Based on this sampling, 1,200 of the Department's 1,300 employees are potential members.
2. Despite the "EXCELLENT" rating, two areas need immediate attention.
3. For example, if we assume a $50,000 sales price and 15%/year cost of capital, it would cost us $3,000/year to retain the drag line. This is besides the cost of insurance, since this is included in the calculation of the net present values.
4. Since in our company only 7.1% of jobs are unskilled–in the Carolinas, only 6.2%–clearly most of the better jobs require some technical background.
5. Since the rear wheels are out of line even though the gauges show in-spec dimensions along the suspension bar, and since this has been true since the car was new, I wonder if some built-in defect prevents the various shops from obtaining proper alignment.
6. Sometimes an established supplier receives reorders without rebid or testing of other sources.

Chapter 19

THE LAST TWO WRONG-POINT-OF-VIEW AGENTS

4. Overuse of the Passive

Defined from a communicative, rather than merely grammatical, point of view, a passive verb is

(1) any form of "to be" plus a past participle, or
(2) a past participle *alone* when it *follows*
    (a) its modificand, or
    (b) a subordinating conjunction ("if," "when" or the like).

Stage 4 now contains ten Type 1's:

2: are / held
5: might be / considered
8: was / decided
11: is / made
13: is / written
14: are / posted
15: is / forwarded
16: to be / deposited
18: is / taken
26: has been / brought

And two 2a's:

12: payroll *made*
21: funds *deducted*

And we had a 2b in Stage 3:

20: As *mentioned*, Smith has purchased no bonds.

The first "half" of a Type 1 may itself be as many as three words, like "should have been," "may have been," "to have been." And it may be "split" by one or more adverbial modifiers, as "then" formerly split "are posted" in 14. And one or more modifiers may separate a 2a from its modificand ("an estimate *almost always* made by the Comptroller's office") or a 2b from its preceding "as" or "when" ("as *previously* mentioned").

But when a "participle" has a *subject*—"the payroll *we* made," "as *John* previously mentioned"—it *isn't* a participle: It's a predicate verb, and the construction is *not* passive.

Also, you're not passive when your verb is any form of

(1) "to *have*" and a past participle ("has held," "had implemented," "should have considered," "to have created")*,

(2) "to be" and a *present* participle ("is holding," "to be implementing," "should be considering"), or

(3) "to be" alone—that is, "to be" when it
   - ends a sentence ("There he was") or
   - is followed by
     - a substantive ("This is Jonathan") or
     - a modifier other than a participle ("They are being difficult [adjective]," "The books will be on the table [prepositional phrase]").

Now first: You must absolutely disregard those who are telling you to *never* use a passive verb. Rather you *should* use one—because it will tell your story *best*, and *not* sound pretentious or artificial, or distort your message, or alienate your reader, or make your message harder to understand—any time that either

(1) who or what did it (or is doing it, or will do it) matters *considerably* less than *what was done* (or is being done, or will be done), or

(2) you want to reduce the force of your message.

And you *may* use one when, and because,

(3) it saves words. Which a Type 1 may do by enabling you to either let your doer go without saying or use an otherwise unusable common element.

But every Type 1 is at least a word longer than its active or intransitive alternative†. So unless your doer or common element is at least two words, the passive, used for this purpose, saves nothing.

And further: When you use it *just* to save words, you can bet it *will* sound—at least somewhat—stilted, pretentious, unnatural. So any time you decide to forgo such a saving you'll probably be absolutely right.

And you should *never* use it *except* for one of these reasons. And if you're like most, you've used it

- every time you should have, virtually without exception;
- often where you needed *no* verb, and
- *very* often where you should have used an active or intransitive verb instead.

---

*But "has *been* held," "had *been* implemented," "should have *been* considered," "to have *been* created" *are* passive; in such cases "to have" is just "auxiliary" to "to be."

†So long as you can recognize a passive verb, you needn't be able to define or distinguish between these others.

Stage 1 contained twenty-five passives, including twelve bad ones. (So Sloane averaged only one overuse of the passive per seventy-four words—which makes him *better* than many in this respect.)

Twelve, including four bad ones, survive. (Though of the four, one is only incidentally passive; we'll eliminate it for another reason in Chapter 21.)

But there are three "standard" ways to eliminate a passive verb (other than by just killing it, as, for example, when it's part of a pointless modifying clause, a pointless third-level modifier or a goes-without saying); and four passives that have dropped out of Sloane illustrate two of them better than any that survive. So let's look at them first. (The line numbers refer to Stage 1.)

Sometimes, to eliminate a passive, you need to shift your point of view only slightly:

16-19: Upon examination of Mr. Smith's deduction card it *was indicated* that . . .	Examination of Mr. Smith's deduction card *indicates* that . . .
34-35: Upon investigation of his individual deduction card it *was ascertained* that . . .	Investigation of his individual deduction card *reveals* that . . .

On the other hand, sometimes you need to shift 180 degrees: to bring in your doer—either from nowhere or from an accompanying prepositional phrase—to be the subject of your verb, and use your original subject, or what your participle or passive infinitive modified, as its object:

67-69: . . . the actions of the above-named personnel in this matter have not been within the intended results *desired to be achieved by the "Buy U. S. Savings Bonds" campaign.* ["Desired," of course, is a past participle following its modificand; "to be achieved" is a passive infinitive.]	. . . the actions of the above-named personnel in this matter have not been within the intended results *we desired the "Buy U. S. Savings Bonds" campaign to achieve.*

But the way Sloane doesn't illustrate, though the least often usable, is when you *can* use it the simplest of all: Sometimes you can just *replace* your passive verb with one that *isn't* passive, leaving the rest of your construction intact (or virtually so):

Maps *attached* to this report are:	*Accompanying* maps are:
U. S. Geological Survey bench marks *were used* as basic vertical control.	U. S. Geological Survey bench marks *provided* basic vertical control.

No funds are provided to cover the additional cost that *will be encountered* if the equipment must be removed in salable form.	No funds are provided to cover the additional cost that *will result* if the equipment must be removed in salable form.

Your addiction to the passive is one more thing you can lay to the schoolmarms. But this one not to those who taught you in grade school or high school or even, especially, your first two years in college; rather to those you met in your "professional" courses, especially in graduate school—and if you personally took no such courses, it doesn't matter: You've been imitating those who did. These are the birds who, since about 1900, have been peddling the neurotic nonsense that there's something improper, unseemly, arrogant, egotistical—something, in short, "unprofessional"—about personal pronouns, and especially first-person pronouns.

These birds are now dead (though clearly they haven't all heard yet that they are, because some are still chirping). Personal pronouns—even "I," "me," "my"—are appearing today where they never did even four or five years ago: not just in intra- and intercompany correspondence, but even in some professional journals. And so increasingly frequently as to promise that by no later than about 1975 *most* writers will be using them as they should.

Now true: *Irrelevant* personal pronouns obtrude, and offend, and you ought not provide any, in *any* kind of writing,

But you *should* put yourself into everything you write to *exactly the extent you belong in it to*—not an inch too far, but not an inch not far enough. And unless you're so unusual as to be virtually unique, *you* have failed to provide *many* personal pronouns that, far from their being irrelevant, you sacrificed communication by *not* providing; if never else, you've done this any time you've written "it is recommended that" or "it is concluded that" instead of "I (or we) recommend" or "I (or we) conclude." Because the judgment and expertise of its author are the *most* important elements in *any* recommendation or conclusion; only an idiot might accept one without knowing whose it was.

True, "it is concluded" and "it is recommended" don't *really* dissociate you from your conclusions and recommendations. Your reader can always figure out who's hiding behind them.

But it costs him a *little* extra energy to do this.

And however often he's seen them—and whether or not he realizes it—they always do sound to him, at least faintly, as if you'd *like* to dissociate yourself from them. Which of course suggests that maybe you're not completely sold on them yourself—and thereby promotes the likelihood that he'll *reject* them.

And as evidence of proper "modesty" and "humility" they're too obviously phony to warrant comment. And as a shield in case a recommendation or conclusion proves unsound, either is like tissue paper.

(Though either *may* "shield" you–from getting *credit*–if one proves *good.*)

But now note that we've so far killed thirteen passives in Sloane without adding even one personal pronoun. And we needed none in the other three examples, and will need none to fix two of Sloane's remaining instances of this agent.

One is in a Type 2 impersonal introduction–this being the type whose trouble is that it *does* involve overuse of the passive:

8: . . . when it *was decided* by Ajax to undertake a campaign . . .	. . . when Ajax *decided* to undertake a campaign . . .

The other is just passive:

17-18: The plan *is taken* advantage of by nearly 1,000 employees.	Nearly 1,000 employees *take* advantage of the plan.

Which illustrates another sad fact: Overusing the passive to avoid personal pronouns is for most of us only a first step. Step 2–which for many comes so quickly that the two sound like one–is to overuse it where *no personal pronouns are involved.*

But I do want to insert a personal pronoun in 26-27:

I *have brought* this improper procedure to Smith's and Wright's attention.

For two reasons:

First: As Sloane wrote that sentence Dawson might have understood it to mean *others* had told Smith and Wright their procedure was improper, and they'd persisted in it nevertheless. Which I'm sure Sloane *didn't* mean.

But I don't think Dawson was fooled, so this reason is relatively minor.

The big reason–as surely you've already decided for yourself–is that the change makes Sloane sound suddenly like a man.

That it saved no words isn't surprising; this agent often costs no words, and lengthens most reports only slightly. But equally where it costs words and where it doesn't, it's a major agent of several diseases, and above all else one of the two *top* agents of weakness.

But the sentence in 18 has been irrelevant from the beginning; having fixed the passive, now kill it entirely.

And if we now reinsert two of Sloane's original words in 8:

> . . . since *July 1,* 1950, when Ajax decided to undertake a campaign . . .

we see that here, too, he must have told a false story; he must have meant:

> . . . since (July 1,) 1950, when Ajax *undertook* a campaign . . .

or, to use a second-time word (though we don't *need* to):

> . . . since 1950, when *we* undertook a campaign.

Do Type 2 impersonal introductions often thus convey untruths?

No—but they sometimes do. Which, of course, is another good reason to avoid them.

39. Failure to Use the Passive

Essentially this appears only in the writing of some new converts to conciseness who are so determined to avoid Agent 4 that they fail occasionally to provide a *good* passive; conceivably, therefore, it has never appeared in your copy till now. But you may need to worry about it—mildly—from now on.

Despite its rarity, Sloane illustrated it—but we have to go back to Stage 1 to see where.

> 47-49: Mr. Wright, the cashier, says that he does not consider himself to have done anything for which anyone can justifiably censure him.

Since from Wright's point of view—which Sloane was relaying—what-shouldn't-have-been-done was *much* more important than who-shouldn't-have-done-it, this should have been:

> . . . does not consider himself to have done anything for which he *can justifiably be censured.*

In fact, this is how Sloane should have written it even if Wright *said* "I do not consider myself to have done anything for which anyone can justifiably censure me." But can you imagine anyone saying that?

For Practice

As you eliminate the passives below you'll expose two hitherto concealed common elements and a long pointless prepositional phrase. Also, 4 contains a just generally wrong point of view—Agent 8—as well as an overuse of the passive.

Where you have to guess who did it, don't mind if you guess wrong.

1. Alicia Skin Tone Cream has been distributed in all markets for 4½ years.
2. An advisory panel will help us prepare the manual . . . It will be composed of:
   - Anslinger, Bloomquist, Brill and Canlis from our Law Enforcement Manual panel . . .

3. Because the equipment RSWs cannot practically store 200, we will ask Ohaus to ship 100 when the order is received, 100 six months later.
4. Dr. Alexander's co-operation on Vizaid Ophthalmic deserves that serious consideration be given to purchasing a quantity of his book, but we must assure ourselves it is in the best interest of our eye-area promotion.
5. I make the additional recommendation that a capital expenditure be considered for a high-pressure corrosion tester on Du Pont's design.
6. In essence, the product was recommended for introduction in practically every market the survey was conducted in.
7. In recent months fifty-to seventy-five complaints concerning extreme bitter taste in TEJAVA were reported to Quality Control Laboratory, many from customers who claimed to be users of TEJAVA for twenty years or more . . . Twenty-five samples were selected at random from retained files of the three batches alleged to be very bitter. They were coded, and instructions were given the panel about how the tests should be conducted.
8. In summary, I recommend:
   - We give Stilley a trial order for each plant for 7/16" seven-ply laminated oak drawer stock.
   - A change authorization be put in for costing purposes.
   - A man be placed in Trim R&G for up to 90 days to work with me to ensure we do the best possible job in utilizing our cutting lengths to the best advantage.
9. It would be premature also because the prospective market for WA-1 is changing rapidly, and by 1971, the earliest year commercial distribution can be achieved, significant changes could invalidate present expansion planning.
10. Most other records can be destroyed in less than ten years because . . .
11. The creditors were advised by Davis that Charles had borrowed $536,000 from the corporation since 1934 and lost it gambling . . . Davis and Charles were then excused so the creditors could discuss the situation privately.
12. The problem is slightly more complex in Peru since Peru has been supplied ex Passaic with WY TONIC Prenatal granulations containing cobalt and such granulations can no longer be shipped from this country.
13. I attach a sheet showing the cost-element details.
14. After a careful study, a 70% "Dacron" Type 65/30% wool blend was chosen because of best performance and aesthetics.

The Answers

The overuses of the passive:

1. has been distributed.
2. will be composed.
3. is received.
4. be given.
5. be considered.
6. was recommended. [Also "was conducted," but we can fix that more easily later.]
7. were reported, were selected, were coded, were given, should be conducted. ["Alleged" was a *good* passive.]
8. be put in, be placed.
9. can be achieved.
10. can be destroyed.
11. were advised, were excused.
12. has been supplied, can be shipped.
14. was chosen.

The one failure to use a passive was in 13 ("attach").

The prepositionitis was in 7; the disregarded common elements were in 7 ("I") and 9 ("we").

1. We *have distributed* Alicia Skin Tone Cream in all markets for 4½ years.
2. An advisory panel will help us prepare the manual . . . It *will consist* of:
   - Anslinger, Bloomquist, Brill and Canlis from our Law Enforcement Manual panel . . .
3. Because the equipment RSWs cannot practically store 200, we will ask Ohaus to ship 100 when they *receive* the order, 100 six months later.
4. In view of Dr. Alexander's co-operation on Vizaid Ophthalmic, we *should give* serious consideration to purchasing a quantity of his book, but we must assure ourselves it is in the best interest of our eye-area promotion.
5. I make the additional recommendation that we *consider* a capital expenditure for a high-pressure corrosion tester on Du Pont's design.
6. In essence, they *recommended* the product for introduction in practically every market the survey was conducted in.
7. In recent months Quality Control Laboratory *has received* fifty to seventy-five complaints concerning extreme bitter taste in TEJAVA, many from customers who claimed to be users of TEJAVA for twenty years or more . . . I *selected* twenty-five samples at random from retained files of the three batches alleged

to be very bitter, *coded* them, and *gave* the panel the necessary instructions. [In this report's context, "the necessary" perfectly replaced "about how the tests should be conducted."]

8. In summary, I recommend we
   - give Stilley a trial order for each plant for 7/16" seven-ply laminated oak drawer stock;
   - *put* in a change authorization for costing purposes, and
   - *place* a man in Trim R&G for up to 90 days to work with me to ensure we do the best possible job in utilizing our cutting lengths to the best advantage.
9. It would be premature also because the prospective market for WA-1 is changing rapidly, and by 1971, the earliest year we *can achieve* commercial distribution, significant changes could invalidate present expansion planning.
10. We *can destroy* most other records in less than ten years because . . .
11. Davis *advised* the creditors that Charles had borrowed $536,000 from the corporation since 1934 and lost it gambling . . . Davis and Charles then *left* so the creditors could discuss the situation privately.
12. The problem is slightly more complex in Peru since Passaic *has been supplying* Peru with WY TONIC Prenatal granulations containing cobalt and we can no longer *ship* such granulations from this country.
13. Cost-element details *are attached.*
14. After a careful study, we *chose* a 70% "Dacron" Type 65/30% wool blend because of best performance and aesthetics.

SLOANE REPORT - Stage 5

September 9, 1957

To : H. B. Dawson

From : N. B. Sloane

AUDIT OF PAYROLL DEDUCTION FUNDS, EXVILLE PLANT

Exville payroll deductions for Savings Bonds are held in the account R. J. Wright, Cashier, at the First National Bank. This account is in balance with the individual accounts. However, there has been a mishandling of the funds which might be considered collusion between
5 Wright and Plant Manager R. W. Smith.

Smith has authorized $100 deductions since 1950, when we undertook a campaign for the purpose of convincing employees to sign up to purchase bonds under the payroll plan. He and Assistant Plant Manager J. J. Blake are on a bimonthly payroll that is made at the main office;
10 all other employees with bond deductions are on a weekly payroll made at the plant. The bimonthly payroll is written--and the deductions are posted to the individual accounts--very early in the payroll period; as you know, the total of the deductions on every payroll is forwarded to the cashier on payday to be deposited. It becomes the cashier's duty
15 to purchase bonds for employees who have accrued enough money.

But Smith has consistently requested Wright to grant him a refund of his $100 before payday, and Wright has always done so, out of funds deducted earlier from other employees' pay. Blake has also taken one or two such advances recently.

20 I have brought this improper procedure to Smith's and Wright's attention. Although both advise that it is admittedly uncommon, Wright says he has merely acted pursuant to Smith's regular instructions, and Smith feels there have been no violations of company rules or policies. I have apprised them I would include the practice in my report. You
25 will surely agree that

- these actions are outside the desired results of the campaign;
- it is possible for additional plant managers to also use this loophole, thereby also improperly obtaining salary advances.

Chapter 20

THE WRONG-KIND-OF-WORD AGENT THAT'S THE MOST IMPORTANT OF ALL

1. Verb Mutilation

Of all thirty-nine, this one not only hurts most per appearance; for most writers—though apparently not Sloane—it also appears the most often. If you pull a thousand sentences at random from your company's files, probably.

- they'll contain altogether about nine hundred mutilated verbs;
- at least about thirty will contain at least three each, and
- at least one will contain six or more.

But now I have to define some terms.

A "verb idea"—to extrapolate from Webster—is one of action, occurrence or mode of being.

A "pure verb idea" is one that's significant strictly *as* an action, occurrence or mode of being.

A "key verb idea" is any pure verb idea except one that—in its author's judgment—is *much* less important than some other or others *in the same construction.* (So provided only that it's purely verblike, even a very unimportant verb idea may be "key"—and in a "typical" report 90% or more of the pure verb ideas *are* "key.")

A "subordinate verb idea" is a pure verb idea that *isn't* "key."

For example: In the following sentence "driving" and "hit" both convey pure verb ideas, but in my judgment—and since it's my sentence, my judgment governs—the idea conveyed by "driving" is much less important than that conveyed by "hit":

Driving home, I hit a traffic stanchion.

A "part-verb idea" is one that's important *partly* as an action, occurrence, or mode of being, but partly also

(1) in that it describes, limits or identifies something or someone:

I tripped over the broken chair [besides describing an action, "broken" tells you *which* chair I tripped over];

She wants a talking doll [besides describing an action, "talking" tells you what *kind* of doll she wants]; or

(2) as a *thing*, in relation to some other idea that's *purely* verblike:

He said swimming would make me healthy [besides being an action, swimming is the thing that may make me healthy];

The Gauls considered surrendering [besides being an action, surrendering is the thing the Gauls were thinking about].

Now to shift from kinds of ideas to kinds of words.

In relation to verb mutilation, every word is

- a pure verb (which from now on we'll call a "verb-verb"),
- a part verb or
- a nonverb,

Your verb-verbs are

- your predicate verbs (if you need to be refreshed about this, see page 109), and
- your infinitives.

Grammatically, an infinitive is a pure verb only when it *is* also a predicate verb; but now that we have that on the record, we'll forget it. And note that the "to" in an infinitive isn't a preposition; it's part of the verb. So you don't eliminate a prepositional phrase when you eliminate an infinitive; rather, usually, you mutilate a verb.

Your part verbs are your participles and gerunds.

A participle, which I defined in Chapter 16, is part verb, part adjective—except that sometimes it doesn't *really* modify, so it's only *grammatically* adjectival, and is communicatively sort of a reduced pure verb. (As in "Driving home, I hit a traffic stanchion.")

A gerund is part verb, part noun.

Every verb's gerund is identical in form with its present participle. This means, of course, you can't distinguish between the two on the basis of how they look. But you'll rarely need to do this anyway; and if ever you must, you can do it quite easily on the basis of how they're used. For example: In "A sleeping child can't get into mischief," "sleeping" modifies "child," so it's a participle; but in "Sleeping is my favorite exercise" it's the subject of the sentence, so it's a gerund.

A nonverb is any *other* kind of word—noun, adjective, adverb, preposition, pronoun, conjunction or interjection.

All right:

You mutilate a verb when you

- **convey a key verb idea through a part verb or nonverb instead of a verb-verb,**
- **convey a part-verb or subordinate verb idea through a nonverb instead of a part verb, or**
- **just *don't* convey an idea you should have conveyed through *some* verb form. (This way is by far the least common.)**

So sometimes you mutilate a verb *by* using a part verb, sometimes by not using one.

Verb mutilation—except in its least common form—is almost always a two-step process. The reason: You must almost always deliver the *container* of your mutilated verb within a clause.

Now sometimes you find a clause right at hand, already equipped with a predicate verb, that, without violating any *grammatical* rule, you can just drop your container into. So as Step 2 you do just drop it in.

But sometimes no such clause is available. So you must make one. And what should have been its predicate verb is now some other part of speech.

So you reach into the pool of what we'll call "coolie verbs"—verbs that do nothing but just *legalize* the constructions they appear in—and pull one out more or less at random, and somehow hitch your real verb idea on behind it.

To illustrate all this in Sloane:

Stage 5, composed of fifteen fairly short sentences—they average 19.9 words—contains at least fourteen mutilated verbs, and some think as many as seventeen. (Several others have fallen out incidentally to other changes.) We'll now fix the fourteen, and see what happens to Sloane's whole tone as a result. While so doing we'll eliminate his Type 1 impersonal introductions ("there has been," 3; "it becomes," 14; "there have been," 23; "it is," 27); this—by far the most common type of impersonal introduction—is the type whose trouble is that it *does* involve verb mutilation.

The italicized words on the left are Sloane's containers; those on the right, the verbs that (I think) he mutilated. The capitalized words are his coolie verbs. Note that four mutilations required no coolie verbs.

3-5: However, there HAS BEEN a *mishandling* [gerund] of the funds that might be considered collusion between Wright and Plant Manager R. W. Smith.	However, the funds *have been mishandled* in a way that might be considered collusion between Wright and Plant Manager R. W. Smith.
6-8: . . . when we undertook a campaign for the purpose of *convincing* [gerund] employees to sign up to purchase bonds under the payroll plan.	. . . when we undertook a campaign *to convince* employees to sign up to purchase bonds under the payroll plan.
13-14: As you know, the total of the *deductions* [noun] on every payroll is forwarded to the cashier on payday to be deposited.	As you know, the total *deducted* on every payroll is forwarded to the cashier on payday to be deposited.
14-15: It BECOMES the cashier's *duty* [noun] to purchase bonds for employees who have accrued enough money.	The cashier *must* purchase bonds for employees who have accrued enough money.

16-17: But Smith has consistently requested Wright to GRANT him a *refund* [noun] of his $100 before payday.	But Smith has consistently requested Wright *to refund* his $100 before payday.
20-21: I HAVE BROUGHT this improper procedure to Smith's and Wright's *attention* [noun].	I *have told* Smith and Wright this procedure *is* [mutilated by omission] improper.
21-23: Although both ADVISE that it is *admittedly* [adverb] uncommon, Wright says he HAS merely ACTED *pursuant* [adverb] to Smith's regular instructions, and Smith feels there HAVE BEEN no *violations* [noun] of company rules or policies.	Although both *admit* it is uncommon, Wright says he has merely *followed* Smith's regular instructions, and Smith feels no company rule or policy *has been violated.*
24: I have apprised them I WOULD INCLUDE the practice in my *report* [noun].	I have apprised them I *would report* the practice.
26: These actions ARE *outside* [preposition] the desired results of the campaign.	These people have *misused* the program.
27-28: It IS *possible* [adjective] for additional plant managers to also use this loophole, thereby also improperly *obtaining* [participle] salary advances.	Additional plant managers *can* also use this loophole *to* improperly *obtain* salary advances.

Some of the revised sentences—especially those in 20-21 and 26—may now convey different messages than Sloane intended them to; this is because some of his containers might each have contained any of several verbs, and maybe I sometimes guessed wrong on *which* one to "unmutilate." (For example: In 20-21 he may have meant rather "I *have spoken* to Smith and Wright about this improper procedure.") But first: If I did misguess some, I think it was more Sloane's fault than mine; if he hadn't mutilated them I wouldn't have had to guess. And second: For our purposes this doesn't matter anyway; all *we* need to note is how much more clearly, interestingly, forcefully and persuasively the new sentences say what they do say, and *why* they do—which is that verb mutilation is a top agent of virtually *every* writing disease. For example: Besides having largely cured Sloane of many others, we've now *completely* cured him of weakness, monotony and ambiguity, to name just a few.

The three cases where *maybe* Sloane mutilated verbs:

2-3: This account IS in *balance* [noun] with the individual accounts.	This account *balances* with the individual accounts.

3-5: However, the funds have been mishandled in a way that MIGHT BE CONSIDERED *collusion* [noun] between Wright and Plant Manager R. W. Smith.

However, Wright and Plant Manager R. W. Smith *have colluded* to mishandle the funds. [Now "mishandle" and "collude" are both expressed through verb-verbs.]

23: Smith FEELS *no* [adjective] company rule or policy has been violated.

Smith *denies* any company rule or policy has been violated.

But in 2-3 I think he was trying to describe a condition, rather than an action, and if he was, "is" is the *right* verb. And I'm just not sure about the others, so I'll settle for the left-side versions.

This is another tough agent, chiefly because there are no objective signals of it: Essentially you just must train yourself to recognize which of your ideas *are* verb ideas, and then find the verbs to convey them.

But if you try, you can begin to cope with it immediately, and can expect to eventually get down from about .9 mutilated verbs per sentence, where I think you are now, to .1, or even .05 or .03. And at such a level you can live with them.

And while there are no objective signals of verb mutilation, there *are* objective signals of *possible* verb mutilation. And you can profit greatly, especially at the beginning, from looking for these.

One set stems from the fact that for most writers—though apparently not Sloane—about 99% of coolie verbs are of five types, of which just the first *two* following provide no less than about 90%.

Type 1 is just "to be" and any of the more "elegant" words we sometimes substitute for it, like "to appear," "to become," "to seem." (For example, Sloane could just as well have said "It *is* the cashier's duty . . . ") Used properly, these are fine verbs; in fact, "to be" is the verb that should appear *most* often in your copy. But you'll nevertheless do well to carefully examine every one of your constructions that contains it.

Type 2 contains at least dozens of verbs, and maybe hundreds, but that doesn't matter. Because their common characteristic is unmistakable: Any of them may be used to describe an actual physical act, but any may also be used nonphysically, more or less figuratively. The most often coolie in this group are "make" and "take," but Sloane showed us also "grant" (meaning "give") and "bring"; within a few more words he might have given us "reach," "hold," "have."

Such a verb is almost certainly *not* coolie when it *does* describe a physical act: "make a desk," "take that chair into the next room," "bring her a napkin," "give him a glass of water," "reach the top shelf," "hold a baby," "pay the cashier," "have a nickel in your pocket." And it *may* not be even in such a construction as any on the left following.

But you mustn't say:	when you mean:
make a decision	decide
take action	act
bring this to his attention	tell him about this
give thought to this matter	think about this
reach a conclusion	conclude
hold a meeting	meet
pay attention	listen
have a tendency	tend

Type 3 is such verbs as "act," "perform," "do." Their common characteristic is that each sort of suggests *something* is moving or happening, but as if in a dark room: You can't tell exactly what or how. So they're likely to be coolie in such constructions as "act pursuant to the instructions of," "act in conformity with," "act in obedience to" or "perform an operation," in which, typically, *specific* actions are conveyed through other words.

Type 4 is such verbs as "occur," "happen," "result," "develop"; and I urge you to suspect "occur," especially, every time you find it in your copy. It won't always be coolie—but we're too likely to say "An explosion occurred in the gas tank" when we mean the gas tank exploded.

Type 5 is such verbs as "note," "mention," "report," "observe," especially in the passive. For example:

A marked DETERIORATION of energy *is observed* below the top of "C" Horizon.	Energy *deteriorates* markedly below the top of "C" Horizon.
A 27% INCREASE in sales *was reported* in the third quarter.	Sales *rose* 27% in the third quarter.

But let me stress: *Any* verb may be coolie; what makes one so isn't that it falls into one of these categories, but just that it merely legalizes a construction in which the *real* verb idea is expressed through some other word.

And your "nonstandard" coolie verbs—like Sloane's "advise," "include," maybe "feels"—you'll have to catch on that basis alone.

The second set of signals stems from the fact that most containers of mutilated verbs are also standard, and classifiable, and soon easily recognized within their classifications.

The most common is the part verb, and especially the "-ing" word, whether as a participle or as a gerund. Sloane showed us "mishandling," "convincing," "obtaining."

Often this form "saves" a word, and sometimes even several. For example, we could change 11-12 to:

The bimonthly payroll is written very early in the payroll period, the deductions then *being posted* to the individual accounts.

But however devoutly you want to save words, you must *never* do so by mutilating a verb, through this kind of construction or any other.

Group 2 is all the countless words that may each be either a verb or some other part of speech, like Sloane's "refund" and "report." And some in this group contain mutilated verbs—at least, as I see them—more often than not:

increase	equal	need
decrease	result	lower
decline	purchase	change
rise	average	wish (for "want" or "like")
fall	reply	desire (for "want" or "like")
request	answer	question (for "ask")
total	return	better (for "improve")
	cost	

We will help you to determine your *needs*, and then to obtain proper financing.	We will help you determine what you *need*, and then to obtain proper financing.
The refund *request* must be sent by the Manager of Surplus Materials to W. J. Baker.	The Manager of Surplus Materials must *request* the refund from W. J. Baker.
Average monthly earnings for the period were:	Monthly earnings for the period *averaged:*
"Expedited refunds" must be handled manually; as a *result* there is an increase in costs.	"Expedited refunds" must be handled manually; this *results* in an increase in costs.

But in the last I've so far "unmutilated" only a coolie verb; the *real* verb idea is in "increase":

"Expedited refunds" must be handled manually; this increases our costs.

Group 3 is

- every noun ending in "-tion," "-sion," "-ment," "-ity," "-ance," "-ancy," "-ence," "-ency" or "-al" (like "withdrawal," "approval," "arrival");
- every adjective ending in "-able," "-ible" and "-ive," and
- many adjectives ending in "-ful."

Not that anything's inherently bad about nouns like "deduction," "attention," "violation"; the trouble is with us, who use them to convey not only noun ideas, but also verb ideas. And "successful" and "unsuccessful" are fine adjectives, and we *should* use them when we want to *describe* things as successful or unsuccessful—but what would a scientist probably mean if he wrote "This experiment was successful," or "This experiment was unsuccessful"?

Group 4 is the following words, which have nothing in common except that each, as I see it, contains a mutilated verb more often than not—and those asterisked *far* more often than not. Those in italics do so especially often in impersonal introductions.

**necessary*, **unnecessary*, necessarily, necessity	need, require
*able, *unable, ability, inability, capacity	can, could
**possible*, possibly (and its "synonyms," like "perhaps" and "maybe"), possibility, **impossible*, impossibility	can, could, may, might
*effect, impact	affect, influence
*effort	try
*statement, *according to	say
**imperative, *essential, mandatory*	must
*aware, awareness, familiar, familiarity	know, realize
*receipt	receive, arrive
important	must, should
purpose, objective	want
*opinion	think, believe

Group 5 is all prepositions. Probably about 5% of yours—meaning, probably, about one in every two hundred of your words—have contained mutilated verbs. But prepositions typically contain their verbs much more subtly than other containers do, and you can never be sure in advance which verb, out of countless possibilities, any preposition will contain. So I urge that before you attack prepositional containers in general, you practice awhile extracting the verbs from your other types.

But I urge that you begin immediately to check every one of your constructions that begins with "because *of*," "due *to*," "*by*," "method *of*" or "means *of*."

"Because of" and "due to" constructions contain mutilated verbs, remarkably consistently, four times in five. And when one does,

the probability is about	*that the container is*	*and the mutilated verb is*
5%	the "because" or due"	"to cause," or some other verb that in some way suggests cause and effect;

10% the "of" or "to"

"to be," or some fancy substitute for "to be";

85% some other word

almost any.

Because *of* the high turbidities, the normal Rayleigh-Debye theory could not be applied.

Because the solutions *were* so turbid, the normal Rayleigh-Debye theory could not be applied.

"Other Division Expense" is expected to be lower, primarily due *to* less interdivision transfer expense.

"Other Division Expense" is expected to be lower, primarily because interdivision transfer expense *will be* less.

We find this accident occurred *because* of the operator's inattention.

We find this accident *was caused* by the operator's inattention.

Due to this unforeseeable incident, the entire project was rescheduled.

This unforeseeable incident *required* us to reschedule the entire project.

Individual crews are no longer practical due to *reduced* crew sizes and workload *fluctuations.*

Individual crews are no longer practical because crew sizes *have been reduced* and the workload *fluctuates.*

Because of the number of trucks *required* to move this quantity, I would appreciate knowing the port of call no later than noon 22 April.

Because so many trucks *will be required* to move this quantity, I would like to know the port of call no later than noon 22 April.

However, fixed charges absorbed in inventory were favorable, due chiefly to *applying* the new adder to inventory balance as of January 1.

However, fixed charges absorbed in inventory were favorable, chiefly because we *applied* the new adder to inventory balance as of January 1.

Note that while all the "due's," "of's" and "to's" disappeared, the only "because's" that did were those that *contained* the verbs. This is typical.

When a "by" phrase contains a mutilated verb, you can usually unmutilate it by replacing either

- the "by" with "if" or "when" (after which you *must* change some following word to a predicate verb):

We can accomplish this *by scheduling* back to back in all areas.

We will accomplish this *if* we *schedule* back to back in all areas.

By checking with the agency I discovered that Jones sometimes did sell United at a special 40% discount.

When I *checked* with the agency I discovered that Jones sometimes did sell United at a special 40% discount.

or

- the verb that the "by" phrase *modifies* with an infinitive:

We *did* this *by estimating* the number of man hours required to fill all positions.

To do this, we *estimated* how many man hours would be required to fill all positions.

When you change "method of" or "means of" to "way to," you've begun to provide an infinitive:

The applied technique provides a *method of determining* the man-power level for the plant maintenance force.

The applied technique provides a *way to determine* the man-power level for the plant maintenance force.

And sometimes you needn't even replace the "method" or "means"—just the "of" with "to":

This device should be investigated further, even if only as a means of reducing the noise level.

This device should be investigated further, even if only as a means *to reduce* the noise level.

When you're ready to attack your actual prepositional *containers*, I suggest you start with the following, checking each for the particular verb or verbs listed after it. They've probably accounted for just about half your cases of verbs-mutilated-into-prepositions. (Though—to repeat—any of them *may* contain the mutilated form of almost *any* verb.)

of:	have, be
with:	have, be
as:	be
above, over:	exceed
after:	follow
before:	precede
in, within:	include, contain
into:	enter

Now, *with* the economy at full employment, neither a big reserve of jobless workers nor unused plant capacity is available.

Now, since the economy *is* at full employment, neither a big reserve of jobless workers nor unused plant capacity is available.

The major control problem is related to the inadequacy *of* the internal-check system.

The major control problem is that the internal-check system *is* inadequate.

There should be a 10-minute critique *after* each showing.

A 10-minute critique should *follow* each showing.

Construction expenditures were $2.0MM *above* last month's.

Construction expenditures *exceeded* last month's by $2.0MM.

Mr. Del Rio cited this *as* more suitable for the Uruguayan sportswear market.

Mr. Del Rio said this *was* more suitable for the Uruguayan sportswear market.

However, the presence *of* water-soluble metabolites would make quantitative determination difficult.

However, this will be hard to determine quantitatively if water-soluble metabolites *are* present.

Then eventually you should be able to feel the mutilation even in most cases like:

This indicates a period *of* 14 months from completion of the first prototype to completion of the first production model.

This indicates it *took* 14 months from completion of the first prototype to completion of the first production model.

He suggested a book *for* our Administrative Library—"Psychological Principles in System Development," by Gagne.

He suggested our Administrative Library *get* "Psychological Principles in System Development," by Gagne.

Operating earnings for the month *at* $2.7MM were 34% below last year.

Operating earnings for the month *were* $2.7MM, 34% below last year.

Less HF *per* vessel reduces the effects of a disaster even though tank-car mishaps are more probable.

Since each vessel *will contain* less HF, individual accidents should be less disastrous even though tank-car accidents are more probable.

We could back up Houston either by outside purchases or *from* Tulsa's excess capacity.

We could back up Houston by either buying outside or *using* Tulsa's excess capacity.

There is a very personal relationship *between* pupils and teachers.

Pupils and teachers *maintain* a very personal relationship.

When a construction contains a standard container *and* a standard coolie verb, it's of course especially likely to contain a mutilated verb.

But the only way to tell for sure is to test it. If your story comes through better with the verb "unmutilated," it was mutilated; if not, it wasn't.

And just as any verb may be a coolie verb, *any* nonverb *may* contain a mutilated verb.

A few more examples of verbs mutilated by omission:

The operator reported a lower viscosity cream.

The operator reported the cream *was* less viscous.

The results of this projection indicate ample capacity.

The results of this projection indicate capacity *is* ample.

In view of this evidence, I recommend a permanent one-shift operation.

In view of this evidence, I recommend we *adopt* a permanent one-shift operation.

We fairly often mutilate a verb and an adjective simultaneously. For example, in some of the sentences we've just fixed:

Because of the *number* of trucks required to move this quantity . . .

The major control problem is related to the *inadequacy* of the internal check system.

However, the *presence* of water-soluble metabolites would make quantitative determination difficult.

Less HF per vessel reduces the effect of a *disaster* even though tank-car mishaps are more probable.

Because of the high *turbidities*, the normal Rayleigh-Debye theory could not be applied.

As you saw in Chapter 16, when the predicate verb in a modifying clause doesn't convey a key verb idea, you need to replace the clause with a better modifier, which often is a participle or participial phrase. On the other hand, to unmutilate a verb you need often to promote a participle or participial phrase *to* a clause.

By so doing you'll often also eliminate an overuse of the passive:

The major fringe benefits *analyzed* were pensions, life insurance, health insurance . . .	The major fringe benefits *we analyzed* were pensions, life insurance, health insurance . . .
This indicates that styles already *developed* by the trade can be used unchanged with Plant yarns.	This indicates they can use Plant yarns in styles *they have already developed.*

Sometimes it turns out that the modifier shouldn't have been a modifier, so the clause that replaces it isn't adjective–in which case the new verb is especially unlikely to be passive:

We had access to the warehouse *accompanied* by the warehouse supervisor.	The warehouse supervisor *accompanied* us through the warehouse.
She then said she wanted it *shipped* to someone else, but *billed* to her.	She then said she wanted us *to ship* it to someone else, but *bill* her.

But sometimes it should be passive:

The impact of the synthetic achievement is significantly reduced by . . . their lengthy theoretical discussion *based* on questionable thermal data.	The impact of the synthetic achievement is significantly reduced by . . . their lengthy theoretical discussion, *which is based* on questionable thermal data.

Since participles and gerunds are equal in their verbness, you don't unmutilate a verb when you go from either to the other.

But you may so use either as to stress either its verb or its nonverb *aspect*, and you mutilate a verb any time you use either in a less verblike *way* than you should. That is:

A participle, first, is less verb and more adjective when it precedes its modificand, more verb and less adjective when it follows. This is why "scowling" and "baked" modify more smoothly on the left below, but the *actions* they describe come through more vividly on the right:

The scowling bully said he'd had enough.	The bully, scowling, said he'd had enough.
My mother's baked apples were delicious.	Apples baked by my mother were delicious.

(In fact, even an adjective may become slightly verblike when it follows what it modifies. For example, "The beggar, still cheerful, thanked the prince" versus "The still-cheerful beggar thanked the prince"; reading the first, can't you almost see the man *being* cheerful?)

And you may modify a gerund either adjectivally, as you would a noun, or adverbially, as you would a verb; and you may or may not let it take an object:

Thank you for your prompt handling of this order.	Thank you for handling this order so promptly.

On the left "handling" is modified by the possessive pronoun "your," the adjective "prompt" and the adjective prepositional phrase "of this order," all of which stress its nounness; on the right it's modified by the *adverb* "promptly" and takes the *object* "this order," both of which stress its verbness.

In context, either version of any of the last three might be right, and the other wrong. It would depend, in each case, on how vividly the author wanted the action to come through.

But we err far more often by being not verblike enough than by being too verblike.

A Type 7 impersonal introduction that was the best alternative to mutilating a verb:

I find *it* difficult to distinguish between ethics and morals.

This *might* have been rewritten as "I find distinguishing between ethics and morals difficult," or "I find the distinction between ethics and morals difficult." But even out of context, I think, you'd have to guess the impersonal way was best.

When a "compared to" construction contains a mutilated verb, it's usually "to be":

These operators now receive \$2.87½/hr., compared to the tri-county average for such jobs of \$2.74.	These operators now receive \$2.87½/hr.; the tri-county average for such jobs is \$2.74. [The container was "of."]

But sometimes it's "compare":

To prove this, he cited last year's production compared to this year's.	To prove this, he compared last year's production with this year's.

And it *can* be almost *any* verb:

On our standard test, she typed only 32 words per minute, compared to our minimum requirement of 40.	On our standard test, she typed only 32 words per minute; we *require* at least 40.

Sometimes the mutilated verb is usable as a common element—in which case it was still mutilated.

The cafeteria can accommodate 75 participants, compared to only 32 for the conference room.	The cafeteria can accommodate 75 participants, the conference room (can accommodate) only 32.

For Practice

Since—again—you can't consult with their authors, you'll do well to bat over .500 on these sentences.

They contain altogether fifty-seven mutilated verbs. One is within a Type 1 impersonal introduction. Thirty-three required a total of twenty-six coolie verbs (two coolie verbs legalized two mutilations each, one legalized six). One preposition contains a different verb than it "normally" does. One participle, one gerund and two predicate verbs are mutilated by omission.

If you correct all twenty-seven as their authors did, you'll shorten fourteen and lengthen nine, including two you'll thereby cure of terseness. This ratio isn't typical; this agent costs words at least three or four times as often as it doesn't. But—as I said before, and as these sentences will illustrate—it hurts even when it "saves" words.

The time has come also to use one more second-time word, and eliminate several more passives, several more goes-without-sayings, two zero words, a club-member phrase, several wrong points of view, a pointless modifying clause and a rather unusual case of adverb mutilation. And your revision of 7 should prove that it did originally (after Chapter 9) contain a long-winded affirmative.

1. A recent situation in which we assisted one customer in relieving his inventories appears to have been correctly managed at first, but not all the way through.
2. Advertising costs were $206,000, or 10.7% of sales, in 1966, as compared with $84,000, or 6.3%, in 1958.
3. After a careful study, we chose a 70% "Dacron" Type 65/30% wool blend because of best performance and aesthetics.

4. Although not critical, the convenience features increase the Hitachi's information output per unit of time.
5. Assuming average delivery distance is 300 miles longer from one plant than from two, freight cost is .7-.8c/bd. ft. more, which is less than the f.o.b. plant price advantage.
6. But for future such visits, please prepare a program of instructions in all phases of our operations, policies and procedures you are concerned with.
7. But some investigators reject them and the lists of side effects may not be complete.
8. In view of Dr. Alexander's co-operation on Vizaid Ophthalmic, we should give serious consideration to purchasing a quantity of his book, but we must assure ourselves it is in the best interest of our eye-area promotion.
9. During this period they are short of cash and obtained bank loans in past years to pay suppliers.
10. However, the pharmacy is where purchases are made, and we should know what factors influence these purchases.
11. I gained an appreciation of the importance of appraisals in employee development.
12. I make the additional recommendation that we consider a capital expenditure for a high-pressure corrosion tester on Du Pont's design.
13. In accord with our telephone conversation November 10, I send herewith copies of reports summarizing the results of consumer panel tests assessing the merits of an experimental bed pillow being developed in Pioneering Research,
14. In essence, they recommended the product for introduction in practically every market the survey was conducted in.
15. In recent months Quality Control Laboratory has received fifty to seventy-five complaints concerning extreme bitter taste in TEJAVA, many from customers who claimed to be users of TEJAVA for twenty years or more. I set up a taste panel to determine whether there was any basis for these complaints.
16. In summary, I recommend we . . .
    - place a man in Trim R&G for up to 90 days to work with me to ensure we do the best possible job in utilizing our cutting lengths to the best advantage.
17. It would be premature also because the prospective market for WA-1 is changing rapidly, and by 1971, the earliest year we can achieve commercial distribution, significant changes could invalidate present expansion planning.
18. Onley, Bender and I have reached these conclusions:
19. Previously the Laboratory examined competitive products and sent completed reports to Wilmington for approval prior to distribution.
20. RECOMMENDATIONS: . . .
    2. Continue co-operation up to $50M with strict prompt payment.

3. Continue efforts to get support, making this mandatory when more yarn becomes available or exposure levels increase above $50M.

21. Sometimes an established supplier receives reorders without rebid or testing of other sources.
22. The COR increases, had they been passed, could well have been the springboard for other regions that would have resulted in further increases.
23. The Joplin code, unique numbers, would be satisfactory were equipment not subject to movement between locations.
24. The proposal would result in shorter loading and unloading time and neater warehouse stacking, but also in
    - increased handling cost (.33c to .995c/lb.) and freight cost;
    - the necessity of breaking down pallets for small orders at warehouses (most sales are to small-quantity customers), and
    - distributors' need for lift trucks for removal from delivery trucks.
25. This is an apt description, too, of our problem in Wilmington.
26. We need your 1968 requirements by October 19 so we can enter our order for the Ohaus scales.
27. Without a proven superior product, our most likely customers are just those we now have, or can establish, favorable relations with.

The Answers

After their verbs were unmutilated, the authors of 10, 11 and 24 decided they also reflected wrong points of view, so other verbs will replace the second "buy," "appreciate" and "sell" in the revised versions.

	The Containers	*The Coolie Verbs*	*The Mutilated Verbs*
1.	relieving [gerund]	---	relieve
2.	compared [participle]	---	were
3.	of [preposition]	---	had
	performance [noun]	---	performed
4.	output [noun]	increase	to provide
5.	average [adjective]	is	averages
	more [adjective]	is	increases
6.	in [preposition]	---	covering
7.	lists [noun]	may be	list
8.	consideration [noun]	give	consider
	interest [noun]	is	will benefit
9.	loans [noun]	obtained	borrowed
10.	purchases [noun]	are made	buy
	purchases [noun]	---	buy
11.	appreciation [noun]	gained	appreciate
	of [preposition]	---	are
12.	recommendation [noun]	make	recommend
	---	---	based
13.	accord [noun]	---	promised
	herewith [adverb]	send	enclosed
	summarizing [participle]	send	summarize
	merits [noun]	assessing	evaluating
	being developed [participle]	---	is being developed
14.	introduction [noun]	---	introduce
	survey [noun]	was conducted	had surveyed
15.	users [noun]	to be	had used
	basis [noun]	was	were justified
16.	utilizing [participle]	do	utilize
17.	distribution [noun]	can achieve	can distribute
18.	conclusions [noun]	have reached	conclude
19.	approval [noun]	---	to approve
	distribution [noun]	---	were distributed
20.	recommendations [noun]	---	recommend
	co-operation [noun]	---	to co-operate
	strict [adjective]	---	require
	efforts [noun]	---	trying
	mandatory [adjective]	making*	require

*A mutilated coolie verb: En route to eliminating it you might have changed the sentence to " . . . and *make* this mandatory when more yarn . . . "

21. reorders [noun]	receives	reorders
---	---	getting
testing [gerund]	---	testing
22. springboard [noun]	could have been	could have led
increases [noun]	would have resulted	to raise
23. subject [adjective]	were	didn't have
movement [noun]	were	to move
24. shorter [adjective]	result	reduce
---	result	permit
increased [participle]	result	increase
increased [participle]	result	increase
necessity [noun]	result	would have
breaking [gerund]	---	to break
sales [noun]	are	sell
need [noun]	result	would need
removal [noun]	---	to remove
25. description [noun]	is	describes
26. order [noun]	enter	order
27. proven [participle–in its less "correct" form]	---	can prove
---	---	is

Some other words that often contain mutilated verbs, though they didn't in these cases (though I hope you at least questioned at least some of them; and since you couldn't check with their authors don't mark yourself down if you even "unmutilated" some):

2. costs.
3. study.
5. cost.
6. instructions.
8. co-operation, promotion.
11. development.
12. expenditure, design.
13. conversation.
15. complaints.
17. changes, expansion, planning.
20. payment, support.
22. increases [the first time].
24. stacking, handling, cost.
26. requirements.

1. A recent situation in which we helped one customer relieve his inventories appears to have been correctly managed at first, but not all the way through.
2. Advertising costs were $206,000, or 10.7% of sales, in 1966; they were $84,000, or 6.3%, in 1958. [The container was a participle preceded by "as"–a Type 2b passive.]
3. After a careful study, we chose a 70% "Dacron" Type 65/30% wool blend; it performed best and had the best aesthetics. [With the verbs unmutilated, "because" goes without saying.]
4. Although not critical, the convenience features enable the Hitachi to provide more information per unit of time.

5. Assuming delivery distance averages 300 miles longer from one plant than from two, freight cost increases by .7-8c/bd. ft.–less than the f.o.b. plant price advantage. [There went the modifying clause.]
6. But for future such visits, please prepare a program of instructions covering all phases of our operations, policies and procedures you are concerned with.
7. But some investigators reject them and they may not list all side effects.
8. In view of Dr. Alexander's co-operation on Vizaid Ophthalmic, we should seriously consider purchasing a quantity of his book, but we must assure ourselves that it will benefit our eye-area promotion.
9. During this period they are short of cash and borrowed from banks in past years to pay suppliers.
10. However, the pharmacy is where people buy, and we need to know why they choose one product over another. [The point-of-view change was from "should know" to "need to know"; "factors" contained the mutilated adverb "why"; "are made" was passive.]
11. It taught me how important appraisals are in employee development.
12. I also recommend we consider a capital expenditure for a high-pressure corrosion tester based on Du Pont's design. [A "that" has disappeared.]
13. The enclosed reports are those I promised you during our telephone conversation November 10. ["Copies of" has disappeared.] They summarize the results of consumer panel tests evaluating an experimental bed pillow that is being developed in Pioneering Research.
14. In essence, they recommended we introduce the product in practically every market they had surveyed. [There went the third passive.]
15. In recent months Quality Control Laboratory has received fifty to seventy-five complaints concerning extreme bitter taste in TEJAVA, many from customers who claimed they had used it twenty years or more. [The second "TEJAVA" has been replaced by "it," and "for" has become zero before "twenty years or more."] I set up a taste panel to determine whether the complaints were justified. [This contained the impersonal introduction.]
16. In summary, I recommend we . . .
    - place a man in Trim R&G for up to 90 days to work with me to ensure we utilize our cutting lengths to the best advantage.
17. It would be premature also because the prospective market for WA-1 is changing rapidly, and by 1971, the earliest year we can distribute it commercially, significant changes could invalidate present expansion planning.
18. Onley, Bender and I conclude that:

19. Previously, the Laboratory examined competitive products and sent completed reports to Wilmington, which had to approve them before they were distributed. [There went "prior to."]
20. I recommend we . . .
    (2) continue to co-operate up to $50M but always require prompt payment;
    (3) keep trying to get support, and require it when more yarn becomes available or exposure levels increase above $50M.
21. Sometimes Purchasing reorders from an established supplier without getting rebids or testing other sources. ["Testing" is still a gerund, but with "of" eliminated, "other sources" becomes its object.]
22. The COR increases, had they been passed, could well have led other regions to raise their rates.
23. The Joplin code, unique numbers, would be satisfactory if we didn't have to move equipment between locations.
24. The proposal would reduce loading and unloading time and permit neater warehouse stacking, but:
    - It would increase handling cost (.33c to .995c/lb.) and freight cost.
    - Small-quantity customers—which most of our customers are—would have to break down pallets at their warehouses [the clause between the dashes replaced "and we sell mostly to small-quantity customers"; "for orders" now goes without saying].
    - Distributors would need lift trucks to remove the pallets from the trucks [now "delivery" goes without saying].
25. This also describes our problem in Wilmington.
26. We need your 1968 requirements by October 19 so we can order the Ohaus scales.
27. Unless we can prove our product is superior, our most likely customers are just those we now have, or can establish, favorable trade relations with.

Chapter 21

THE LAST THREE MEMBERS OF THE WRONG-KIND-OF-WORD FAMILY

27. Noun Mutilation

While we mutilate nouns much less often than we do verbs and modifiers, any 500-word report is likely to contain at least one example of this agent.

Till now probably most of your mutilated nouns have been contained in modifiers, mostly nonce adjectives.

You can usually change a nonce adjective back to a noun by just crossing out what it modifies:

> Plastics proposes, beginning about 1970, to load HFL for research *purposes* in 3-pound instead of 7-pound containers.

> If sales *volume* in any market does not warrant registering the new formulations, we will have to delete the products when the current stocks are exhausted.

When your container is a "pure" adjective, or an adverb, the change must be somewhat more drastic. But it's rarely really difficult:

> The most important personality trait for success in this company is, you must be *willing* [adjective] to take reasonable risks.

> The most important personality trait for success in this company is a *willingness* to take reasonable risks.

> Since that month was abnormally heavy *productionwise* [adverb], we felt a one-shift operation was possible.

> Since *production* that month was abnormally heavy, we felt a one-shift operation was possible.

Sometimes you may *reciprocally* mutilate a noun and a modifier:

> *Sociological pessimists* could see no future for the community.

> *Pessimistic sociologists* could see no future for the community.

But from now on your zeal to avoid verb mutilation may lead you somewhat more often to mutilate nouns into verbs and part verbs.

Surprisingly, Sloane mutilated no nouns into modifiers but did mutilate one into a verb. In 14, the act of depositing was clearly inconsequential; the "total deducted" was "forwarded to the cashier" for a *purpose*, which he could have expressed beautifully through a noun:

> . . . is forwarded to the cashier on payday *for deposit.*

(Which incidentally eliminates his last bad passive.)

An example of a noun mutilated into a gerund:

We should be able to plan more confidently after we have the results of this *testing*.	We should be able to plan more confidently after we have the results of these *tests*.

One mutilated into a participle:

Lot 1061 was used first and was being used when the woman *supervising* the production line first questioned the hand-cream quality.	Lot 1061 was used first and was being used when the production-line *supervisor* first questioned the hand-cream quality. [The supervisor's sex was totally irrelevant.]

An idea that needs to be conveyed through a verb the first time you convey it may be a noun idea in some later appearance or appearances:

The new program requires that each machine *be inspected* four times a year. The reason we have decided *to inspect* them more often is that this should enable us to spot potential trouble before it arises.	The new program requires that each machine *be inspected* four times a year. The more frequent *inspections* should enable us to spot potential trouble before it arises.

(Or vice versa—but only *very* rarely.)

29. Failure to Use Prepositions

Almost always this is a simple verb-for-preposition substitution: One conveys through a verb an idea too trivial or goes-without-saying to justify a verb, that a preposition would have conveyed perfectly. In 7-8, for example, obviously anyone who "signs up" for bonds will "purchase" them, and the important act here, I think, is the signing up. So replace "to purchase" with "for."

(If "to purchase" *was* important, "to sign up" went without saying, so Sloane shouldn't have provided it.)

But once in a while you may convey through a *noun* an idea that warranted only a preposition. As in the title of a recent talk: "*Comparison* of U. S. and Canadian Liability Policies" instead of "U. S. *Versus* Canadian Liability Policies."

And when a verb has appeared so recently that you can still feel its effect, a preposition can sometimes replace it as sort of a second-time word:

Since you should use part verbs *to convey* part-verb and subordinate verb ideas, but not *to convey* key verb ideas, you sometimes mutilate a verb by using one, sometimes by not.	Since you should use part verbs *to convey* part-verb and subordinate verb ideas, but not *for* key verb ideas, you sometimes mutilate a verb by using one, sometimes by not.

21U. "Unusual" Modifier Mutilation

This, too, usually reflects an overreaction to verb mutilation: A writer is so determined to convey no key verb ideas through part verbs that he occasionally conveys through verb-verbs ideas he should have conveyed through participles. As in:

> The Patent Proposal System *recognizes* this but provides check points to ensure we operate within Company rules to consistently obtain good protection for our discoveries.

The first step in editing this was to change "recognizes" to a participle, but not move it:

> The Patent Proposal System, recognizing this, provides check points to ensure we operate within Company rules to consistently obtain good protection for our discoveries.

But then, to further reduce its verbness—and thereby, by contrast, further stress the other verbs in the sentence—it was moved up ahead of its modificand:

> Recognizing this, the Patent Proposal System provides check points to ensure we operate within Company rules to consistently obtain good protection for our discoveries.

Wrapping Up This Family

Basically, you fight all members of this family at once—by just resolving to always use

- verbs to convey verb ideas,
- nouns to convey noun ideas,
- modifiers to convey modifying ideas, and
- prepositions for ideas so trivial or goes-without-saying that prepositions can convey them perfectly.

And if I was right to change "to be deposited" and "to purchase," the proof is *not* that I thereby saved two more words; I could have saved still more—to repeat—by mutilating some of Sloane's verbs. If these were good changes, it's only because they made Sloane still easier to read and understand.

For Practice

The clause that contains the "unusually" mutilated modifier also represents a wrong point of view.

1. Absecon Point has rejected our recommended procedures for off-spec G-3783.
2. Advertising costs were $206,000, or 10.7% of sales, in 1966; they were $84,000, or 6.3%, in 1958. The principal reason for the increased cost was the spending for space, radio, literature and

mailings (primarily for "Astor" and "Topquality"), which amount to $150,000 in 1967, up $100,000 from 1966.

3. At the last session of the Tenth Triennial meetings, when we were all very tired, we may have approved certain minutes without realizing what complications might develop as we seek funds to increase our general budget (and the American Section general budget) as well as to begin new projects which we can undertake when we find funds and personnel.
4. Based on this sample, 1,200 of the Department's 1,300 employees are potential members.
5. I recommend we . . .

   (3) keep trying to get support, and require it when more yarn becomes available or exposure levels increase above $50M.
6. In recent months Quality Control Laboratory has received fifty to seventy-five complaints concerning extreme bitter taste in TEJAVA, many from customers who claimed they had used it twenty years or more.
7. The proposal would reduce loading and unloading time and permit neater warehouse stacking, but . . .
   - small-quantity users—which most of our customers are—would have to break down orders at their warehouses . . .
8. The rate for the second five-year period is half the normal rate, or 22.5%.
9. This would be a management training program for the latter, and give us a pool of trained sales-management manpower.

The Answers

The failure to use a preposition was in 3 ("to begin"); the "unusually" mutilated modifier—and slightly wrong point of view—were in 7 ("are").

The mutilated nouns were in:

1. recommended [participle].
2. increased [participle].
4. based [participle].
5. exposure [nonce adjective].
6. bitter [adjective].
8. (five)-year [adjective].
9. (sales)-management [nonce adjective].

1. Absecon Point has rejected our *recommendations* for off-spec G-3783.
2. Advertising costs were $206,000, or 10.7% of sales, in 1966; they were $84,000, or 6.3%, in 1958. The principal reason for the *increase* was the spending for space, radio, literature and mailings (primarily for "Astor" and "Topquality"), which amount to $150,000 in 1967, up $100,000 from 1966.
3. At the last session of the Tenth Triennial meetings, when we were all very tired, we may have approved certain minutes without realizing what complications might develop as we seek funds to increase our general budget (and the American Section general budget) as well as *for* new projects which we can undertake when we find funds and personnel.
4. On this *basis*, 1,200 of the Department's 1,300 employees are potential members.
5. I recommend we . . .

   (3) keep trying to get support, and require it when more yarn becomes available or *exposure* increases above $50M.
6. In recent months Quality Control Laboratory has received fifty to seventy-five complaints concerning extreme *bitterness* in TEJAVA, many from customers who claimed they had used it twenty years or more.
7. The proposal would reduce loading and unloading time and permit neater warehouse stacking, but . . .

   - small-quantity users—*meaning* most of our customers—would have to break down orders at their warehouses.

     [Or, to italicize the word that really was italicized in this sentence:

     The proposal would reduce loading and unloading time and permit neater warehouse stacking, but . . .

     - small-quantity customers—meaning *most* of our customers—would have to break down orders at their warehouses.]
8. The rate for the second five *years* is half the normal rate, or 22.5%.
9. This would be a management training program for the latter, and give us a pool of trained sales *managers*.

Chapter 22

IN WHICH WE POLISH UP

We can change 6-8 first to:

> Smith has authorized $100 deductions since 1950, when we undertook a bonds campaign*.

And then, because it's what Sloane must have meant, to:

> Smith has authorized $100 deductions since 1950, when we undertook the [or "our"] bonds campaign.

Which replaces an adjectival-infinitive-phrase-that-followed-its-modificand with a nonce-adjective-that-precedes-it. And thereby eliminates a case of Agent 6, and shows that "prepositionitis" is really just a kind of nickname for this agent: To *really* describe it I'd have had to call it "The Pointless Second-Level Modifier." But you mismodify so rarely with infinitives, and so often with prepositional phrases, that just *thinking* the extra syllables, every time you spot this agent, would cost you more effort than the greater accuracy would be worth.

But probably "when we undertook the bonds campaign" goes without saying; and if it doesn't, it's probably irrelevant; and if it's not that, it's *surely* trivial. So kill it. And on the same basis, kill also:

> 13-15: as you know, the total deducted on every payroll is forwarded to the cashier on payday for deposit. The cashier must purchase bonds for employees who have accrued enough money.

I think there's arrogation in 10-11: Insert "Exville" before "employees." But probably "with bond deductions" inaccurately limits the scope of this statement; wouldn't you bet *all* other Exville employees were on the weekly payroll? And if it wasn't zero, I think it should have gone without saying; so kill it, too, for whichever reason you prefer.

"Although both admit it is uncommon," 21, is unquestionably irrelevant. And without it, "and," 22, is zero; replace it with a period.

For accuracy, change "a," 9, to "the," and "the," 11 (before "payroll period"), to "each."

"Bimonthly payroll," 9 and 11, is a zigzag; and so is "I have told them," 20, and "I have apprised them," 24. Redo their sections as:

> 7-12: He and Assistant Plant Manager J. J. Blake are on the bimonthly payroll that is made at the main office. This payroll is

---

*So I fixed this sentence the wrong way in Chapter 13: The agent wasn't fractional anticipation, but repetition plus. My reason: I wanted to save Sloane's only example of the construction I'm about to discuss.

written—and the deductions are posted to the individual accounts—very early in each payroll period. All other Exville employees are on a weekly payroll made at the plant.

20-24: Wright says he has merely followed Smith's regular instructions. Smith feels no company rule or policy has been violated. I have told them that the procedure is improper and I would report it.

"To improperly obtain salary advances," 28, is repetition plus of "use this loophole." And "use this loophole," a second-time phrase, can become the *better* second-time phrase "do the same."

Since Blake, as well as Smith, had already crawled through the loophole, Sloane, in 27, must have meant not "additional plant managers," but "some top people at other plants." But since the practice required a co-operative cashier, and maybe no other cashier *would* have co-operated, "can," 27, had better be "might be able to."

And now we need neither dots nor the typographical breakdown in the last sentence; it can become just:

> You will surely agree that these people have misused the program, and some top people at other plants might be able to do the same.

With which—except that we'll expose some more superfluous words while we're curing him of pretentiousness and disorganization—we've completely (I think) cured Sloane of wordiness.

We've also, in this chapter, finished curing him of inaccuracy and hypercomplexity.

We've not yet completely cured him of arrogation or pretentiousness, and certainly not of disorganization, so his report still isn't *good*.

But I think it's a lot better than it was 153 pages ago.

SLOANE REPORT - Stage 6

September 9, 1957

To : H. B. Dawson

From : N. B. Sloane

AUDIT OF PAYROLL DEDUCTION FUNDS, EXVILLE PLANT

Exville payroll deductions for Savings Bonds are held in the account R. J. Wright, Cashier, at the First National Bank. This account is in balance with the individual accounts. However, the funds have been mishandled in a way that might be considered collusion between
5 Wright and Plant Manager R. W. Smith.

Smith has authorized $100 deductions since 1950. He and Assistant Plant Manager J. J. Blake are on the bimonthly payroll that is made at the main office. This payroll is written-- and the deductions are posted to the individual accounts-- very early in each payroll
10 period. All other Exville employees are on a weekly payroll made at the plant.

But Smith has consistently requested Wright to refund his $100 before payday, and Wright has always done so, out of funds deducted earlier from other employees' pay. Blake has also taken one or two such
15 advances recently.

Wright says he has merely followed Smith's regular instructions. Smith feels no company rule or policy has been violated. I have told them that the procedure is improper and I would report it. You will surely agree that these people have misused the program, and some
20 top people at other plants might be able to do the same.

Subsection 2 – THE DISEASE OF HYPERCOMPLEXITY

Chapter 23

GENERAL

First: You must absolutely disregard those who are telling you you must *never* write a long sentence, a grammatically complex sentence or a long paragraph. True: Short, simple sentences and paragraphs are the easiest to understand. But you don't write so your reader can understand your sentences; you write to convey a *message.* And often the only alternative to a certain amount of complexity is to fail to point out how your facts and ideas *relate* to one another, which is typically the *most* important part of your message. And if your reader doesn't get your message, it doesn't matter that he could understand all your sentences: You've failed to communicate.

Further–as you saw in relation to common elements–often you can make your reader's job easier, over all, by writing somewhat *more* complexly than you must.

And still further: A sentence's length is just *one* of the factors that determines how tough it is; even a fifty- or sixty-word sentence may not be really tough.

But you've been *hyper*complex any time that

(1) you've been more complex than you needed to be, and
(2) whatever extra value the incremental complexity contributed–if any–was too little to compensate for
    - the additional effort your reader had to expend to get it, and
    - the additional probability it created that he wouldn't understand you at all, or would *mis*understand you.

And a construction needn't be *really* complex to be hypercomplex; it just needs to be more complex than it should have been. And hypercomplexity, I think, is the fourth most serious writing disease.

Sentences, paragraphs and even whole reports may be hypercomplex. But hypercomplex paragraphs and reports essentially reflect disorganization rather than just hypercomplexity, so in this section we'll attack only the agents that produce hypercomplex sentences.

A sentence is one or more complete clauses followed by a "final" punctuation mark, plus maybe

- one or more conjunctions to tie some clauses together, and/or
- one or more other words or phrases–interjections, for example–that are within the sentence but not within any of its clauses.

Your "final" punctuation marks—each of the last two being final only when it's bounded on at least one side by what would otherwise have been a complete sentence (maybe preceded by a conjunction)—are your

periods,
question marks,
exclamation points,
semicolons and
colons.

Stretching only a little, we'll regard all five as equally "final." In fact, I urge you to regard semicolons and colons as special kinds *of* periods, and use

- a semicolon where you feel a period would separate two sentences *too* sharply, and
- a colon where your reader can't completely understand a preceding sentence till he's read the next.

Whether a sentence is hypercomplex depends—except rarely—on one or more of five factors.

Since one is just the number of words it contains, *every* agent of wordiness is also an agent of hypercomplexity, at least to a certain extent.

But some of these, either always or in particular manifestations, each reflect also one of the other factors, and these we'll look at again in the next chapter.

Hypercomplexity has also four other agents, all major. But these vary much less in importance than the agents of wordiness do, so I'll give you letters, instead of numbers, to identify them with. And don't be surprised if you don't find them all in your thousand-word sample; while I'm sure each has been invading your copy at least from time to time, none appears nearly as often as most of the agents of wordiness do.

The practice sentences for hypercomplexity will be at the end of Chapter 26.

Chapter 24

THE AGENTS OF WORDINESS THAT ARE ESPECIALLY AGENTS OF HYPERCOMPLEXITY

Every sentence is one of four types.

A *simple* sentence is a single clause.

John came home.

It may have a compound subject—that is, two or more substantives sharing the same predicate:

John and Mary came home.

Or a compound predicate:

John came home and went to the movies.

Or both:

John and Mary came home and went to the movies.

But compoundness of subject is generally only a minor factor in hypercomplexity, and a compound *predicate* may even make a sentence *easier* to understand.

A *compound* sentence is two or more clauses, but all "co-ordinate"—that is, joined by *co*-ordinating conjunctions, like "and," "or," "but." Separately, each clause would have been a complete simple sentence:

John went to the movies and Mary knew it.

A *complex* sentence is one "main" clause and one or more "subordinate" clauses, which exist only as modifiers or substantives within or in relation to the main clause. I've already defined the two types of modifying clause. *Almost* every noun clause is

- the subject of its main clause ("*That John was going to the movies* was known to Mary"),
- the object of a verb ("Mary said *John was going to the movies*"), or
- in apposition to a preceding substantive ("Mary relayed the message *that John was going to the movies*").

A clause that's subordinate to *the* main clause may also be a main clause to one or more subordinate clauses of its own:

John, *who wasn't hungry* [adjective; modifies "John"] *when he came home* [adverbial; modifies "wasn't"], went to the movies.

A *compound-complex* sentence is at least three clauses; at least two are co-ordinate, but at least one of these is main or subordinate to at least one other.

John, who wasn't hungry, went to the movies, and Mary knew it.

Another factor in whether a sentence is hypercomplex is how many clauses it contains. So any compound sentence is tougher than two simple ones to convey the same ideas.

So a zero word or goes-without-saying is especially an agent of hypercomplexity when it hooks together two constructions that should have been separate sentences. Sloane several times illustrated the zero connective; this illustrates the goes-without-saying type:

> However, it is our opinion that while satisfactory for use for the immediate purpose of the Valley survey, the somewhat limited operating range of the model makes it an unsatisfactory instrument for the Department's use in Chile, *where* the extreme north-south spread of the country, as well as the elevation ranges, calls for as wide an operating range as is economically feasible.

But a third factor is how the clauses in a sentence are *related* to one another. And while not even a complex or compound-complex sentence has to be really *tough*, either, on the average, is significantly tougher than one that's merely compound.

So when an agent of wordiness produces an extra clause in a complex or compound-complex sentence, it's still more serious, as an agent of hypercomplexity, than a zero or goes-without-saying connective.

So—since every modifying clause is a subordinate clause—Agent 13 is always a major agent of hypercomplexity.

But such superfluous clauses are often produced also by

all the sheer superfluities,
all the repetitive agents,
disregard of common elements,
the wrong point of view,
failure to use second-time words,
zigzagging,
the impersonal introduction,
the elegant variation,
noun mutilation, and
failure to use summary words.

For example, the sentence in 6-11, Stage 1, contained eight clauses; the predicate verbs, in order, were

has been,
represents,
might be considered,
advise,
have been engaging,
is,
fails,
can be considered.

"Represents what" was zero, and "in which they have been engaging" went without saying.

"While the procedure is admittedly not a very common one" was irrelevant, and "both of them advise (that)" was pointless attribution. (We moved these before we killed them—but we killed them.)

From "each of them fails to see" through "deserving of censure"—two clauses—was fractional anticipation.

So only two of the eight survive in Stage 6. And while the sentence is still *grammatically* complex, no normal reader could have trouble with it.

Rarely, even some other agent may produce a superfluous clause. For example, "if it had not been," 42, was a long-winded negative.

* * *

If you can tell a story from the point of view of

- "because" or some equivalent ("since," "due to the fact that" or the like), you can also tell it from a "so" or "therefore" point of view:

Because he's only six feet four, he'll play backcourt.	He's only six feet four, so he'll play backcourt.

- "although" or some equivalent ("even though," "while," "despite the fact that" or the like), you can also tell it from a "but" or "however" point of view:

Although he's only six feet four, he'll play forecourt.	He's only six feet four, but he'll play forecourt.

- "in order that" or "so that," you *sometimes* can tell it from a "then" point of view:

I want to be six feet eight so (that) I can play forecourt.	I want to be six feet eight; then I can play forecourt.

In a particular context, any of those sentences might provide the right emphasis, implication or overtone, and its alternative a wrong one. And you want to so tell every story—forgive me for repeating—that its significance comes through most clearly.

But:

"Although," "because," "so that" and their equivalents—even when "that" is "understood" after "so"—all are, or include, subordinating conjunctions, and therefore produce grammatically complex constructions, while

"but" is a *co*-ordinating conjunction, and so produces at worst a *compound* construction (and often, as you'll see, even separate simple ones), and

"therefore," "however," "then" and "so" (when it means "therefore") are adverbs, and so always—theoretically—produce simple constructions. (The most common exception: When "so" follows a comma, rather than a semicolon, the construction is for all practical purposes compound.)

So any time you provide a "because," "although" or "in order that" construction *without good reason*, the wrong point of view is a major agent of hypercomplexity.

* * *

Another major factor in a sentence's relative difficulty is its "engine-to-cargo ratio"–its engines being its verbs, its cargo being its other words. So verb mutilation, too, is in every appearance at least a moderately important agent of hypercomplexity.

But we'll regard it as *major* only when

(1) the mutilated verb should have been a verb-verb (because while a part verb has *some* driving power, it hasn't much), *and*

(2) the construction required no coolie verb. (Because while a coolie verb is a pretty sorry engine, at least a construction that contains one has as *many* engines as it should.)

You're especially likely to have needed no coolie verb when your container is

- a part verb or preposition, or
- within a prepositional phrase.

For example, Sloane needed no coolie verbs to mutilate "convince" into "convincing" or "obtain" into "obtaining"; and of the twenty-four sentences illustrating preposition-connected verb mutilation on Pages 145-147, nineteen required no coolie verbs. And you're almost *certain* to have needed none when your container follows the "to" in a "compared to" construction; this is illustrated in the example sentences on Pages 149-150.

But when hypercomplexity is the product of verb mutilation, you do *not* fix it by eliminating a clause. Rather:

First: If the mutilated verb should have been

- an infinitive (other than one that should have been the predicate verb in an infinitive clause) or
- part of a compound predicate,

your "decomplicated" construction contains exactly as many clauses as its predecessor did:

Providing this service free of charge will pay us in the long run.

In the long run, it will pay us *to provide* this service free of charge.

"To provide, etc.," is a noun phrase in apposition to "it"; each sentence is a single clause, with "will pay" as the predicate verb.

. . . when we undertook a campaign for the purpose of *convincing* all our employees . . .

. . . when we undertook a campaign *to convince* all our employees . . .

"To convince, etc.," is an adjective phrase modifying "campaign"; each version is part of a single clause, with "undertook" as the predicate verb.

The only reason we handled the powder costs as a separate item is that Lamb insisted, since he believed this would decrease the total cost of the survey in the eyes of the Government, thereby *reducing* the tax on the value of the contract, which is for their account.

The only reason we handled the powder costs as a separate item is that Lamb insisted: He believed this would decrease the total cost of the survey in the eyes of the Government and thereby *reduce* the tax on the value of the contract, which is for their account.

"(Would) reduce"—the "would" carries over, as a common element, from in front of "decrease"—is an additional predicate verb in the clause beginning "this would decrease," and each version contains six clauses; the other predicate verbs are "handled," "is," "insisted," "believed" and "is." "Since," in the third line of the original, was of course a goes-without-saying connective.

And second: If the mutilated verb should have been an *independent* predicate verb, you give yourself one *more* clause when you fix it. And sometimes also one more *sentence*—in which case you've cured the *most* hurtful kind of hypercomplexity produced by verb mutilation:

Because of the high turbidities, the normal Rayleigh-Debye theory could not be applied.

Because the solutions were so turbid, the normal Rayleigh-Debye theory could not be applied. [From "because" through "turbid" is an adverbial clause modifying "could be applied."]

These operators now receive \$2.87½/hr., compared to the tri-county average for such jobs of \$2.74.

These operators now receive \$2.87½/hr.; the tri-county average for such jobs is \$2.74.

Verb mutilation by omission virtually *must* cost a clause:

I have brought this improper procedure to Smith's and Wright's attention.

I have told Smith and Wright this procedure is improper. ["This procedure is improper" is a noun clause, the direct object of "have told."]

* * *

Since a passive verb has much less motive power than an active or intransitive verb, and an unnecessarily difficult verb less than its simpler alternative, Agent 4—when the passive verb should be *replaced*, rather than just killed—and Agent 17 are also in every appearance major agents of hypercomplexity. In fact, both are considerably more important in this aspect than in relation to wordiness.

And since every infinitive clause is just naturally tougher than an indicative clause, pointless use of infinitives especially is.

Chapter 25

THE OTHER AGENTS OF HYPERCOMPLEXITY THAT INVOLVE WORDS (RATHER THAN PUNCTUATION OR TYPOGRAPHY)

A. The Wrong Kind of Clause

An adjective clause is sometimes the smoothest and most economical way to convey a message whose significance is *not* really adjective–that is, one that *doesn't* really describe, limit or identify. And just so long as it's *grammatically* adjective–that is, so long as it contains a "relative" word that "refers," grammatically, to some preceding substantive–such a clause is a fine communicative device, and perfectly "correct."

But since every modifying clause is a subordinate clause, you've been hypercomplex any time you've used one to convey a message you could have conveyed as clearly and meaningfully–and at least *almost* as efficiently–through a *co*-ordinate clause or a separate sentence.

Sometimes the relative word that introduces such a clause–if you need to be refreshed about this, see Page 109 –is just a goes-without-saying connective; then all you must do to simplify your construction is just kill it. This was the case in the sentence beginning "However, it is our opinion that," on Page 169. And sometimes the relative word is *part* of a goes-without-saying connective:

> These trends appear to be based on the over-all economic "slow-down" and the severe austerity programs instituted by the oil companies over the past two years, both *of which* were brought about by an oversupply of oil, some politics and a necessary period of catching up with an overly forward-moving economy during the past ten years.

But *usually* to pull such a clause out of its sentence you must *replace* the relative word:

if it's	*with*
a pronoun,	some other kind of pronoun or a noun;
an adjective,	a demonstrative adjective ("this," "these," "that" or "those");
an adverb,	some other adverb (like "then" for "when," "here" or "there" for "where").

We have this recent telegram from Shaw asking us to do different things to the drills *which* we have either tended to or are still investigating, *which* I am	We have this recent telegram from Shaw asking us to do different things to the drills; we have either tended to *these* or are still investigating *them*. I am

sure you will continue to follow through on and seek Webster's advice if necessary.

sure you will continue to follow through on *these* and seek Webster's advice if necessary.

If you have no objection, we feel it would be to our mutual advantage to replace our party chief, John Davis, in Panama with Richard Ramsey, *whom* we had hoped to send to this crew originally but *who* was not available at the time.

If you have no objection, we feel it would be to our mutual advantage to replace our party chief, John Davis, in Panama with Richard Ramsey. We had hoped to send *Ramsey* to this crew originally, but *he* was not available at the time.

There is a tendency for the positive and negative charges to accumulate at the boundary between the P and N materials, *where* they are attracted to one another and combine to cause current flow.

There is a tendency for the positive and negative charges to accumulate at the boundary between the P and N materials. *Here* they are attracted to one another and combine to cause current flow.

When your relative word was an adjective, you may find that just one pronoun perfectly replaces your new adjective *and its modificand:*

Indeed, many dip interpretations are made on the basis of a single Δt determination across a split record without much concern for the magniture of dip on either half of the record, *which* procedure seems to imply planeness of reflector and practically that the sub-surface coverage is very nearly one half of the surface spread.

Indeed, many dip interpretations are made on the basis of a single Δt determination across a split record without much concern for the magnitude of dip on either half of the record. *This* (procedure) seems to imply planeness of reflector and practically that the sub-surface coverage is very nearly one half of the surface spread.

Sometimes after you've split your sentence you may decide the original reflected also a wrong point of view.

1. During the period May 5 to June 3, *when* the stage of the river was still high and a large amount of river water was being discharged through Southeast Pass, sufficient water was flowing to lower the temperature of the water for several miles into the Gulf by as much as three degrees (Figure 2).
2. During the period May 5 to June 3 sufficient water was flowing to lower the temperature of the water for several miles into the Gulf by as much as three degrees (Figure 2). The stage of the river *then* was still high and a large amount of river water was being discharged through Southeast Pass.
3. During the period May 5 to June 3 the stage of the river was still high and a large amount of river water was being discharged through Southeast Pass. *Therefore* sufficient water was flowing to lower the temperature of the water for several miles into the Gulf by as much as three degrees (Figure 2).

B. Overuse of Common Elements

First: If a common element is just one word—or you can convey it the second time through one word—you save *no* words by using it if to do so you must insert a conjunction. And you may complicate a construction greatly by doing this.

This is not a healthy situation for us *and* must be corrected through the efforts of each of you to treat the locals with more respect and to exercise more tact and diplomacy in your dealings with them.	This is not a healthy situation for us. *It* must be corrected through the efforts of each of you to treat the locals with more respect and to exercise more tact and diplomacy in your dealings with them.
The Δt, therefore, may not be a reliable indication of the emergence angle of a ray at any point *or* may not even be a significant average when wave fronts from various sources are arriving simultaneously *as* is commonly the case in steep-dip areas. It implies nothing about the planeness or inclination of the arriving wave except as it may be assumed to arrive vertically for purposes of correction to reference plane *and* does not even discount the possibility that several waves, with different angles of emergence, are arriving simultaneously.	The Δt, therefore, may not be a reliable indication of the emergence angle of a ray at any point; *it* may not even be a significant average when wave fronts from various sources are arriving simultaneously (*this* is commonly the case in steep-dip areas). It implies nothing about the planeness or inclination of the arriving wave except as it may be assumed to arrive vertically for purposes of correction to reference plane; *it* does not even discount the possibility that several waves, with different angles of emergence, are arriving simultaneously.

But you don't want to save words just to save words: You want to only when, and because, you thereby save your reader time and energy. So if by using a common element you'd require him to expend *more* time and energy, you mustn't use it even if you *would* thereby save words:

It was installed, incidentally, to give us a time break on track 12 so we could plot MAEed records through the EIC Plotter, and is in addition to the time break placed on track 27, but since it was installed has developed random time lags of from .001 to .007 seconds.	It was installed, incidentally, to give us a time break on track 12 so we could plot MAEed records through the EIC Plotter, and is in addition to the time break placed on track 27, but since it was installed *it* has developed random time lags of from .001 to .007 seconds.
While acknowledging that the "Carolina Plan" would entail relatively high initial costs, especially during the initial 6-9	Dobson acknowledged that the "Carolina Plan" would entail relatively high initial costs, especially during the initial 6-9

months (we would have to move considerable equipment, some operators and families, and many first-line supervisors and theirs), Dobson argued that it could be expected ultimately to yield significantly higher returns in terms of production costs and good public relations and offered long-range tax advantages, and you and I had overstated the added transportation costs.

months, *when* we would have to move considerable equipment, some operators and *their* families, and many first-line supervisors and theirs. But *he* argued that it could be expected ultimately to yield significantly higher returns in terms of production costs and good public relations, *that it* offered long-range tax advantages, and *that* you and I had overstated the added transportation costs.

When to use a common element you must convey a key verb idea through a participle—like "acknowledging," in the second example above—this agent and verb mutilation are jointly responsible for the resulting hypercomplexity.

Chapter 26

THE AGENTS OF HYPERCOMPLEXITY RELATED TO PUNCTUATION AND TYPOGRAPHY

The fifth major factor in hypercomplexity is the presence or absence of punctuative and typographical "visual aids."

C. Failure to Use the "Most Nearly Final" Punctuation Marks

You should regard punctuation marks exactly as you should words: You should want to give every reader every one you can think of that will help him get your message, but none that won't. Because any that won't help will hinder.

Now often if you didn't provide a particular punctuation mark–or provided one that you shouldn't–you'd seriously distort your *story:*

John says the boss is an idiot.

John, says the boss, is an idiot.

But often whether to punctuate, or with what, is optional. And it's this kind of situation we'll be (chiefly) concerned with here.

You can so punctuate as to separate two ideas (1) "finally," (2) "semi-finally," (3) slightly or (4) not at all.

I listed the "final" punctuation marks in Chapter 23. The "semifinal" are

dashes,
parentheses, and
colons and semicolons when they're *not* "final."

Generally, the only proper "semifinal" use for a semicolon is as a sort of double comma, to separate items that *include* commas. As in:

> In the process we'll eliminate his Type 1 impersonal introductions ("there has been," 3; "it becomes," 14; "there have been," 23; "it is," 27) . . .

Essentially, dashes and parentheses differ only in that parentheses downgrade the importance of–in fact, sort of invite a reader to skip–what they surround. So you ought never provide them around anything you want to be sure he doesn't skip.

At the third level, all by itself, is the comma.

And at the lowest is *no* punctuation mark.

Now sometimes you'd just clutter your copy by moving from any level to a higher one.

But often, without changing any words, you can make a construction easier by doing this.

For example: In the next three sentences–besides going from commas to parentheses in the second–we'll go from no punctuation to

- a comma in the first (after "up-dip velocity"),
- dashes in the second, and
- a period in the third:

If the velocity of 23,500 feet observed on Stations 91 to 158 from Shot Point 272 is from the same refractor, it is also an up-dip velocity and the refractor is dipping eastward at the east end of the line.

If the velocity of 23,500 feet observed on Stations 91 to 158 from Shot Point 272 is from the same refractor, it is also an up-dip velocity, and the refractor is dipping eastward at the east end of the line.

When it was announced that Snyder was taking a trip to Milan to not only place in operation BKF's geological field parties but also to have discussions with Smith, who will be the manager of the Sahara operation, concerning what contractor should be assigned the geophysical work, it was decided that it would be advantageous for us to have not only a representative from our London office but to have Taylor from the New York office in Milan.

When it was announced that Snyder was taking a trip to Milan–to not only place in operation BKF's geological field parties but also to have discussions with Smith (who will be the manager of the Sahara operation) concerning what contractor should be assigned the geophysical work–it was decided that it would be advantageous for us to have not only a representative from our London office but to have Taylor from the New York office in Milan.

It is possible that construction of a concrete vault anchored on bedrock might reduce or eliminate this effect but a conclusion on the basis of data available would lead to an all-out hard rock site for the best location.

It is possible that construction of a concrete vault anchored on bedrock might reduce or eliminate this effect. But* a conclusion on the basis of data available would lead to an all-out hard-rock site for the best location.

Here we'll promote one comma to a period, one to a colon:

Another set of rules we were advised to peruse begins on Page 181 of Bullen's Introduction to the Theory of Seismology, and we were to find occasion to apply one of these rules to an event we analyzed, namely, that one of the errors most frequently made in the reading of seismograms is "the identification of

Another set of rules we were advised to peruse begins on Page 181 of Bullen's Introduction to the Theory of Seismology. And we were to find occasion to apply one of these rules to an event we analyzed: namely, that one of the errors most frequently made in the reading of seismograms is "the identification of

*You certainly may begin a sentence with a conjunction–"but," "and" or any other.

PP and PS as P and S when Δ is about 115°-120°, leading to a false estimate of about 80° for Δ."

PP and PS as P and S when Δ is about 115°-120°, leading to a false estimate of about 80° for Δ."

Here we'll go from commas to a semicolon and a period (in the first, the original punctuation was *incorrect*):

The east end of the line, marked Stake 1, is located 336 meters west of Reflection Shot Point 11, the west end of the line, marked Stake 185, is located at Reflection Shot Point 73.

It was installed, incidentally, to give us a time break on track 12 so we could plot MAEed records through the EIC Plotter, and is in addition to the time break placed on track 27, but since it was installed it has developed random time lags of from .001 to .007 seconds.

The east end of the line, marked Stake 1, is located 336 meters west of Reflection Shot Point 11; the west end of the line, marked Stake 185, is located at Reflection Shot Point 73.

It was installed, incidentally, to give us a time break on track 12 so we could plot MAEed records through the EIC Plotter, and is in addition to the time break placed on track 27. But since it was installed it has developed random time lags of from .001 to .007 seconds.

D. Failure to Separate Ideas Typographically

On Page 166 I gave you this sentence:

But you've been *hyper*complex any time that (1) you've been more complex than you needed to be, and (2) whatever extra value the incremental complexity contributed—if any—was too little to compensate for the additional effort your reader had to expend to get it, and the additional probability it created that he wouldn't understand you at all, or would *mis*understand you.

It contains sixty-two words in eight clauses. Seven clauses are subordinate, but only two, which are co-ordinate with each other, are subordinate to *the* main clause, and one of these is the main clause to a subordinate clause of its own, and the other is to three subordinate clauses, and still another is subordinate to one of the three that are subordinate to one of the co-ordinate clauses that are subordinate to *the* main clause.

Yet I don't think you found it terribly difficult. The reason: I broke it down typographically, and thereby helped you (1) read it in segments, (2) properly relate each segment to every other. (Which—to show the difference—I did *not* do in the second sentence of the preceding paragraph.)

And often such a breakdown will be your best alternative to

*over*simplifying: to so conveying a message that your reader *can't* see clearly and easily how its segments relate to one another.

For Practice

All these sentences except 1 and 2 are new to you, and most suffer seriously from wordiness as well as hypercomplexity. But you're "supposed" to

first eliminate from them only the agents specifically mentioned in Chapters 24-26: that is, A through D and whatever examples you can find of

zero or goes-without-saying connectives,

any agents of wordiness that produced superfluous clauses in complex or compound-complex sentences,

verb mutilation (but only of verbs that should have been verb-verbs in constructions containing no coolie verbs),

overuse of the passive,

the unnecessarily difficult verb, and

the wrong point of view when it involved "although," "because" or "so that";

then check yourself against the "Answers" on Pages 182-185, and then eliminate the other agents of wordiness.

14 needs three more words to cure it of terseness, and two more—as it stands—to make it say what its author meant.

1. Although this policy may benefit the Arnold operation, it lessens the quality of the receivables portfolio.
2. During this period they are short of cash and borrowed from banks in past years to pay suppliers.
3. As we have discussed before, I believe it would be good if Varden and Powers can get together for a day or two at Sentinel Street so that Powers can be apprised of the vendors, our method of handling business in general, etc., and then I feel that it would be best for Powers to go over to the Newark branch and stay there several weeks so that he can really become acquainted with their particular projects and the project engineers.
4. Because of the surface offset of the refracted ray from its subsurface emergence point on the refractor, it is not possible to make the subsurface interpretation for the entire 13,800 meters, so a surface overlap of one spread (3,450 meters) is used to ensure complete subsurface coverage and to establish ties between the various segments of the interpretation.
5. However, as the average value of the earth's gravitational attraction in 980 gals (1 gal = 1 centimeter per second squared) and it has been established that in order to be geologically significant the meter readings of a survey must be accurate to .01 milligal (1 milligal = .001 gal) the accuracy of the meter must be of the order of one part in 100 million.

6. I will sincerely appreciate your thoughts and suggestions as soon as possible on drawing up a more specific reporting procedure on the condition of equipment of our crews, including recording instruments, cables, surveying gear, and the actual vessel itself, particularly the engine room, in order that proper allowance can be made for the time and expense on repairs.
7. If sufficient attenuation could be realized, the cross-correlation could be eliminated and it is felt this can be done with a delay-line filter, which would contain fewer points in the operator and provide the necessary attenuation only at the frequencies where it is needed and not at all frequencies on either side of the harmonic under investigation as present filters do.
8. In the future, especially on contracts involving a large volume of sales or contracts with clients with whom we already have a large volume of sales, we should make fairly frequent calls on the client, making a sincere effort to answer satisfactorily any questions he may have concerning our proposal and, if necessary, follow this client into the field and be on the ground with him during discussions at the time the contractor is being selected.
9. It was agreed by all the experts that the major stable results would be that the tides in the ocean would cease except for the small effects of the sun, earthquakes and other major crust disturbances would possibly be decreased, excursions of people from the "no-moon" side of the earth might have to be arranged until succeeding generations became accustomed to no-moon nights, the net result would be an appreciable decrease in the length of the earth day so a revision of all clocks and time standards would be required.
10. Of course, we could make up two sets of cables for this but it would be desirable if we could design three sections of cable which were identical (or two identical and one different) which would allow us to plug two sections together to shoot the 1,800′ spreads or plug three sections together and use every other connector to shoot the 2,700′ spreads.
11. The front brake assembly still consists of two single action wheel cylinders, activating two primary or self-energizing shoes, but the brake drum cylinder, front and rear, has increased from 230 mm to 250 mm and the brake lining width has increased in the front from 50 mm to 55 mm and in the rear from 40 mm to 45 mm.
12. The N layer on the left is called the emitter, the center P section (which is a very thin layer of material which is actually only about .001 inch thick) is called the base and the N layer on the right is called the collector.
13. The reduction indicated by R. P. Hawkins for payroll may not be possible to meet, since we in some cases have personnel who are already costing us well above the amount Hawkins allows, and we would not expect to change these people during the term of their contract to have them replaced by people making lower salaries.
14. This accounts for the fact that the engine's output falls somewhat below the regular type 3/1500 (53 SAE hp) which is equipped with the 32 PHN carburetor, improved intake manifold and horizontal fan assembly (internal parts remaining the same).

15. To name a few prize winners in the day's games, the fastest sack in the race was in Tony Santo's possession, who, from the velocity at which he clocked in, must've had an Ajax engine tucked away in his sack—as we tell our customers, that Ajax engine really has get-up-and-go power. Victors in the three-legged race were . . .
16. We realize that you cannot possibly forecast exactly what you will be selling when you submit your monthly order, but with your assistance in limiting emergency orders to emergency items and keeping on hand an adequate supply of such items as wiper blades, overriders, etc., we will be able to offer the very best service to all our dealers.

The Practice Sentences Cured Only of Hypercomplexity

The superfluous connectives were the zero "and's" in 3 and 12, the goes-without-saying "since" in 13.

The superfluous clauses, and the agents that produced them:

3. it would be good . . . [a Type 1 impersonal introduction]; I feel that [pointless attribution]; it would be best . . . [a Type 1 impersonal introduction].
4. it is not possible . . . [a Type 1 impersonal introduction, but superfluous because it fractionally anticipated the last part of its sentence].
5. it has been established that [a Type 2 impersonal introduction and pointless attribution]; 1 milligal = .001 gal [went without saying].
7. as present filters do [went without saying].
8. with whom we already have a large volume of sales [a pointless modifying clause].
10. it would be desirable [an impersonal introduction, and became Type 3 when the sentence's wrong-kind-of-clause was eliminated]; which were identical [a pointless modifying clause].
12. which is a very thin layer of material [a pointless modifying clause].
13. we in some cases have . . . [disregard of common elements].

The containers of the mutilated verb-verbs whose mutilations required no coolie verbs:

3. handling.
4. offset; coverage.
6. reporting.
8. involving; making.
9. effects.
11. activating.
13. indicated; term.

14. remaining.
16. limiting; keeping.

The overuses of the passive:

3. can be apprised.
6. can be made.
7. could be realized; could be eliminated; is felt; can be done.
8. is being selected.
9. was agreed; would be decreased.
13. replaced.

The unnecessarily difficult verbs:

7. could be realized; could be eliminated.
8. is being selected.
10. could make up; could design.
13. are costing; would not expect to change.
16. will be selling.

The pointless "although" and "because" constructions were in 1, 4 and 5; "because" was expressed as "as" in 5. The other "because" and "so that" constructions reflected *right* points of view.

The wrong-kind-of clauses:

7. which would contain . . .
10. which would allow us . . . [Which as "*this* would allow us . . . " represented a wrong point of view resulting in a superfluous clause.]
12. which is actually . . .
14. which is equipped . . .
15. who, from the velocity . . .

The overused common elements (in 8 and 11 this agent collaborated with verb mutilation to produce the hypercomplexity):

2. they.
4. a surface overlap.
8. we.
11. two single-action wheel cylinders.

Commas needed to be inserted in 6 (around "as soon as possible"), 7 (after "could be eliminated"), 9 (after "earth day") and 11 (after "250 mm"); also, you might have inserted others en route to other changes, and still others came in sort of incidentally. The other failures to use most nearly final punctuation marks:

4 needed a period, instead of a comma, before "a surface overlap." (And the new sentence reads more smoothly with "therefore" instead of "so.")

9 needed semicolons, instead of commas, after "effects of the sun," "possibly be decreased" and "no-moon nights."
10 needed a period after "cables for this."
11 needed a period, instead of a comma, after "self-energizing shoes."
12 needed semicolons after "the emitter" and "the base."
15 needed a colon after "the day's games," and a period, instead of a dash, after "tucked away in his sack."
16 needed a period, instead of a comma, after "your monthly order."
9 and 15 needed to be broken down typographically.

The words that needed to be added in 14 are italicized.

1. This policy may benefit the Arnold operation, but it lessens the quality of the receivables portfolio.
2. During this period they are short of cash; they borrowed from banks in past years to pay suppliers.
3. As we have discussed before, I believe Varden and Powers should get together for a day or two at Sentinel Street so that Varden can apprise Powers of the vendors, how we handle business in general, etc. Then Powers should go over to the Newark branch and stay there several weeks so that he can really become acquainted with their particular projects and the project engineers.
4. But the refracted ray is offset on the surface from its subsurface emergence point on the refractor. Therefore a surface overlap of one spread (3,450 meters) is used; this ensures that we cover the entire 13,800 meters of subsurface and enables us to establish ties between the various segments of the interpretation.
5. However, the average value of the earth's gravitational attraction is 980 gals (1 gal = 1 centimeter per second squared), and in order to be geologically significant the meter readings of a survey must be accurate to .01 milligal. Therefore the accuracy of the meter must be of the order of one part in 100 million.
6. In order that we can make proper allowance for the time and expense on repairs, I will sincerely appreciate your thoughts and suggestions, as soon as possible, on how we can report more specifically the condition of equipment on our crews, including recording instruments, cables, surveying gear, and the actual vessel itself, particularly the engine room.
7. If we can realize sufficient attenuation, we can eliminate the cross-correlation, and we feel we can do this with a delay-line filter. This would contain fewer points in the operator and provide the necessary attenuation only at the frequencies where it is needed and not at all frequencies on either side of the harmonic under investigation.
8. In the future, especially on contracts that involve a large volume of sales or contracts with major present clients, we should make fairly frequent calls on the client. We should make a sincere effort to answer satisfactorily any questions he may have concerning our

proposal and, if necessary, follow this client into the field and be on the ground with him during discussions at the time he selects the contractor.

9. All the experts agreed that the major stable results would be that
   - the tides in the ocean would cease except as the ocean was pulled slightly by the sun;
   - earthquakes and other major crust disturbances would possibly decrease;
   - excursions of people from the "no-moon" side of the earth might have to be arranged until succeeding generations became accustomed to no-moon nights;
   - the net result would be an appreciable decrease in the length of the earth day, so a revision of all clocks and time standards would be required.
10. Of course, we can make up two sets of cables for this. But if we can design three identical sections of cable (or two identical and one different), we can plug two sections together to shoot the 1,800′ spreads or plug three sections together and use every other connector to shoot the 2,700′ spread.
11. The front brake assembly still consists of two single action wheel cylinders, which activate two primary or self-energizing shoes. But the brake drum cylinder, front and rear, has increased from 230 mm to 250 mm, and the brake lining width has increased in the front from 50 mm to 55 mm and in the rear from 40 mm to 45 mm.
12. The N layer on the left is called the emitter; the center P section is called the base; the N layer on the right is called the collector. The P section is a very thin layer of material which is actually only about .001 inch thick.
13. The reduction that R. P. Hawkins proposes for payroll may not be possible to meet. In some cases personnel already cost us well above the amount Hawkins allows, and we cannot change these people till their contract expires to replace them by people making lower salaries.
14. This accounts for the fact that the engine's output falls somewhat below *that of* the regular type 3/1500 (53 SAE hp); the latter is equipped with the 32 PHN carburetor, *an* improved intake manifold and *a* horizontal fan assembly. (*Its* internal parts remain the same.)
15. To name a few prize winners in the day's games:

    The fastest sack in the race was in Tony Santo's possession; from the velocity at which he clocked in, he must've had an Ajax engine tucked away in his sack. (As we tell our customers, that Ajax engine really has get-up-and-go power.)

    Victors in the three-legged race were:
16. We realize that you cannot possibly forecast exactly what you will need when you submit your monthly order. But if you limit emergency orders to emergency items, and keep on hand an adequate supply of such items as wiper blades, overriders, etc., we will be able to offer the very best service to all our dealers.

The Practice Sentences Cured Also of Wordiness

To cure these sentences of wordiness, you had to somewhat recomplicate some. But since in each case the additional complexity served a worth-while purpose at only a reasonable cost, it wasn't *hyper*-complexity.

The other agents:

Sentence	*Agent*	
3	5	before; that; over; that; really; particular
	6	in general
	2	the . . . branch; go to . . . and
	3	Newark + there; their + the
4	1	ties [the fix eliminates "between," which should have been "among"]
5	1	average
	5	in order; the . . . of a survey
	21	accuracy
	18	of the order of
6	18	in order
	1	allowance
	5	the; actual
	25	thoughts and suggestions
	6	of our crews
7	8	if we can realize sufficient attenuation
	2	necessary
	5	the; and
	1	attenuation [the second time]; investigation
	3	frequencies + where
	16	on either side
8	16	contracts that involve; sales; contracts; clients
	3	contracts + that + contracts; involve + with
	24	large
	1	calls; effort
	2	satisfactorily
	9	this client [the second time]
	5	on the ground; during discussions
	6	at the time
9	5	that [the second time; replaceable by a colon]; the net result would be
	6	in the ocean
	1	possibly; revision
	2	of people
	18	succeeding generations
	21	decrease
10	2	for this; of cable
	3	plug together + plug together

11	39	has increased [twice]
	3	has (been) increased + has (been) increased; mm + mm [three times]
12	11	very thin
	3	is called + is called + is called; the P section + a very thin layer of material + which
	5	actually
13	1	reduction
	6	in some cases
	8	already cost us
	9	the amount; Hawkins; these people
	11	change
	16	their contract expires
	14	making lower salaries
	2	by lower-salaried people
14	18	accounts for
	3	the fact + that the engine's . . .
	9	the engine's
	1	output
15	2	in the day's games; in the race
	1	possession; get-up-and-go
	33	at which
	9	his sack
16	5	that; possibly
	8	we will be able to
	30	to all our dealers

3. As we have discussed, I believe Varden and Powers should get together for a day or two at Sentinel Street so Varden can apprise Powers of the vendors, how we handle business generally, etc. Then Powers should spend several weeks in Newark so he can become acquainted with their projects and project engineers.
4. But the refracted ray is offset on the surface from its subsurface emergence point on the refractor. Therefore a surface overlap of one spread (3,450 meters) is used; this ensures that we cover the entire 13,800 meters of subsurface and enables us to tie together the various segments of the interpretation.
5. However, the earth's gravitational attraction averages 980 gals (1 gal = 1 centimeter per second squared), and to be geologically significant, meter readings must be accurate to .01 milligal. Therefore the meter must be accurate within one part in 100 million.
6. So that we can properly allocate time and expense for repairs, I will sincerely appreciate your suggestions, as soon as possible, on how we can report more specifically the condition of our equipment, including recording instruments, cables, surveying gear and the vessel itself, particularly the engine room.
7. If we can increase attenuation sufficiently, we can eliminate the cross-correlation, and we feel we can do this with a delay-line filter. This would contain fewer points in the operator and attenuate only

where attenuation is needed, not at all frequencies on both sides of the harmonic being investigated.

8. In the future, especially if a contract involves a large sale or a major present client, we should call on the client fairly frequently. We should try sincerely to answer any questions he may have concerning our proposal and, if necessary, follow him into the field and be with him when he selects the contractor.
9. All the experts agreed that the major stable results would be:
   - The ocean's tides would cease except as the ocean was pulled slightly by the sun.
   - Earthquakes and other major crust disturbances might decrease.
   - Excursions from the "no-moon" side of the earth might have to be arranged until people became accustomed to no-moon nights.
   - The earth day would become appreciably shorter, so all clocks and time standards would have to be revised.
10. Of course, we can make up two sets of cables. But if we can design three identical sections (or two identical and one different), we can plug together
    - two sections to shoot the 1,800′ spreads, or
    - three sections, and use every other connector, to shoot the 2,700′ spread.
11. The front brake assembly still consists of two single-action wheel cylinders, which activate two primary or self-energizing shoes. But the brake drum cylinder, front and rear, has been increased from 230 to 250 mm, and the brake lining width from 50 to 55 mm in front and from 40 to 45 in the rear.
12. The N layer on the left is called the emitter; the center P section, the base; the N layer on the right, the collector. The P section is only about .001 inch thick.
13. We may not be able to reduce the payroll as R. P. Hawkins proposes. Some personnel have contracts calling for well above what he allows, and we cannot replace them till their contracts expire.
14. This is why it produces somewhat less horsepower than the regular type 3/1500 (53 SAE hp); the latter is equipped with the 32 PHN carburetor, an improved intake manifold and a horizontal fan assembly. (Its internal parts remain the same.) [With the verb unmutilated, we *don't* need "that of."]
15. To name a few prize winners:

    The fastest sack belonged to Tony Santo; from the velocity he clocked in at, he must've had an Ajax engine tucked away in it. (As we tell our customers, that Ajax engine can really get up and go.)

    Victors in the three-legged race were . . .
16. We realize you cannot forecast exactly what you will need when you submit your monthly order. But if you limit emergency orders to emergency items, and keep on hand an adequate supply of such items as wiper blades, overriders, etc., you will help us offer all our dealers the very best service.

Subsection 3 – THE DISEASE OF PRETENTIOUSNESS

Chapter 27

THE DISEASE AND ITS AGENTS

This–in my judgment the third most serious writing disease–is the one that makes your reports sound as if your chief reason for writing them was not to communicate, but to show off. And actually, you almost certainly *have* been choosing and arranging your words chiefly to show off, though almost certainly without realizing it.

And for this, too–as I said earlier–you can chiefly blame your schoolteachers. From fifth grade on they *trained* you to write to show off–chiefly, to miss no opportunity to prove you knew all the "elegant" words that "educated" people are "supposed" to use when they write, like "inform" for "tell," "observe" for "see," any of maybe two dozen alleged synonyms for "get." They trained you to prefer even an inaccurate "elegant" word to its simpler alternative, provided only it wasn't *too* inaccurate–like "indicate" for "show," "anticipate" for "expect," "frequently" for "often." They said, and imagined, they were requiring you to "build your vocabulary," which would have been fine, had they really been. But since they took a word from you for every one they gave you, all they *really* gave you was a *substitute* vocabulary, to be used only in writing, through which you could convey only the very same messages that you could through your everyday spoken words. And by defining a great many fine, precise words as mere "synonyms" for less precise ones, they prevented you from learning what they *really* meant, and how to use them *properly,* and thereby seriously limited your ability to convey the subtler, more precise messages that the less precise ones can't convey.

And the result of your writing "elegantly" is exactly the opposite of what you want it to be: Rather than admiring your reports, and you for having written them, your readers *dis*like them, and as they read look continuously for anything they can find that will show you're *not* as bright as you think you are, and excuses for *not* doing what you think they should: errors of fact, logic, interpretation, even of grammar and word usage. And usually–as surely you've found many times by now–they can find such excuses whether or not they exist.

Pretentiousness has

- five major agents, among them verb mutilation, overuse of the passive, the club-member phrase and failure to use second-time words;

- two—prepositionitis and the elegant variation—that are almost major, and
- twenty-three that range downward from fairly important to minor.

The last include twenty-one that are agents also of wordiness and one other agent of hypercomplexity, but of these the only one that warrants individual mention is "preposition first." Per appearance, it hurts at least as much as any of the others; it's minor only because it appears so seldom.

Its other minor agent is pointless use of Roman numerals.

Roman numerals aren't *always* pretentious. For example: When you've two numbered series running concurrently you can sometimes *help* a reader by using Roman numerals for one, Arabic for the other. And Roman numerals may help when you need to *sub*numerate, as within an outline. And in a few contexts—chiefly after the names of kings and queens, as in "George VI," "Elizabeth II"—they're so standard that you'd jar most readers by *not* providing them.

But most use them far more often than they need to or should. For example, the notion that a chemist must write "Figure III" to distinguish it from "Table 3" is nonsense.

And when you use them pointlessly, their only apparent purpose is to prove to your readers that you know them.

Which brings us to its other major agent.

S. The Sesquipedalium

We have very few—if any—real synonyms in English. Rather we have pairs of words, in each of which, typically, one is "bigger," the other "smaller" (you'll see in a moment why those words are in quotes). And the two typically differ, in that the "bigger" has a narrower, more precise, more exclusive meaning *within* the meaning of the "smaller." For example: "Receive," "obtain," "acquire," "procure," "secure" and maybe a dozen other words have each a particular meaning within the meaning of "get," while "get" means just "come into possession of," by whatever means and in whatever way.

And you can identify the "bigger" quite objectively—but not just by counting letters. Rather it's the one that "outscores" the other—by 3-0, 2½-½ or even just 2-1—on three counts:

1. It contains more *syllables.*
2. It's less colloquial—that is, however often you see it on paper, you *hear* it less often.
3. It's derived from Latin or Greek whereas the other is from Anglo-Saxon*. (And if you've never studied Latin or Greek, don't

*If you want to know *why* a word's ancestry affects the way readers react to it, I can't tell you, and I don't think anyone can. But believe me: It does.

worry; you can almost always *feel* which of these three languages a word is derived from.)

If they tie, you decide on the basis of how *much* longer one is, and/or how *much* less colloquial. But they'll seldom tie.

Now a word that would tell your story *best* is *not* a sesquipedalium, however big or unusual it is. Rather it's the one you *should* use. (Which means, of course, you must disregard those who've been telling you you must *never* use a big or unusual word.)

But a bigger word *won't* tell your story best unless it satisfies *all four of four conditions*. And a sesquipedalium—as we'll define it: Webster defines it a little differently—is a bigger word that, in a particular context, does *not* satisfy one or more of the four.

1. Its special, precise meaning is the one you really want to convey.

   So before you use a bigger word you need to be sure *you* know what it means. And for many of the more popular "elegant" words this may require some *real* vocabulary building, involving a good deal more than just looking it up in a pocket dictionary—which if you undertake, I suspect, you'll often find they *don't* mean quite what you thought they did.

   And I hope you'll often undertake it; the more words you know, the better you can communicate. But any time that, for whatever reason, you decide not to, you'll be wise to settle for the smaller word. True, your message may come through a little less sharply—but compared with what the bigger word would cost if it *didn't* mean what you thought it did, this is a very small loss indeed.

2. Its special, precise meaning is relevant.

   For example, suppose I've been pestering someone to let me do something, and finally, just to get me off his back, he lets me. If I then report that he acquiesced, I'll be using the word quite accurately.

   But this alone does *not* justify me in using it. Unless it *matters* that he only acquiesced, I should *report* only that he *agreed.*

3. Its special, precise meaning doesn't go without saying.

   For example, "to purchase" doesn't mean just "to buy"; it means "to buy" either

   - as a result of negotiations—bids and counterbids, offers and counteroffers—or
   - for or on behalf of a company or organization rather than an individual.

   So your company purchases—in the second special meaning—every time it buys. So the only time you need to *report* that it did is when you want to stress the *first* special meaning.

4. There's at least *some* chance—your judgment tells you—that *your reader will catch* its special significance and relevance: that it won't convey to him only exactly the same message that the smaller one would.

For example: Even if you do mean "purchase," and its special meaning *is* relevant, and *doesn't* go without saying, there's no point in your writing it if all it will mean to your reader is "buy" in eight letters. And so many of us, for so many years, have so grievously misused so many fine words that the special meanings of some no longer leap out as they should.

Now clearly: This means a reader is more likely to catch the special significance of a really unusual word than that of a "standard" fancy one, like "receive," "indicate," "approximately."

But even as to words like those last: The more carefully *you* use them—even within a single report, even to readers who've never read you before—the more likely it is that any of *your* special meanings *will* come through.

Now clearly, on the basis of this definition a word needn't be *really* long or uncommon to be a sesquipedalium. In fact, the shortest standard sesquipedalium in English—not counting the sesquipedalian abbreviations "i. e." and "e. g.," which I think can *never* be justified—is just two letters: It's "re," which is sesquipedalian by 2-1 anywhere that "about" would have done the job as well or better. And similarly, "due (to)" outscores "because (of)" by 2-1. And in relation to the number of times it appears, the English word that's *most* often a sesquipedalium is a four-letter Anglo-Saxon-derived word that appears twice in Sloane: It's "upon," which outscores "on" by 2½-½. In fact—as Sloane is about to show us—even a *one-syllable Anglo-Saxon-derived* word can be a sesquipedalium.

Stage 1 contained at least seventy-three sesquipedalia (some think more than eighty, but I've shut my eyes to all marginal cases). So Sloane averaged at least one sesquipedalium per 12.2 words. And while probably most who read this have been averaging fewer than half that many, probably *some* have been averaging *more.*

The seventy-one following involved simple one-word-for-one-word substitutions. Those in italics didn't satisfy even the first condition. (Probably some others didn't either, but again I've chosen to be conservative.) Seven have survived to Stage 6; these are identified by line numbers in the right-hand column.

1:	employees	people
3:	*indicated*, these, funds are	showed, the, money is
6:	however	but (3)
8:	although, *advise*	though, say
9:	procedure	practice
11:	censure	criticism

Both words come to us from Latin, and "censure" is shorter—but it's *much* less colloquial.

13:	informed	told
14:	undertake, *concentrated*	start, big

If "big" *is* what Sloane meant, and we can't be sure. But whatever he meant, wouldn't you bet it was a smaller word than "concentrated"?

15:	*purchase, convincing*	buy, getting

If he didn't mean "getting," he meant "persuading."

16:	upon	on
17:	*indicated*, although	found, while
19:	*purchased*	bought
21:	forwarded	sent
22:	becomes	is

This assumes we've already killed the zero "then."

23:	*purchase*, whenever	buy, when
24:	*indicate*	show
26:	therefore	so

Since "therefore" is an adverb, it needed to be preceded by a semicolon, so the original sentence was mispunctuated. But with "so," the comma is fine.

28:	however	but

We must move "but" to the beginning of the sentence, but that's no great chore. And "as was mentioned in the above paragraph" needed to come out anyway.

29:	never, *purchased*	not, bought

After which we still need to fix the long-winded negative.

30:	payroll [the first time]	pay (9)
31:	every	each
32:	payroll	pay
34:	however, upon	but, on
35:	ascertained, *consistently*, requested	found, always (12), asked (12)

Actually, I suspect Sloane really meant "told," and this will be relevant later. But meanwhile I'll settle for "asked."

36:	grant	give

40:	actually, obtaining	really, getting
41:	payroll	pay
43:	funds	money
45:	procedure	practice (18)
47:	consider	think

After which, of course, "himself to have done" must still become "he has done."

48:	justifiably, censure	properly, criticize
49:	merely, pursuant, instructions	just (16), according, orders (16)

Whereupon, in Stage 6, "Smith's regular" goes without saying.

50:	regularly, received	always, had

Had this been my report, I'd have changed "received" to "got," but I'm in a special position, and in 1969 I can't recommend this to others. I'll explain why shortly.

But whether with "had" or with "got," there's a wrong point of view here; the message would have been at least as meaningful—and a word shorter—as "that the plant manager has regularly *given* him."

But even in that form, the clause represents Agent 13; and the rest of the construction—in Stage 1—still contains all the other agents we've eliminated since Stage 1. So these two changes make no difference in Stage 6.

53:	apprised	told
56:	complication	fact
57:	*indicate*	show
58:	utilized	used
59:	procedure, frequently, "occassions," during	loophole, often, times, in

Yes, "on one or two times in the past several months" sounds ridiculous. But this is a *plus* for the simpler words; "on one or two occasions during the past several months" is equally ridiculous, but the "elegant" words somewhat conceal the fact.

And Sloane could hardly have misspelled "times."

60:	another	other
61:	likewise	also
63:	whereas	while
64:	employees	people
66:	*conclusions*	facts
67:	personnel	people
68:	desired	wanted

Again by changing to a simpler word we show clearly how ridiculous the original construction was.

71:	additional	other
71-72:	perhaps	maybe
72:	follow, procedure, obtaining	use, method, getting

This assumes "the Smith" has become "Smith's."

73-74:	actually	really
74:	becomes	is

And with the two simpler words substituted, the last ten words almost scream to be crossed out.

Note that "funds" and "employees"—at least in my judgment—were sometimes sesquipedalia, sometimes not. This sort of thing often happens; a word that satisfies the four conditions in one sentence may fail to in the very next.

A word may qualify as a sesquipedalium also by outscoring two or more other words combined. This is why I urge that—all else being equal—you prefer "there is" to "exists" or "occurs." Sloane's example is "whenever," 38; it ties "every time" in derivation and number of syllables ("every" is two syllables), but "every time" is more colloquial.

But the one word will tell your story *better*—so it's *not* a sesquipedalium—

- always, when it's a case of a verb versus a verb-plus-adverb or verb-plus-preposition and the key verb idea in the latter is in the adverb or preposition. As, generally, with "advance" versus "move up," "approach" versus "move toward," "accompany" versus "go with."

  But if all else is equal, the two-word alternative *is* better when the key verb idea is in its *verb* "half." As, generally, with "make up" versus "compose," "talk to" versus "address."

- usually, when the two or more words include a preposition, as with "in the past" versus "previous" or "previously." The reason: Adjectives (when they precede their modificands) and adverbs (always) are first-level modifiers, prepositional phrases only second-level.

  But if the one word is *especially* heavy—for example, "simultaneously" versus "at the same time"–it may be worth your while to settle for the less desirable modification.

Similarly, two words may outscore three, and so on–so "financially embarrassed," 60-61, is sesquipedalian for "short of cash." (Which also Sloane wouldn't have misspelled.)

As to "bimonthly":

Its first meaning, in all dictionaries, is "every two months"; and this *should* be its *only* meaning. But unhappily, most dictionaries now say it may also mean "twice a month," and some companies do use it to mean this; and if "Ajax" was one such–and I've assumed it was–Dawson might have wondered what Sloane was talking about had he referred to the "semimonthly" payroll.

So I'll not beat Sloane for using it.

But I think the dictionaries, by listing both meanings, have just destroyed the word for most people. Me, I expect never to use it again.

Of all our good English words, the one the schoolmarms have beaten the *most* mercilessly for so many years is "get." One result is that most writers are terrified to use it. Another is that middlemen are very sensitive to it; any time you must write through a middleman your readers will probably never see your "get's" even if you do provide them. A third is that most *readers* are jarred by it in its *perfect* tenses ("have got," "had got") or in the passive ("was got," "have been got").

But for all their efforts, that's *all* the schoolmarms have achieved in relation to it. Any time you use it in one of its "g-*e*-t" forms ("get," "gets," "getting") or in the *past* tense (as in "I got a letter from him yesterday"), if it really does tell your story, not one reader in a hundred will even notice it. I've proved this countless times in the past ten years.

And this is why you *should* use it: The words that tell your stories best are those that tell them *without* sticking out individually. In fact, the trouble with "receive," "acquire," "obtain"–except where one of them does satisfy the four conditions–is that they do stick out, and thereby impede communication.

And if we're lucky, by the year 2000 or so even the little effect that the schoolmarms have had will have disappeared, and you'll be able to use "get" freely in any of its forms.

But suppose you do eliminate all the pointless "elegant" words from your reports, and strive always to communicate through the very simplest words you can think of that will tell your stories accurately and meaningfully:

Won't you sound illiterate, unintelligent, unsophisticated?

You will not.

Won't your reports be dull, monotonous, uninteresting?

They will not.

May not your readers feel you're writing down to them?

They will not.

But should you just accept *my* answers to these questions?

Absolutely not, any more than you should have accepted your teachers'. Rather it's time you decided for yourself.

All right. As a first step, would you look now at Stage 7, on Page 213, and see whether *you* think

- it sounds as if its author was illiterate, unintelligent, unsophisticated;
- it's dull, monotonous, uninteresting;
- it might have led Dawson to suspect he was being written down to.

And it contains not even *one* word that—unless I just missed it—is any bigger or fancier than it has reason to be.

Not that it contains no big words. There's "deductions," ten letters and derived from Latin; there's "authorized," ten letters and derived from Greek. People like us, writing about the kinds of things we write about, can't help using words like these, and bigger ones.

But those we *should* use are more than enough to prove we're "educated." Those we provide merely to impress *do* impress—but not as we want them to.

For Practice

Many sesquipedalia have already fallen out of these (and our other) example sentences, for many reasons. But at least fifty-eight survive in these:

1. A recent situation in which we helped one customer relieve his inventories appears to have been correctly managed at first, but not all the way through.
2. All the experts agreed that the major stable results would be:
   - The ocean's tides would cease except as the ocean was pulled slightly by the sun . . .
   - Excursions from the "no-moon" side of the earth might have to be arranged until people became accustomed to no-moon nights.
3. Although not critical, the convenience features enable the Hitachi to provide more information per unit of time.
4. As we have discussed, I believe Varden and Powers should get together for a day or two at Sentinel Street so Varden can apprise Powers of the vendors, how we handle business generally, etc. Then Powers should spend several weeks in Newark so he can become acquainted with their projects and project engineers.

5. At the last session of the Tenth Triennial meetings, when we were all very tired, we may have approved certain minutes without realizing what complications might develop as we seek funds to increase our general budget (and the American Section general budget) as well as for new projects which we can undertake when we find funds and personnel.
6. Because the equipment RSWs cannot practically store all 200, we will ask Ohaus to ship 100 when they receive the order, 100 six months later.
7. Davis advised the creditors that Charles had borrowed $536,000 from the corporation since 1934 and lost it gambling.
8. For example, if we assume a $50,000 sales price and 15%/year cost of capital, it would cost us $3,000/year to retain the drag line.
9. However, the earth's gravitational attraction averages 980 gals (1 gal = 1 centimeter per second squared), and to be geologically significant, meter readings must be accurate to .01 milligal.
10. However, the pharmacy is where people buy, and we should know what makes them choose one product over another.
11. I think we should omit the bottom 25% of the population, because its "Tridil C" potential is small.
12. In essence, they recommended we introduce the product in practically every market they had surveyed.
13. In recent months Quality Control Laboratory has received fifty to seventy-five complaints concerning extreme bitterness in TEJAVA, many from customers who claimed they had used it twenty years or more . . . I selected twenty-five samples at random from retained files of the three batches alleged to be very bitter, coded them, and gave the panel the necessary instructions.
14. In summary, I recommend we
    - place a man in Trim R&G for up to 90 days to work with me to ensure we utilize our cutting lengths to the best advantage . . .
15. In the future, especially if a contract involves a large sale or a major present client, we should call on the client fairly frequently. We should try sincerely to answer any questions he may have concerning our proposal, and, if necessary, follow him into the field and be with him when he selects the contractor.
16. In view of Dr. Alexander's co-operation on Vizaid Ophthalmic, we should seriously consider purchasing a quantity of his book, but we must assure ourselves that it will benefit our eye-area promotion.
17. Pile height and drape of existing samples are impressively uniform.
18. Previously, the Laboratory examined competitive products and sent completed reports to Wilmington, which had to approve them before they were distributed.
19. Since subfreezing temperatures can damage most adhesives—and carriers are not liable for frozen goods unless we can prove they were involved—from now on please allow suppliers sufficient lead time to take proper precautions.

20. So that we can properly allocate time and expense for repairs, I will sincerely appreciate your suggestions, as soon as possible, on how we can report more specifically the condition of our equipment, including recording instruments, cables, surveying gear and the vessel itself, particularly the engine room.
21. Some personnel have contracts calling for well above what he allows, and we cannot replace them till their contracts expire.
22. The enclosed reports are those I promised you during our telephone conversation November 10.
23. The fastest sack in the race belonged to Tony Santo; from the velocity he clocked in at, he must've had an Ajax engine tucked away in it.
24. The Joplin code, unique numbers, would be satisfactory if we didn't have to move equipment between locations.
25. The principal reason for the increase was the spending for space, radio, literature and mailings (primarily for "Astor" and "Top-quality"), which amount to $150,000 in 1967, up $100,000 from 1966.
26. The proposal would reduce loading and unloading time and permit neater warehouse stacking, but: . . .
    - Distributors would need lift trucks to remove the pallets from the trucks.
27. . . . the latter is equipped with the 32 PHN carburetor, an improved intake manifold and a horizontal fan assembly. (Its internal parts remain the same.)
28. The U. S. formulation is altered as foreign regulations require; each time it is, a different suffix is added.
29. This would contain fewer points in the operator and attenuate only where attenuation is needed, not at all frequencies on both sides of the harmonic being investigated.
30. Unless we can prove our product is superior, our most likely customers are just those we now have, or can establish, favorable trade relations with.
31. We realize you cannot forecast exactly what you will need when you submit your monthly order. But if you limit emergency orders to emergency items, and keep on hand an adequate supply of such items as wiper blades, overriders, etc., you will help us offer all our dealers the very best service.

The Answers

In these contexts, these words—plus some others that you might have questioned—were *not* sesquipedalia:

2. excursions
3. provide
5. certain, undertake, personnel
13. alleged
14. place
18. previously, examined
19. precautions
20. allocate
28. formulation

But these were:

1. situation, one, appears, managed	case, a, seems, handled
2. major, cease, until, became, accustomed	chief, stop, till, got, used
3. although	though
4. we have discussed, believe, apprise, etc., become	I have told you, think, brief, and so forth, get
5. funds, funds	money, money
6. receive	get
7. advised	told [whereupon "that" is zero]
8. retain	keep
9. however	but
10. however	but
11. omit	forget
12. practically	just about
13. received, concerning, claimed, selected, retained	had, about, said, took, our
14. utilize	use
15. in the future, large, frequently, concerning, selects	from now on, big, often, about, chooses
16. purchasing	buying
17. existing	present
18. completed	its
19. allow, sufficient	give, enough
20. expense, vessel, particularly	money, ship, especially
21. personnel	people
22. telephone	phone
23. velocity	speed
24. satisfactory	all right

25. principal, primarily	chief, chiefly
26. remove from	take off
27. remain	are
28. altered	changed
29. contain	have
30. superior, favorable	best, good
31. forecast, submit, etc., offer	know, send us, and so forth, give

In 22, "during our (tele)phone conversation" represented also a slightly wrong point of view.

1. A recent case in which we helped a customer relieve his inventories seems to have been correctly handled at first, but not all the way through.
2. All the experts agreed that the chief stable results would be:

   - The ocean's tides would stop except as the ocean was pulled slightly by the sun . . .
   - Excursions from the "no-moon" side of the earth might have to be arranged till people got used to no-moon nights.

3. Though not critical, the convenience features enable the Hitachi to provide more information per unit of time.
4. As I have told you, I think Varden and Powers should get together for a day or two at Sentinel Street so Varden can brief Powers on the vendors, how we handle business generally, and so forth. Then Powers should spend several weeks in Newark so he can get acquainted with their projects and project engineers.
5. At the last session of the Tenth Triennial meetings, when we were all very tired, we may have approved certain minutes without realizing what complications might develop as we seek money to increase our general budget (and the American Section general budget), as well as for new projects which we can undertake when we find money and personnel.
6. Because the equipment RSWs cannot practically store all 200, we will ask Ohaus to ship 100 when they get the order, 100 six months later.
7. Davis told the creditors Charles had borrowed $536,000 from the corporation since 1934 and lost it gambling.
8. For example, if we assume a $50,000 sales price and 15%/year cost of capital, it would cost us $3,000/year to keep the drag line.
9. But the earth's gravitational attraction averages 980 gals (1 gal = 1 centimeter per second squared), and to be geologically significant, meter readings must be accurate to .01 milligal.
10. But the pharmacy is where people buy, and we should know what makes them choose one product over another.
11. I think we should forget the bottom 25% of the population, because its "Tridil C" potential is small.

12. In essence, they recommended we introduce the product in just about every market they had surveyed.
13. In recent months Quality Control Laboratory has had fifty to seventy-five complaints about extreme bitterness in TEJAVA, many from customers who said they had used it twenty years or more . . . I took twenty-five samples at random from our files of the three batches alleged to be very bitter, coded them, and gave the panel the necessary instructions.
14. In summary, I recommend we
    - place a man in Trim R&G for up to 90 days to work with me to ensure we use our cutting lengths to the best advantage . . .
15. From now on, especially if a contract involves a big sale or a major present client, we should call on the client fairly often. We should try sincerely to answer any questions he may have about our proposal, and, if necessary, follow him into the field and be with him when he chooses the contractor.
16. In view of Dr. Alexander's co-operation on Vizaid Ophthalmic, we should seriously consider buying a quantity of his book, but we must assure ourselves that it will benefit our eye-area promotion.
17. Pile height and drape of present samples are impressively uniform.
18. Previously, the Laboratory examined competitive products and sent its reports to Wilmington, which had to approve them before they were distributed.
19. Since subfreezing temperatures can damage most adhesives—and carriers are not liable for frozen goods unless we can prove they were involved—from now on please give suppliers enough lead time to take proper precautions.
20. So that we can properly allocate time and money for repairs, I will sincerely appreciate your suggestions, as soon as possible, on how we can report more specifically the condition of our equipment, including recording instruments, cables, surveying gear and the ship itself, especially the engine room.
21. Some people have contracts calling for well above what he allows, and we cannot replace them till their contracts expire.
22. The enclosed reports are those I promised you over the phone November 10.
23. The fastest sack in the race belonged to Tony Santo; from the speed he clocked in at, he must've had an Ajax engine tucked away in it.
24. The Joplin code, unique numbers, would be all right if we didn't have to move equipment between locations.
25. The chief reason for the increase was the spending for space, radio, literature and mailings (chiefly for "Astor" and "Topquality"), which amount to $150,000 in 1967, up $100,000 from 1966.
26. The proposal would reduce loading and unloading time and permit neater warehouse stacking, but:
    - Distributors would need lift trucks to take the pallets off the trucks.

27. . . . the latter is equipped with the 32 PHN carburetor, an improved intake manifold and a horizontal fan assembly. (Its internal parts are the same.)
28. The U. S. formulation is changed as foreign regulations require; each time it is, a different suffix is added.
29. This would have fewer points in the operator and attenuate only where attenuation is needed, not at all frequencies on both sides of the harmonic being investigated.
30. Unless we can prove our product is best, our most likely customers are just those we now have, or can establish, good trade relations with.
31. We realize you cannot know exactly what you will need when you send us your monthly order. But if you limit emergency orders to emergency items, and keep on hand an adequate supply of such items as wiper blades, overriders, and so forth, you will help us give all our dealers the very best service.

Subsection 4 – THE DISEASES OF DISORGANIZATION AND ARROGATION, AND HOW TO ATTACK EVERY WRITING JOB FROM NOW ON

Chapter 28

DISORGANIZATION AND ITS SIMPLEST AGENT

While less hurtful to most writers than wordiness, disorganization is *far* more serious than any *other* writing disease. And organizationally, your chief trouble has been that you've been organizing every report exactly as your teachers taught you to: into three sections called "introduction," "main body" and "conclusion." You need to ditch this pattern completely.

But first let's look at the simplest agent of this disease.

Failure to Outline in Advance

You really begin to organize a report the moment you know you'll have to write it. Your tentative–and usually subconscious–organization affects even the way you gather your material.

And you never stop organizing till you finish it.

But the *most* important moment in the organizing job comes just before you start to actually put it on paper. At this point you need to outline what you're going to say. And unless your story is so simple that you can tell it in a sentence or two, you need to outline it *on paper.*

The outline needn't be minutely detailed, or grammatically correct, or physically attractive. It may suffice, in fact, just to scribble on the back on an old envelope the points you think you'll have to cover, in the order in which–at this point–you think you'd cover them best.

But however skeletal or unattractive it is, you should have completed it before you start to write, and have it at your elbow while you write, and stick to it *exactly* . . .

Unless, and until, *you find a reason to depart from it.*

And you'll often find such a reason. Because while you're writing a report you're *very* likely to get insights into your subject that you just couldn't have had before you started to write.

But any time you get such an insight you must *not* just toss the outline aside and go on *without* an outline. Rather you should *revise* the outline, so that it, too, reflects the new insight; and then check the revision to ensure–so far as you can–that it still includes everything you want to say, and everything still seems to hang together . . . and only *then* resume writing.

You may need to revise an outline twice, three times, maybe a dozen times or more; this doesn't matter. What matters is just that when you've finished writing, you have a report and an outline that are perfectly parallel.

The usual excuse for not outlining–"I haven't time"–is a bad one; outlining will rarely, if ever, cost you time, and will usually save you time. And if ever it doesn't, you can bet it's saved your *readers* time.

* * *

The exercise for this disease will be at the end of Chapter 32.

Chapter 29

THREE MORE AGENTS OF DISORGANIZATION INCLUDING THE TWO MOST IMPORTANT

L. Failure to Start With the Proper "Lead"

You must resolve to never again willingly start a report with an "introduction," but instead–ground rules permitting–to start every one, without exception, with its proper "lead."

To see why, let's consider how the job of reading a report differs from that of "reading" a picture.

First: The picture tells its story instantaneously, or just about so; you look at it, and you have it. (Or, at least, as much as you're likely to want or need.)

Second: You can understand it perfectly without understanding even one of its brush strokes.

Third: You can look at the individual brush strokes in any order you like–in fact, the order you look at them in will probably correlate at just about zero with the order the painter put them there in.

The report, on the other hand, unfolds its "picture" a "brush stroke" at a time, and the only way you can "see" the whole is by reading each "brush stroke"–or at least almost each–individually. Further: To understand the whole you must *understand* each individual "brush stroke," or at least almost each. And finally: You must look at the individual "brush strokes" in exactly–or at least almost exactly–*the order the writer put them there in.*

Which means . . . and if this isn't enough to scare the daylights out of any writer, I don't know what is . . .

That a writer, *at best*, is in the position a painter would be in if the painter had to say to every prospective viewer: "If you want to see my picture, you must sit there and *follow me through its creation, brush stroke by brush stroke*–and *understanding* every brush stroke."

And in relation to the introduction . . .

Since the introduction is that part of a report, at the very beginning, where you "set the stage," for your reader, for your "main body," which will follow (I've tried to quote your teachers) . . .

That any time you *do* start with an introduction you put yourself into the position that the painter would be in if he had to say to every prospective viewer: "If you want to see my picture, not only must you watch me paint it, but also, before I *start* to paint it, you must sit there and *watch me build a frame for it*."

This being so, isn't it surprising that people have read your reports at all?

Not really. People have *had* to read your reports—or at least some of them, at least in part. Their bread and butter have depended on it, and people are willing to make some sacrifices to go on eating.

But surely no reader has ever been *grateful* for this treatment.

Whereupon it's time to define "lead":

> **The lead is that part of your story, at the *very* beginning, where you sketch in for your reader, as quickly and completely as you can but without going into detail, all the essential elements in your story, in such a way that he can see immediately what's in it for him, and thereby decide whether to read on.**

Now this differs markedly from the way your teachers defined "introduction." Is it possible, though, that all I'm really urging is that from now on you *call* your introductions "leads," and define "lead" differently than you did "introduction," but still begin every future report exactly as you've begun every past one?

No. The two concepts are *very* different.

In Sloane, for example: I defy anyone to tell me that the first sixty-one words in Stage 1 didn't perfectly "set the stage," for Dawson, for Sloane's "main body," which did follow. (And all Sloane needed to worry about was whether Dawson would still be there when the main body got there.)

Whereas his *lead*—as I see it—would have been something like:

> A loophole in our Savings Bonds procedure has enabled Exville Plant Manager R. W. Smith to get two salary advances every month out of other employees' deductions. Assistant Plant Manager J. J. Blake has also taken one or two such advances recently.

That is: If your essential elements are a man, a woman and the moon, you must not start by describing the bench that the man and woman are sitting on. If you do, your intended reader—the one who needs your story, and would probably have hung around to hear it had you begun it properly—may not recognize in time what it *is* about, and may leave you. And further, though less important: You may hold a reader who's interested in the *bench*, whom you *don't* want to hold.

Rather, starting no later than in your first sentence—and preferably even *earlier*: in your *subject line*—you must first sketch in the man, the woman and the moon.

And further: You must sketch in *all* your essential elements before providing any *details* about *any* of them—or, for that matter, about anything else. That is: Once you've begun your lead, you must provide nothing *but* lead till the lead is *complete.**

And your *most* important point must appear *before your first period.*

Once in a great while you may even be able to provide your whole lead in your subject line. All right: In such a case don't repeat it in your first sentence; just go on to whatever comes next. But this will happen only *very* seldom, and you must never let yourself imagine you've provided your whole lead when really you've only begun to provide it.

Sloane's subject line, of course, was only a label; it maybe helped Dawson's file clerk, but it surely did nothing for Dawson. Let's replace it with one that's lead-type: "Loophole in Bond-Deduction Program."

(Some are now starting even every *letter* with a subject line, between the "salutation" and the first paragraph—and I think this is a great idea.)

Your lead may or may not be preceded by a subhead. If you choose to use one—or ground rules require you to—the best are "Abstract" and "Summary," because you can write anything you like under either of these; but even "Introduction" will usually do, if you don't let the label trap you into actually *writing* an introduction. "Conclusions," or "Conclusions and Recommendations," is good only when your conclusions and/or recommendations *are* your essential elements; and while they *almost* always are—when you have any—they don't absolutely have to be.

But if you write your lead under a subhead, don't write the rest of the report as if your reader won't read the lead, or, having read it, will immediately forget it; it's fine to *elaborate* later on what you say in the lead, but don't just *repeat* it†. Scientists often do this in reports that begin with "abstracts," on the basis that "some who'll read the abstract may not read the whole report." This is absurd: The point is that no one will read the *report* without having read the *abstract*.

After your subject line, your lead may be a sentence, a paragraph, several paragraphs, even a whole chapter; it depends entirely on how many essential elements you have *to* sketch in.

But however long it is: Wherever it ends, a paragraph should end.

If, as I hope, you've now resolved that from now on you *will* write

---

* Except that—I have to admit, reluctantly—you may sometimes find it economical to drop in one or two *very* small details—requiring, say, up to three or four words each—that won't clutter it *much*.

†By definition, it is *not* fractional anticipation—or zigzagging—to say something briefly in the *lead* and elaborate on it later, provided

(1) the brief statement *belongs* in the lead, and

(2) the elaboration doesn't.

leads rather than introductions, I must warn you it won't be easy. However enthusiastically you *think* you embrace the idea, in particular cases you'll find all sorts of (what seem to be) good reasons for making exceptions.

For example, when you're answering the letter that was addressed to your boss: You're likely to say to yourself "This man doesn't know me from Adam. So before I answer his questions I need to identify myself, and explain why he's hearing from me instead of the boss." First, you do *not* need to do this—and second, you can usually achieve both objectives at once anyway. For example, this is an introduction:

> Dear Mr. Breckenridge:
>
> My boss, John P. Jones, has asked me to answer your letter of May 15, in which you asked the following questions:

This is a lead:

> Dear Mr. Breckenridge:
>
> To answer the questions you asked May 15 in your letter to John P. Jones, I suggest you tell your customer that . . .

Or "If I start right in by telling this guy we've decided not to hire him, he'll hate us. So first I'll butter him up—and *then* I'll drop the bomb." Actually, this way you'll make him *really* hate you; comparatively, he'll be *grateful* for a forthright "We're sorry, but . . ."

Or—as, for example, in a report on an especially exotic scientific experiment—"I guess the essential elements in this one are my findings, but if I start with them my reader won't understand them. So, obviously, I need to background him first." He doesn't need to understand them immediately; he needs to understand them *when he's finished the report.* And at that point he'll be most likely to if you provide them first, and *then* background him.

Or "This recommendation will infuriate my reader; if I start with it he'll just snort and swear and throw the report aside after the first sentence. So I'll ease in; I'll first show him how I arrived at it." Well, first, I've never even once heard of a reader tossing a report aside after the first sentence because it began with a lead and he hated it, and I'll be greatly surprised if I ever do. And second: Unless you start with your recommendation, your reader may *never reach it.* And third: Till he knows what you're recommending, he may agree with everything you say while you're justifying it but not see how it *relates* to your recommendation; so when—or if—he finally does find out, he may not realize you *have* justified it.

All right. I'd like you now to go back and reread the first sentence in this chapter, but this time, please, mentally underline "without exception."

Preferably, you also start every section, subsection and paragraph by sketching in its essential elements. (Which does *not* mean you can't write a one-sentence paragraph; more on this later.)

But you can have good reason *not* to do this with a section, and somewhat more often with a subsection, and still more often with a paragraph.

Back to the outline for a moment.

Since every report should start with a lead, you can write the first two words of any outline without even thinking:

1. Lead.

But then you do have to start thinking. And the first thing to think about is whom, exactly, you'll be writing to communicate *to*.

And this person, or these people, may *not* be exactly the ones you'll *ostensibly* be writing to. For example, some on your addressee list may be there just for reasons of "courtesy," or "protocol," and even if some of these *are* interested in your story, you don't really care whether they get it or not. And you may *really* be aiming it at some who officially *won't* get it—for example, your boss, who officially will see it only to OK it before it goes out.

Having thus identified your readers, you forget about everyone else in the world, and figure out exactly what you want to tell *them*.

And the best way to do this, I'm convinced, is now to stop outlining and actually *compose* your lead, and go on to Point 2 of your outline only after you've satisfied yourself—as well as you can, at this point—that it's the *right* lead.

Now however conscientiously you try to do this—since, to repeat, you're likely to get new insights into your story while you're writing it—this first lead will *not* necessarily be exactly the one you end up with.

But at least it will get you started in a particular direction. And *almost* always, at least, this should be the right direction, and the lead you end up with at least *fairly* close to your first lead.

SL. Failure to Follow the "Straightest Possible Line"

Your objective in organizing must be to try to ensure that your report will move continuously forward: that each word will serve as a firm substructure for the next, and each following word rest securely on the one that preceded it, and your reader can read from Word 1 through Word *n* without ever looking back, or having to consciously recall anything you said earlier, or wonder what you'll say later, and you'll never have to *remind* him of anything you've said, or tell him you'll say something later—and when he's finished, he'll understand it perfectly.

And you need to think in these terms twice while you're preparing a report.

The first time is when you're outlining it. And at least in *almost* every case, your forward motion will be most nearly continuous if you follow the order:

1. Lead.
2. Background (if any).
3. Elaboration of the lead.
4. Anything else.

Your background, of course, will always include anything your reader may need to understand your lead—the kinds of things you used to think you had to start with. And your "anything else," essentially, will be whatever *you* don't think he really needs, but are willing to provide in case *he* thinks he does.

But sometimes your judgment will tell you your background should come third or fourth instead of second, so you put it third or fourth. (Though in such a case, obviously, it *won't* include anything your reader may need to understand your lead.) And sometimes—more on this in the next chapter—you'll do best to scatter your "anything else" around within your background and/or elaboration sections.

So of the four sections, the only one whose position you'll *never* have good reason to change is the lead.

But I recommend that when you outline, you always try this pattern first, and depart from it *only* when your judgment tells you to.

To illustrate it in Sloane:

We already have the lead, which in Stage 6 was the second sentences in Paragraphs 1 and 3 and part of the first sentence in 3.

The background is the first sentence in 2 and what's left of the first sentence in 3; let's put these together as Paragraph 2 of Stage 7. (Except that, because I can't believe Smith merely *asked* Wright for the "refunds," I'm going back to Sloane's "requested," but with quotes around it to signal to Dawson not to take it literally; and for the same reason I'll also quote "refund." And we can substitute "he" for the second "Smith.")

> Smith has authorized $100 deductions since 1950. But he has always "requested" Cashier R. J. Wright to "refund" his $100 before payday, and Wright has always done so.

Then, to elaborate on the lead, we must point out:

1. Exactly what the loophole is.

2. How Smith and Wright feel about what they've done. (Because other plant managers and cashiers may feel as they do; this is why Sloane fears the practice may spread.)
3. That Sloane has properly notified both men that he'd report what they've been doing.

Which, sticking to Sloane's words as closely as we can, we do like this:

The practice is possible because:

- Smith and Blake are on the bimonthly payroll that is made at the main office. This payroll is written—and the deductions are posted to the individual accounts—very early in each pay period.
- All other Exville employees are on a weekly payroll made at the plant. But all deductions are held in the account R. J. Wright, Cashier, at the First National Bank.

Wright says he has just followed orders. Smith feels no company rule or policy has been violated.

I have told them that the practice is improper and I would report it.

And now, it seems to me, the fact that "this account is in balance with the individual accounts" is exposed

(1) as a goes-without-saying (because unless something *else* is wrong at Exville, that Sloane hasn't told us about, it couldn't be otherwise), and

(2) whether or not it goes without saying—now that we really know what we want to say—as *irrelevant.*

And so is the account's name now clearly irrelevant. So replace the second sentence in the second dotted paragraph with "But all deductions at each plant are held in one bank account."

But now we can see something's *missing*: the fact that the balance in this account has *always exceeded $100*. Because if it hadn't, there'd have been times when Smith *couldn't* have got his "refund."

And you'll often thus expose previously concealed irrelevancies, and/or arrogation, when you reorganize a report along these lines.

Now let's show you the whole report.

SLOANE REPORT - Stage 7

September 9, 1957

To : H. B. Dawson

From : N. B. Sloane

LOOPHOLE IN BOND-DEDUCTION PROGRAM

A loophole in our Savings Bonds procedure has enabled Exville Plant Manager R. W. Smith to get two salary advances each month out of other employees' deductions, and some top people at other plants might be able to do the same. Assistant Plant Manager J. J. Blake has also taken one or two such advances recently.

Smith has authorized $100 deductions since 1950. But he has always ''requested'' Cashier R. J. Wright to ''refund'' his $100 before payday, and Wright has always done so.

The practice is possible because:

- Smith and Blake are on the bimonthly payroll that is made at the main office. This payroll is written-- and the deductions are posted to the individual accounts-- very early in each pay period.
- All other Exville employees are on a weekly payroll made at the plant. But all deductions at each plant are held in one bank account, and the balance in this account has always exceeded $100.

Wright says he has just followed orders. Smith feels no company rule or policy has been violated.

I have told them that the practice is improper and I would report it.

The second time to think in terms of "continuous forward motion" is when you're editing.

Sometimes, at this point, you may decide you can straighten your line by moving sentences around within paragraphs, or even paragraphs or whole sections within the report.

But the way you'll *most* often eliminate this agent is by moving *words or phrases within sentences.* And while misplaced words and phrases typically hurt much less than misplaced sentences or paragraphs, their *total* effect can be *very* significant.

For example, in a made-up sentence that I gave you earlier:

On July 13 I'm going to the ball game.	I'm going to the ball game (on) July 13.

And in two of the example sentences, which I didn't make up:

During this period they are short of cash; they borrowed from banks in past years to pay suppliers.	During this period they are short of cash; in past years they borrowed from banks to pay suppliers.
The tax for the second five years is half the normal rate, or 22.5%.	The tax for the second five years is 22.5%—half the normal rate.

FGO. Failure to Get Off at the End of the Line

First: Once in a great while, at the end of a report, you may need to tie some loose ends together, or do something else that makes the report end with what your teachers would have called a "conclusion" section.

Fine. If ever you need to do this, do it.

But you should need to rarely, if ever.

And if ever you do, the section should almost certainly *not* contain any *conclusions*. Because—to repeat—when you have conclusions, they should virtually always be in your lead; and to repeat them at the end would almost any time be Agent 19.

And second: You should *never* tie up a report with a pink ribbon at the end—for example, an automatic "If we can be of any further assistance, do not hesitate to let us know."

Now such a sentence is *not* a pink ribbon if

(1) you really *want* your reader to ask for more help if he needs it, and

(2) you really believe that unless you invited him to, he might not.

And in such a case you *should* include it, though not necessarily at the end—and, of course, without mutilating the verb "help" into the noun "assistance."

But the only "section" you must necessarily "conclude" any report with is a *period after the last sentence*—or maybe a question mark. When you've finished telling a story, just quit. And don't worry if you seem to have ended "abruptly"; if you've really told it, the end *won't* seem abrupt to your reader.

Chapter 30

THE OTHER AGENTS OF DISORGANIZATION

Zigzagging and fractional anticipation are also agents of disorganization; in fact, the first is always—and the second is sometimes—more important in this respect than in relation to wordiness.

But I think I've already said all I need to about both.

FHS. Failure to Help a Reader Skip

Even when you're writing to just one reader, you can't always be sure whether he knows something or doesn't. And when you're writing to many, you often *can* be sure that some will know some things, others other things.

The overriding rule, in relation to this problem, is that you must *always* provide *everything* that *any* of your readers are likely to need: Something goes without saying only if you can reasonably assume *all* your readers know it, or *any* of them could figure it out.

But any time you make anyone read something he does know, you waste his time and energy, and he has a right to resent it.

So you must also always make it as easy as you can for any reader to *skip* anything *he does* know.

To illustrate, let's pretend you're at a point in a report where a reader, to understand your message, must know about the Johnstown flood. And you're pretty sure some of your readers do, but suspect others don't—or, if you're writing to just one reader, you aren't sure whether he does or doesn't.

In view of the overriding rule, you *will* now tell about the Johnstown flood.

Now you *could* preface this section with something like "The next *n* paragraphs are only for those who don't already know about the Johnstown flood; all others please skip them." Or "The next *n* paragraphs, about the Johnstown flood, are only for Brown, who I suspect doesn't already know about it; Smith, Jones and Robinson please skip them." Or "The next *n* paragraphs are included only in case you don't already know about the Johnstown flood; if you do, skip them."

But of course you'd rather do it more subtly. And you can, with any of many devices—some of which you probably have used, but not consciously for this purpose, so probably not as effectively as you might have. And most of them also serve other purposes—for example, any of those below may be a way to drop an "anything else" into your background or elaboration section.

The most often useful are:

section headings, subheads, read-ins
"section separators"
typographical variations
footnotes
parentheses
appendixes and exhibits

Whichever you choose, the basic principle is simple: You must show clearly where each marginal section begins, and *where it ends*.

On Page 215, "Chapter 30—The Other Agents of Disorganization" is a section heading, and "Failure to Help the Reader Skip" is a subhead. (That the "section" is a chapter doesn't matter.) I defined "read-in" on Page 68, in relation to zero numbers.

I recommend that in typed copy,

section headings generally be capitalized and centered, but not underlined;
subheads generally be flush left, underlined, capital and small letters.

When you use all three in one report, you should use

subheads within sections introduced by section headings;
read-ins within sections introduced by section headings or subheads.

Using only any two of them, you just mustn't reverse any of these relationships. The reason:

Whether as section heading, subhead or read-in, the words "The Johnstown Flood" clearly mark the beginning of the section that—presumably—tells about the Johnstown flood. As soon as a reader sees them he knows whether he wants to read the section or skip it.

And he also knows—whether or not he realizes it—that

- a section introduced by a section heading *continues through any intervening subheads or read-ins* and ends at the next section heading;
- one introduced by a subhead *continues through any intervening read-ins* and ends at the next section heading or subhead, whichever comes first;
- one introduced by a read-in ends *no later* than the next read-in, subhead or section heading; and if it ends earlier, the end will be signaled by some other typographical device. (For example: On Page 68 I showed you where the "MOST IMPORTANT" section ended by reverting to "normal" typography.)

So—provided only *you* know what *he* knows—he knows exactly where to skip *to*.

(And note: This means you'd better *not* convey in this section any significant information about anything *else*—say the Chicago fire. If you do, a reader who knows about the Johnstown flood may never find out about the Chicago fire.)

Read-ins are almost necessarily just labels, but section headings and subheads may be either label- or lead-type. (For example, I could have called this section just "Chapter 30.") You should greatly prefer the lead type.

Lead-type section headings and subheads—and over nonmarginal as well as marginal sections—can also

- significantly help a reader follow your "line," and
- help keep *you* on the organizational beam. For example: Had I said anything in this section that didn't somehow relate to "Failure to Help a Reader Skip," I'd have digressed. And when I edited the report, to spot the digression I'd have needed just to read the section with the subhead in mind.

Also, all three of these devices—and especially the subhead—can "dress up" your report beautifully. (Though if you provide *too* many, they'll *detract* from your report's appearance.)

"Section separators" include such things as the extra white space that surrounds this section. Suppose you'd wanted to skip it; where would you have skipped to?

But used for this purpose, white space alone is likely to be adequate only for short sections—in fact, *really* adequate only when both its appearances are on the same page. For longer ones, you'd better use something like the asterisks on Pages 170 and 171. (Suppose you hadn't been interested in engine-to-cargo ratio: Where would you have skipped to?)

Typographical variations are another fine way to set a section apart.

For example: The first three words in the paragraph above told you what this section would be about. And either you wanted to read it or you didn't.

All right; suppose you'd wanted to skip. Where would you have skipped to?

Since all the footnotes in this book have been intended, at least chiefly, to serve another purpose—you'll see which under the next subhead—they don't really illustrate the use of footnotes to help readers skip. But on Page 109, suppose you hadn't wanted to know about "most words that can serve as subordinating conjunctions": Where would you have skipped to?

(As I said earlier, parentheses actually invite a reader to skip; and they especially do around whole paragraphs and groups of paragraphs. And you can use them either by themselves or with section separators and/or typographical variations.

(Note, by the way, how you parenthesize plural paragraphs: Each begins with a parenthesis, but only the last ends with one.)

Finally: Probably the *most* effective way to help a reader skip anything is to provide it in an appendix or exhibit (even if you do tell him, in your text, that he can find it there). In fact, most readers usually *do* skip appendixes and exhibits, and when they don't, usually just skim them. So you must never convey through one anything you *don't* want anyone to skip.

GTW. Inefficiency in "Going Two Ways at Once"

However earnestly you strive for a perfectly straight line, you almost always must settle for one that's just "optimally" straight. Partly this is because you sometimes *must* give your reader a preglimpse of something that's coming, or remind him of something you said earlier. But often it's because–for example–en route from A to Z you must stop off at X, which you can reach only from N–which is also the only point from which you can reach O:

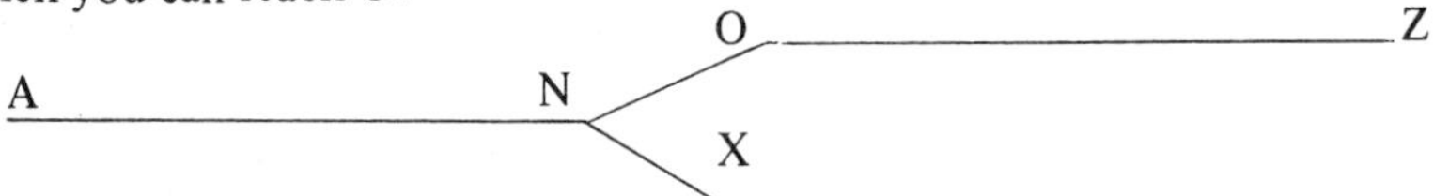

Usually you best take your side trip via a footnote, dashes, parentheses or brackets (the last being essentially just a special kind of parentheses). The end of the footnote, or the second dash, parenthesis or bracket, signals your reader to return to N, from which he can continue with you through O to Z.

Since dashes can be used for this purpose only within sentences, they can contain only fairly short sections. (I urge, by the way, that you ask your typist to type a dash as *two* hyphens, the first immediately following the preceding word, the second followed by a space. She probably learned it differently in business school.)

So you must usually use one of the others for a longer section.

But parentheses (and brackets) downgrade the importance of what they surround.

And many readers loathe footnotes.

So generally you must choose chiefly on the basis of which, in your particular context, seems less *un*desirable.

Incidentally: When you *want* a reader to read a footnote, be sure to put it on the same page with your asterisk (or whatever you used to send your reader to it). *All* readers loathe flipping back and forth between pages—and many just won't do it.

P. Poor Paragraphing

Probably your teachers defined a paragraph as "a group of sentences all on one topic," and probably this is how you'd still define it. I'll propose a new definition shortly. But if you're like most, you need a new *attitude* toward paragraphs much more than a new definition.

What chiefly reflects your present attitude—if you're like most—is that your paragraphs are consistently too long.

The point is: Where any "topic" ends and another begins is clearly a judgment question, on which any two people may differ. Otherwise you'd have to write every report, however long, as one paragraph, because what's a report but "a group of sentences all on one topic"?

Your teachers realized this. But they clearly felt *your* judgment needed a crutch. The proof: Their definition included the word "group," lest you ever decide *one* sentence could cover a "topic" completely.

But apparently many feared you needed a stronger crutch, because they superimposed on the definition of "paragraph" their personal definitions of "group." Of these, probably most said it meant at least three—but I've met, and maybe you also have, some who said it meant at least four.

But whatever their minimums, surely most of them made it clear that they *preferred* substantially *more*: The longer a paragraph, the more "elegant" it was.

So you trained yourself not just to ensure that every paragraph contained at least a "group" of sentences, but also to so define your "topics" that you could write the longest paragraphs *possible*.

You need to

(1) start to regard a paragraph not as a group, but as a *number*, of sentences. The difference: One is a number, and so is any fraction. And you can cover many a topic completely in one sentence—many even in incomplete sentences.

(2) resolve to hereafter define your "topics" more narrowly—in fact, to start a new paragraph every time you've a *reasonable excuse.*

Even at best, too-inclusive paragraphs just don't help your reader see what direction your "line" is moving in. And at worst, they

- invite zigzags. Having defined as one topic what's really two or more, you still *can* move from each to the next as you should. But you don't have to; your definition licenses you to bounce back and forth among them at will.
- conceal zigzags. The more broadly you define a topic, the more

sentences you need to cover it; and a lot of sentences that more or less relate to each other may serve as a kind of screen around one that's totally unrelated.

- disguise zigzags. Even if you do look through the screen, an out-of-place sentence tends to take on the coloration of those that surround it.

On the other hand, you must never break a paragraph *without* a reasonable excuse; and if this ever requires you to write a very long paragraph, do. Excessively short paragraphs—paragraphs that cover not topics, but only fractions of topics—also invite zigzagging. Because unless you paragraph together two sentences that should have been adjacent in the same paragraph, you promote the likelihood that they won't even be adjacent—even that they'll appear pages apart.

And even if every sentence appears exactly where it should in relation to every other, "subtopical" paragraphs make it harder for a reader to see "intersubtopical" relationships, and may cause him to miss some.

Chapter 31

THE DISEASE OF ARROGATION

This is the disease you suffer from when you fail to provide in a report facts and/or ideas that *don't* go without saying to your reader, and that he must have to really understand your story. Usually this is background material, elaboration or definitions—but it *may* be something you just *forgot to include.*

Its agents are all the agents of wordiness and disorganization, because each of these hinders you from *spotting* your omissions. For example: If while editing one of your reports you come to a spot where you said "$x = 7$; therefore $xy = 21$," you virtually must see that you left something out. But if a lot of words intervene between those sentences, you may not.

So the best time to cure a report of arrogation is after you've cured it of wordiness and disorganization. That is, just before you turn it loose, you need to check it—quickly—one last time, questioning everything you've said to decide whether you need to explain it, and everything you've omitted to decide whether you shouldn't have included it.

While doing this, of course, you must remember whom you're writing to. You might need to define for a sales manager—for example—terms and concepts you'd better *not* define for a financial vice-president.

But remember that a *multiple*-reader report must include *everything* that *any* of its readers may need to know.

Chapter 32

HOW TO ATTACK EVERY WRITING JOB FROM NOW ON

So now you know about all the agents of the most important writing diseases. But if you plan to be concerned about them, *please* believe what I say in this chapter. For the sake of not only your comfort, but also my conscience; because if you believe what else I've said, but disregard me here, I'll have hurt you, rather than helped, by writing this.

You must regard every report as a three-step project.

Step 1 is to organize it, as carefully as you can, in the light of the agents discussed in the last four chapters.

Step 2 is to get the words on paper, as fast as you can, however they occur to you first, *not* letting yourself think about any agents of any writing diseases.

Step 3 is to edit it.

Even if you do it this way, writing may never again be as easy for you as it used to be. But it won't be *unbearably* tough. And every time you edit a bad construction out of your writing you'll advance the day when the words that occur to you first will be its alternative *right* construction. And as each bad construction drops out, you'll more easily spot those that remain; so one at a time these, too, will drop out; so the editing will get easier and easier, and your first drafts better and better, till finally you're writing much better first drafts with no more pain than your poor ones used to cost you.

(But you'll *never* write a first draft so good that you can afford to turn it loose *un*edited. Reconcile yourself to second drafts forever.)

On the other hand, if you try to edit *while you write*, your writing life *will* be unbearably tough. You'll write a sentence, cross it out, write it again, cross it out, and write it again; then after you've gone on to the next you'll decide you still don't like it, and go back and cross it out one more time. And when–or if–you ever do finish a report, it won't even be good; and no succeeding report will be much better than the last.

And you'll hate me.

The more conscientiously you edit yourself, the more strikingly your writing will improve. But how much time and energy you should invest in any *particular* report depends on

(1) how important it is;
(2) how much time you can *afford* to give it.

That is: Since you'll never write a perfect report anyway, you never require yourself to. Rather you just work on each till you can conscientiously say to yourself "I know this isn't perfect, but it's as good as it deserves to be," or "I know this isn't perfect, but it's good as I have time to make it"—and then *stop* working on it, and send it off.

And *no* report can be so important that it justifies your looking for the agents in it one at a time.

Sure: If you look for them all at once, you'll miss some. (I know, for example, I've missed some in this book.)

But you'll also miss some if you look for them one at a time.

For Practice

The report following is a very slightly doctored version of one turned in for an in-company writing course. Your job is to cure it of *all* the diseases it suffers from.

I suggest you start by outlining it according to the pattern on Page 211.

You can't possibly revise it exactly as the author and his editors did; especially, you're likely to provide more information than they decided to. But otherwise, I think, you might get fairly close.

The "From," "To" and "Date" are uneditable; they were printed on the page.

FROM : Lou Barber
TO : Mr. Michael Sennett
DATE : June 19th, 1968 cc. Mr. Jim McGovern

This is in reply to your memo of June 16th, 1968, inquiring about the main roof and North Wall of the Morris Avenue facility, 227 Morris Avenue, New Brunswick,

A field inspection of this facility was conducted on June 13th, 1968, at the request of Mr. W. Walton. Purpose of the inspection was to investigate the reported water seepage through the main roof and the North Wall. As a result of the investigation, the following corrective measures are recommended:

Main Roof - resurface the entire roof (approximately 2,200 square feet) with an approved, guaranteed, built-up roofing material.

North Wall - apply waterproofing to exterior masonry wall, plaster patch and paint damaged interior walls.

In general, the existing main roof is in poor condition. The roof is approximately 12-15 years old and of minimum quality. Roofing appears to be one ply of approximately 30 lb. asbestos felt material, lapped 16 inches (sample of existing roofing material is enclosed). Copper flashing at parapet walls appears to be in good condition. Mr. E. Gordon stated that roof has required periodic patching over the last five years. It is highly improbable that any guarantee exists.

The third floor is used as a storage area and the roof leak has not caused serious damage.

However, the leak has on occasion worked its way through the ceiling of the recording studio on the second floor. To date, technical equipment has not been affected, but the potential threat of water damage is critical.

The North wall is of painted brick construction. The paint has peeled considerably and is possibly the cause (or effect) of the saturated condition.

The second-floor Men's Room is the most extensively affected area. Configuration of interior wall damage indicates that the moisture is permeating directly through the wall. The storage room damage on the first floor however, appears to be caused primarily by water threading down from the Men's Room. The North wall is inconspicuously located and appearance would not be a factor in selecting a waterproofing material.

Photographs of the main roof and North wall are enclosed for reference.

Estimated cost to resurface existing roof, waterproofing North wall, plaster patching and painting would be on the order of $3,000.

Mr. Walton has received a proposal from a local roofer (New Brunswick Roofing) to repair the main roof (copy enclosed).

However, it is suggested that quality of new roofing be in accordance with standards established by Facilities Engineering.

If you have any other questions, please feel free to call me.

The "Answer"

The lead extends through the dots. It came from various places in the original. The author convinced me that the new first sentence really does convey his most important point (I'd guessed, in advance, this would be his recommendations).

The background is the short paragraph after the dots; the elaboration is the next three paragraphs; the "anything else" is the last paragraph. Everything else in the original—the author decided—was trivial or irrelevant or went without saying.

FROM : Lou Barber
TO : Mike Sennett cc: Jim McGovern
DATE : June 19, 1968

WATER SEEPAGE AT MORRIS AVENUE FACILITY

I have inspected the main roof and north wall at this facility and confirm that water is seeping through them. I recommend we

- resurface the whole roof (about 2,200 square feet);
- waterproof the outside wall, patch and paint the interior;
- require bidders to guarantee that roofing quality will meet standards established by Facilities Engineering;
- invite additional bids. (New Brunswick Roofing is the only bidder so far.)

The roof is about fifteen years old. I doubt it was guaranteed.

Ed Gordon says that though it has been patched periodically, water has leaked through it for five years. This water has slightly damaged the third floor (used as a storage area) and the second-floor recording studio, and threatens the recording equipment.

The north wall is in the rear, so appearance is not a factor in the waterproofing material.

Total cost would probably be about $3,000.

I enclose photos of the roof and wall, and a copy of the New Brunswick Roofing proposal.

Subsection 5 – THE DISEASE OF UNATTRACTIVENESS

Chapter 33

THE DISEASE AND ITS AGENTS, AND YOU AND YOUR TYPIST

You can lose a reader at any point in a report. But there are four spots where you're most likely to: at the first period, at the end of the first paragraph, at the bottom of the first page, and *before he starts to read.* And if it isn't read, the "best" report ever written is a total failure: It's failed to communicate.

Now how a report looks is rarely the only factor in whether a potential reader starts to read it. But it's always one factor–and usually an important one.

True, your typical reader does *not* say to himself–usually–"This report is ugly, so I won't read it." But if it's unattractive, it's likely to remind him of some other job–or jobs–that he must take care of *first.* So he puts it aside "temporarily"–just till he can read that other report, write that letter, make that phone call or whatever. Whereupon you're in trouble; the odds leap that he'll never pick it up again.

And even if he does start to read it: The less attractive it is, the more likely it is to remind him, *while* he's reading it, of something else that he "needs" to just "take time out" for. The trouble is that if he does this, time may never be in again.

And finally: Even if he reads it all the way through, its appearance will have predisposed him–without his realizing it–to dislike it. And therefore to skip and skim, not understand it, *mis*understand it, and reject its conclusions and recommendations.

So if you've taken the attitude that "How my reports look is my typist's business–I've more important things to worry about," you've hurt yourself. How a report looks is an important factor in how well–and whether–it will communicate.

This disease has three major agents. We'll attack the most important last.

Failure to Provide Enough White Space

The more paragraphs on a page, of course, the more white space. But *most* of your white space must always be in your margins, which of course will be widest as your *lines* are shortest.

Now some investigators have reported that readers get lost in lines containing more than fifty-two letters and spaces each, but I suspect they overlooked some other factors. I'm convinced that—unless your *paragraphs* are too long—sixty characters is safe, even with a standard typewriter, which has 12-point type. And using one with 10-point type, I feel free to provide up to seventy.

Further, it will usually pay you to cheat a little on margins to reduce two pages to one, or three to two. (When you get beyond two, the number of pages matters *relatively* little.)

But generally, a report presented as a loose page, or loose pages, should have at least 1½ inches of space at the top, left and right of each page—which my 70-character lines do provide—and a little more at the bottom. And any time you can provide more—which in a one-pager you distribute around all *four* sides—great.

(The reason for the more at the bottom: Your typical reader likes to hold such a report with his thumb extending either due north from some point at the bottom or northwest from the lower right corner; or, if he's left-handed, northeast from the lower left. And he's uncomfortable when he must either

- hold a page in his fingertips to avoid covering some of its words—which, oddly, he's likely to do even while reading the *top* of the page—or
- shift his grip when he gets to the bottom.)

A bound or stapled report, or one presented in a binder or the like, may have a *little* less margin at the bottom (because readers hold these kinds differently) and at the right; and a printed report may have less on all sides. But the *lines* in any of these should be no longer than those in a loose-page typed report.

Failure to Provide Sharp Black-Versus-White Contrasts

Provided that your typist changes her ribbon often enough, this means chiefly that every report that's typed to be *read*—as opposed to first drafts, which are typed to be edited—should be single-spaced.

(But it's also an additional reason to shorten your paragraphs, and to prefer 10-point to 12-point type. The argument that some have trouble reading 10-point type doesn't impress me; I think you have to be almost blind to have trouble with it. And it saves pages.)

The argument that readers get lost in single-spaced paragraphs—which so far as I know is the only one offered for double-spacing—holds only where lines, or paragraphs, or both, are too long. Which yours aren't—or, at least, won't be from now on.

Double-space between paragraphs, of course, and provide an extra line of space above each section heading and subhead. (And *below* each section heading, if *each* starts a new page.)

Failure to Give an Over-All Impression of "Orderly Variety"

Accent both words equally in "orderly variety." You always want to provide absolutely all the typographical variety you can–*short* of letting your reports look frilly, whimsical or haphazard.

(If one does look frilly, whimsical or haphazard, readers will hate it.)

Chiefly, you achieve orderly variety by

- indenting paragraphs, and
- varying your typography for special sections, including special sections *within* paragraphs.

But you can also capitalize section headings and read-ins, underline subheads, and provide occasional "pictures": graphs, charts, or even drawings or (in printed reports) photographs. And it may *sometimes* help to use the red half of a two-color typewriter ribbon–though I urge that you do this *very* sparingly, at most, and only for *extraordinarily* important passages.

Probably your typist has *not* been indenting your paragraphs. (In fact, she's probably been *taught* not to.) All right: Bribe her, cajole her or beat her, whichever you must to get her to start–but get her to start. And insist on a *ten*-space indent.

The only justification for the so-called block style–except that some also find it more attractive, which I can't understand–is that it's "more efficient": It saves typing time, and maybe sometimes paper. This is ridiculous. It takes one peck at a tab key to indent ten spaces–a fraction of a second per paragraph, maybe one second per page. And a ten-space difference in one line of each paragraph–even if you *don't* ever compensate for it by stretching another line a little or squeezing an extra line onto a page–will on the average produce the first extra page after about twenty-five pages, and one extra page per fifty after that.

Now if there were no reasons *to* indent, this "efficiency," trivial though it is, might govern.

But there *are* reasons to indent.

For example: Unless you indent, if a page ends with a period at or near the right margin, there's no way by which a reader can tell whether the first sentence on the next page *begins a new paragraph or continues the old one*. And this matters; he should read it differently in one case than in the other.

And the same holds when a sentence starts directly under a chart or table, or after a specially indented section.

If he does try to figure out whether he's starting a new paragraph or still in the old one—even if he figures it out right—he's likely to resent *having* to figure it out. And it costs him some energy; and the more energy he must devote to figuring out where your paragraphs begin and end, the less he has left for the job of understanding your words.

And if he figures it out wrong—or doesn't even try—he'll probably miss some of the intertopical or intersubtopical relationships your paragraphing was intended to show.

Aesthetically, the indentions provide an extra "line" down your page, parallel to the left margin and just far enough removed from it—and just sufficiently broken—to make the page look more interesting to most readers.

But good a reason as this is to indent, it's *much* less important than the communicative reasons.

I've already discussed the typographical variation as a device to help readers skip. And while I've not discussed variations within paragraphs, I've surely illustrated them—with and without dots and numbers.

With a ten-space paragraph indent, I suggest you normally spot dots or numbers four or (preferably) five spaces from the margin, and *block* the text following them at eight spaces. (The dots, or numbers, themselves provide a kind of indention—a "hanging" indention.) This way you get *four* interesting lines down the left side of your page.

But when you can center your dotted items without going to a second line for any, I urge that you do—provided you can spot each dot (or number) at least *thirteen* spaces from the left margin. (This to avoid their seeming to be on the same "line" with the first letters in your paragraphs.)

You and Your Typist

Your typist is probably every bit as bright and capable as you or I. In fact, except that we happened to take different professional paths—which we did *mostly* because we had different *opportunities*—you might now be typing her reports instead of vice versa, or I might be reading what she wrote about how to write.

And she believes she was trained properly. And she takes pride in her work.

So when you ask her to change, you can expect her to resist you.

But the fact is that the reports she types for you are *your* reports; *you'll* rise or fall with them. So it's up to you to decide how they should look.

Well, I think you can exercise that right without causing her to quit, or burst into tears, or hate you, or even seriously resent your "meddling" in her job.

And I think you should.

PART 4 – THE "ANYTHING ELSE"

Chapter 34

GRAMMATICAL GLOSSARY

ACTUAL PRESENT TENSE: See Page 21.

ADJECTIVE: A word of a type that substantives should be modified by, except that (1) a gerund may be modified by either an adjective or an adverb, and (2) when a substantive *clause* should be modified by a single word, the word should almost always be an adverb.

ADJECTIVE CLAUSE: See Page 109.

ADJECTIVE PHRASE: As used in this book, either an adjective plus one or more modifiers of its own (see Page 108), or an adjective prepositional phrase (see Page 107).

ADVERB: A word of the type that verbs, adjectives, adverbs, phrases (except substantive phrases) and clauses (except the few substantive clauses best modified by adjectives) should be modified by. (For modification of gerunds and substantive clauses, see under ADJECTIVE.)

ADVERBIAL CLAUSE: See Page 109.

ADVERBIAL PHRASE: As used in this book, an adverbial prepositional phrase.

APPOSITION: The relationship of two words or phrases of the same type–for example, two substantives or two predicates–when the second comes right after the first and explains or elaborates on it. Here, for example, the capitalized words are in apposition to those in italics:

George Washington, OUR FIRST PRESIDENT, was born in 1732.

He *did what anyone would have done under the circumstances*: POURED HIMSELF A DRINK.

APPOSITIVE: In apposition.

ARTICLE: A term used, for no good reason, to describe the adjectives "the," "an" and "a": "The" is the "definite article," "an" and "a" the "indefinite articles."

AUXILIARY VERB: A verb whose function is just to help "inflect"—that is, show the voice, tense or mood of—some other verb. For example, "had" in "had deducted" (the past perfect tense of "to deduct"), "is" in "is required" (the present tense, third person singular, passive voice of "to require"), "would" in "would apply" (the conditional mood of "to apply").

BIPHRASAL VERB: A verb and an adverb that, though spelled as two words, are in speech a single verb. Like "make up" in "I think you made that story up," or "shake down" in "He shook his victim down for several thousand dollars."

CHARACTERISTIC PRESENT TENSE: See Page 21.

CLAUSE: See Page 108.

COMPARATIVE ADJECTIVE: One that expresses a greater degree, but not the greatest possible. Some English adjectives are made comparative by the addition of "-er" ("warmer," "greater"), others by being modified by "more" ("more probable," "more intelligent").

COMPLEX SENTENCE, COMPOUND-COMPLEX SENTENCE, COMPOUND PREDICATE, COMPOUND SENTENCE, COMPOUND SUBJECT: See Page 168.

CONJUNCTION: A word that joins two other words, phrases and/or clauses.

CO-ORDINATE CLAUSE, CO-ORDINATING CONJUNCTION: See Page 168.

DIRECT OBJECT: Of a verb, the word, phrase or clause that identifies the object of the action.

EMPHATIC PRESENT TENSE: See Page 21.

FIRST-PERSON PRONOUN: "I" or "we" (nominative case), "me" or "us" (objective case), "my," "mine," "our" or "ours" (possessive case).

FUTURE TENSE: The form in which a verb tells what *will* happen.

GERUND: The form in which a verb is supposed to be used as a substantive. See Page 138 and discussion under ADJECTIVE.

IMPERATIVE MOOD: The form in which a verb expresses a command or request, as in "Do this" or "Please do this."

IMPERFECT TENSE: The form in which a verb describes an action as past and performed at a time when something else was also happening, formed by prefixing "was" or "were" to the verb's present participle. As in "I was shaving when you phoned," "You were still growing then."

INDIRECT OBJECT: Of a verb, the word or phrase that identifies the recipient or beneficiary of an action rather than its direct object ("He bought *his wife* a present," "He told *me* a story").

INFINITIVE: See Page 24.

INFINITIVE CLAUSE; One in which the predicate verb is an infinitive, as in "He wanted *his son to be president.*" (Which is also a noun clause, the direct object of "wanted.")

INFINITIVE PHRASE: See Page 108.

INTENSIVE PRESENT TENSE: See Page 21.

INTERJECTION: A word or phrase that's within a sentence but not within any of its clauses, like "hey" ("Hey, you're going the wrong way"), "well" ("Well, if that's the way you feel about it . . . ") or the like.

IRREGULAR VERB: A verb that's not regular (see REGULAR VERB).

LINKING VERB (sometimes called "copulative verb"): One that, instead of expressing an action, "links" its subject to a predicate noun or adjective (which see). Our most often used linking verb is "to be" ("They are hungry," "Some day he will be president"); others are "to seem," "to appear," "to become" and so forth.

MAIN CLAUSE: See Page 168.

MODIFICAND: What a modifier modifies.

MODIFIER: A word, phrase or clause that modifies.

MODIFY: Describe, limit or identify.

MOOD (or MODE): The "manner" in which a statement is expressed; see IMPERATIVE MOOD, INDICATIVE MOOD, SUBJUNCTIVE MOOD.

NONCE ADJECTIVE: See Page 49.

NOUN CLAUSE: See Page 168.

PARSE: Analyze grammatically.

PARTICIPIAL PHRASE: See Page 108.

PARTICIPLE: See Page 107.

PASSIVE VOICE: See Page 127.

PAST PARTICIPLE: See Page 107.

PAST PERFECT TENSE: The form in which a verb reports that an action (1) is past and (2) *preceded some other* past action; formed by prefixing "had" to the verb's past participle ("I had spoken to them before you came"). May be pointlessly difficult even when used "correctly," and *should* be used only when a simple past tense wouldn't do the job. See Page 23.

PAST TENSE: The form in which a verb simply describes an action as past, as in "I *spoke* to them before you *came*."

PERFECT TENSE (sometimes called PRESENT PERFECT TENSE): The form in which a verb describes an action as either (1) having been performed within a period that includes the present, or (2) begun in the past but continuing into the present. See Page 23.

PHRASE: For our private definition, see Page 34.

POSSESSIVE PRONOUN: "My," "mine," "your," "yours," "its," "his," "her," "hers," "our," "ours," "their" or "theirs."

PREDICATE: See Page 109.

PREDICATE ADJECTIVE: An adjective that follows a linking verb and modifies the verb's subject.

PREDICATE NOUN: A noun that follows a linking verb and "equals" the verb's subject: "Shakespeare was an *Englishman*," "Lincoln became *president*."

PREDICATE VERB: See Page 109.

PREPOSITION, PREPOSITIONAL PHRASE: See Page 107.

PRESENT PARTICIPLE: See Page 107.

PRONOUN: A word that "stands for" a substantive, or for a group of words that may be regarded as jointly a substantive: "*He* is president," "Guess *who*'s coming to dinner," "*That*'s the idea."

PROPER NOUN: One that identifies a *particular* person, place or thing, every word in whose name (usually except articles and prepositions) must begin with a capital letter. For example: "John," "Seattle," "the First National Bank of Concordville," "the Renaissance."

REFERENT: The word, phrase or idea that a second-time word or phrase refers to.

REGULAR VERB: One whose past tense and past participle are itself plus "-d" or "-ed," like "bake" ("baked"), "gallop" ("galloped"), "transmit" ("transmitted"). (Note that the last letter may be doubled.)

RELATIVE ADJECTIVE, RELATIVE ADVERB, RELATIVE PRONOUN: See Page 109.

SIMPLE SENTENCE: See Page 168.

SPLIT INFINITIVE: An infinitive whose first and last components surround an adverbial modifier or modifiers, like "to quickly eat," "to be completely eaten."

SUBJECT: See Page 108.

SUBJUNCTIVE MOOD: The form in which a verb describes an event or condition as contrary to fact ("If I were king, you'd be queen") or suggests some sort of request, obligation or the like ("I asked that he leave," "It is important that he stay"). In the latter use the subjunctive is usually undesirable communicatively even when it's correct grammatically, and can usually be replaced ("I asked him to leave," "You should stay"). A verb's "future subjunctive" is its present infinitive without the "to" (like "leave," above); its present subjunctive is the same as the plural form of its past indicative (like "were," above); its past subjunctive is the same as its past perfect indicative ("If I *had been* king, you'd have been queen," or "*Had* I *been* king, you'd have been queen").

SUBORDINATE CLAUSE: See Page 168.

SUBORDINATING CONJUNCTION: See Pages 65 and 109.

SUBSTANTIVE: A noun, pronoun or other word or phrase that plays a noun role in its sentence.

TENSE: The form of the verb that shows the time of the action.

TOPIC SENTENCE: As we were taught it in school, the first sentence in a paragraph, which (our teachers said) must identify the paragraph "topic."

VERB: A word that expresses action, occurrence or mode of being.

VOICE: The form of the verb that shows whether its subject is the doer (in which case the verb is active or intransitive) or the object of the action (in which case it's passive).